FOR CAUSE
and COMRADES

FOR CAUSE
and COMRADES

———◇———

WHY MEN FOUGHT IN
THE CIVIL WAR

James M. McPherson

OXFORD UNIVERSITY PRESS

NEW YORK   OXFORD

Oxford University Press

Oxford   New York
Athens   Auckland   Bangkok   Bogotá   Bombay
Buenos Aires   Calcutta   Cape Town   Dar es Salaam
Delhi   Florence   Hong Kong   Istanbul   Karachi
Kuala Lumpur   Madras   Madrid   Melbourne
Mexico City   Nairobi   Paris   Singapore
Taipei   Tokyo   Toronto   Warsaw

and associated companies in

Berlin   Ibadan

Library of Congress Cataloging-in-Publication Data
McPherson, James M.
For cause and comrades: why men fought in the Civil War
James M. McPherson.
p. cm.   Includes bibliographical references (p.) and index.

1. United States.   Army—History—Civil War, 1861–1865.
2. Confederate States of America.   Army—Biography.   3. Soldiers—
United States—Psychology—History—19th century.   4. United
States—History—Civil War, 1861–1865—Psychological aspects.
5. Combat—Psychological aspects—History—19th century.   I. Title.
E492.3.M38   1997
973.7—dc20   96-24760
ISBN-13 978-0-19-512499-6 (Pbk.)

20 19 18
Printed in the United States of America

To

LUTHER OSBORN
Private, Corporal,
and Sergeant, Co.
B, 93rd New York
Volunteer Infantry,
1862–63
    and
Lieutenant, Co. G
Captain, Co. H
22nd U.S. Colored
Infantry, 1863–65

and to

JESSE BEECHER
Private, Co. E
112th New York
Volunteer Infantry,
1862–65

PREFACE

HARRIET BEECHER STOWE insisted that she did not write *Uncle Tom's Cabin*; God did. I cannot make the same claim for this book. It would be close to the truth, however, to say that Civil War soldiers wrote it. They articulated their motives for fighting far above my poor power to add or detract. Their uncensored letters and diaries provide fuller and more candid explanations for their decisions to enlist and fight than we have for soldiers in any other war. Many historians have used such sources to explore the thoughts, emotions, and actions of these men. But none has read their diaries and letters with the same questions about why they fought as I have done.

Three million soldiers fought in the Union and Confederate armies. How does an historian discover and analyze the thoughts and feelings of three million people? Modern pollsters claim a margin of error of no more than 4 percent when questioning a sample of one thousand people to analyze the opinions of, say, one hundred million voters. But they do so by selecting a *representative* sample that stands as an exact epitome of the whole. I cannot construct such a sample of Civil War soldiers, nor can I submit a questionnaire to them. The best I can do is to select a quasi-representative group of soldiers whose letters or diaries have survived and read those documents with a discerning eye toward answering the questions posed in this book. By "quasi-representative" I mean a sample that comes as close as possible to representativeness. My sample consists of 1,076 soldiers: 647 Union and 429 Confederate. This proportion of 40 percent Confederates overrepresents the actual 29 percent of all Civil War soldiers who were Confederates, but this overrepresentation seems desirable in order to broaden the base for generalizations about Southern soldiers.

The average age at enlistment of Union soldiers in the sample (25.8 years) is identical with the average age at enlistment for all Union soldiers, while the sample's median age of 23.9 years at enlistment is almost the same as the median for all Union soldiers (23.5). The average and median ages of the Confederate sample at the time of enlistment were 26.5 and 24.2 respectively.[1] In the Union sample 29 percent of the men were married when they joined the army, which conforms almost exactly with the estimate of 30 percent of all Union soldiers in the only study of the marital status of Civil War soldiers that I am aware of.[2] Reflecting the mobilization of a larger proportion of the eligible white male population into the Confederate than into the Union army, 36 percent of the Confederate sample were married. Soldiers in both samples hailed from the various states in roughly the same proportions as did all white soldiers. In the Union sample Massachusetts, Michigan, and Iowa are somewhat overrepresented and New York and the border states underrepresented, while in the Confederate sample South Carolina is overrepresented and Tennessee underrepresented. (See Appendix.) Three percent of the Union sample fought in the navy, compared with about 5 percent of actual Union personnel. Of the Union army sample, 82 percent served in the infantry, 11 percent in the cavalry, 6 percent in the artillery, and 2 percent in the engineers, which slightly underrepresents the cavalry. Of the Confederate sample, only one-half of 1 percent were in the navy, which may underrepresent even that tiny branch of the Confederate service. Of the Confederate army sample 78 percent were infantry, 15 percent cavalry, and 7 percent artillery, which conforms closely to the actual percentages in these branches.

With respect to age, marital status, geographical distribution, and branch of service, therefore, the samples are fairly representative. In other respects, however, they are not. By definition the 10 or 12 percent of all white soldiers who were illiterate are not represented. Black Union soldiers and sailors are radically underrepresented: 1 percent of the Union sample were blacks compared with almost 9 percent of all

Union personnel. (Note, however, that some 70 percent of black soldiers were illiterate.) In both the Union and Confederate samples,
foreign-born soldiers are substantially underrepresented. In the Union
sample only 9 percent of the men were born abroad compared with
24 percent of all Union soldiers. Unskilled and even skilled laborers
are underrepresented in both samples. Nonslaveholding farmers are
underrepresented in the Confederate sample. Indeed, while about
one-third of all Confederate soldiers belonged to slaveholding families,
slightly more than two-thirds of the sample whose slaveholding status
is known did so. Men of professional and white-collar occupations are
equally overrepresented in the Union sample. Officers are overrepresented in both samples. While some 10 percent of Civil War soldiers
served as officers for at least half of their time in the army, 47 percent
of the Confederate sample and 35 percent of the Union sample did
so. Both samples are also skewed toward those who volunteered in
1861–62 and therefore contain disproportionately few draftees, substitutes, or those Union soldiers who enlisted in 1863–64 for large
bounties.

The biases in the sample toward native-born soldiers from the middle and upper classes who enlisted early in the war are unavoidable.
These soldiers were more likely to write letters or keep diaries and
their descendants were more likely to preserve them than were
working-class, foreign-born, black, or slaveless soldiers. But in one
crucial respect these biases may turn out to be a blessing in disguise.
The purpose of this book is to explain the motives of Civil War soldiers for fighting. I am less interested in the motives of skulkers who
did their best to avoid combat. My samples are skewed toward those
who did the real fighting. What is the evidence for that assertion? The
best way to tell who fought is to look at casualty figures. The fighting
regiments were those with the highest casualties; the fighting soldiers
were those most likely to get killed. While 5 percent of all Union
soldiers were killed or mortally wounded in combat, a startling 17
percent of the soldiers in the Union sample were killed or mortally
wounded. Some 11 or 12 percent of all Confederate soldiers suffered
this fate, compared with 29 percent of the Confederate sample.

Two possible explanations for this phenomenon suggest themselves; both may be right. First, the groups overrepresented in the
sample probably did a disproportionate amount of the fighting. Second, the families and descendants of men killed in action may have
been more likely to preserve their letters for posterity than the families

and descendants of those who were not killed. In any event, the letters and diaries of these 1,076 Civil War soldiers speak to us across the generations to tell us why they fought.

From such writings I have come to know these men better than I know most of my living acquaintances, for in their personal letters written in a time of crisis that might end their lives at any moment they revealed more of their inner selves than we do in our normal everyday lives. These letters and diaries have enabled me to answer many of my questions about what they fought for, how they coped with the fear and stress of combat, and why Civil War armies could sustain a far higher level of casualties than any other armies in American history and keep on fighting.

This book challenges some of the conventional wisdom about the motives and mentalité of Civil War soldiers. It offers some interpretations that differ from those of other historians. I do not expect readers to take my word alone for these interpretations. That is why I tell the story of why they fought as much as possible in the words of the men who did the fighting. In doing so I have proceeded on the "iceberg principle." Only one-seventh of an iceberg is visible above the water's surface. Likewise the evidence for soldiers' motivations and opinions and actions presented in the following pages represents only the iceberg tip of the evidence accumulated in my research. For every statement by a soldier quoted herein, at least six more lie below the surface in my notecards.

In 1993 I delivered the Walter C. Fleming Lectures at Louisiana State University. These three lectures were published the following year in a small book entitled *What They Fought For, 1861–1865*. That book focused on the political and ideological issues that Confederate and Union soldiers perceived to be at stake in the war. *For Cause and Comrades* incorporates these themes of the Cause *for which* Civil War soldiers professed to fight but goes well beyond them to analyze the full range of causes *why* they fought and *how* they coped with the enormous stresses and emotions of combat.

Although I have come to know these soldiers and their families familiarly by name, few of them were famous people, and to scatter hundreds of different names over these pages would overwhelm and confuse the reader. Thus I have normally identified a quoted soldier by his rank, regiment, state, and branch of service. Unless otherwise indicated, such references are to infantry units: for example, a captain in the 51st New York, a private in the 33rd Virginia, a sergeant in the

8th Illinois Cavalry. Readers interested in the names of these soldiers and in the names or identities of the recipients of their letters will find this information in the endnotes.

While most Civil War soldiers could make their meaning quite clear in words on paper, and many wrote vigorous, colorful prose, their spelling, grammar, punctuation, and capitalization did not always conform to the rules. Because their departures from these rules sometimes reveal insights into their personalities, education, or state of mind when writing, I have quoted their words exactly as they wrote them, without the intrusive [sic] to indicate their mistakes. In a very few cases, where it was necessary for clarity, I have silently corrected punctuation or have added the correct spelling of a word in brackets. In other cases, when such words as don't or can't appear as dont or cant, they are not typographical errors. I can assure the reader that I know the difference between there and their, though soldiers sometimes mixed them up. And as the runner-up in the Freeborn County spelling championship in eighth grade, I can also assure the reader that I know how to spell such words as separate and altar, so when they appear as seperate and alter they are not my mistakes or the printer's, nor are the many other misspelled words in the letters of soldiers whose orthography was often delightfully original and creative.

ACKNOWLEDGMENTS

I COULD NOT have written this book without the help of a great many people. As always with a work of history, libraries and curators of manuscript collections are essential to research. Individuals who facilitated my research are too numerous to name, though a few stand out for having rendered services above and beyond the call of duty: Richard J. Sommers, archivist of the United States Military History Institute at Carlisle Barracks, Pennsylvania; Peter Michel and his staff at the Missouri Historical Society in St. Louis, who gave me access to the Society's collections during a distracting move into a new building; Paul Romaine, curator of the Gilder-Lehrman Collection, and Lori Gilbert, curatorial assistant at the Pierpont-Morgan Library in New York City, which houses this rich collection of soldiers' letters and diaries, for special efforts to make some of this material available to me; John H. Rhodehamel, curator of American History at the Huntington Library in San Marino, California, who arranged access to an important collection of letters before it was cataloged; and John Henneman, History Bibliographer at Firestone Library, Princeton University, for obtaining the microfilm set of the Library of Congress's collection of soldiers' letters and diaries.

Dozens of other skilled professionals at the following institutions also provided courteous and efficient service: the Filson Club Historical Society in Louisville; the Department of Special Collections at Firestone Library, Princeton University; the Hill Memorial Library at Louisiana State University; the Huntington Library; the Illinois State Historical Library in Springfield; the Kentucky Historical Society in Frankfort; the Lincoln Shrine at the Albert K. Smiley Library in Redlands, California; the Maryland Historical Society in Baltimore; the Minnesota Historical Society in St. Paul; the State Historical Society of Missouri in Columbia; the Museum of the Confederacy in Richmond; the Ohio Historical Society in Columbus; the Perkins Library at Duke University; the Southern Historical Collection at the University of North Carolina; the Tennessee State Library in Nashville; the Virginia Historical Society in Richmond; the Wisconsin Historical Society in Madison; and the Woodruff Library of Emory University in Atlanta.

Despite the numerous published volumes of soldiers' letters or diaries held by the Firestone Library and the Huntington Library, where I did most of the research for this book, even these outstanding repositories do not possess several volumes that turned out to contain important material. For those volumes I turned to Professor Gary Gallagher of Pennsylvania State University, who has one of the finest private Civil War libraries that I know of. Many conversations with Gary also helped me clarify and refine some of the themes treated in this book. Professor Mark Grimsley of Ohio State University also shared sources and ideas with me. Other friends and scholars whose conversations or correspondence have proved valuable are: Peter S. Carmichael, John Whiteclay Chambers III, Eric T. Dean, Earl J. Hess, Frances H. Kennedy, John Lynn, Louis Masur, Reid Mitchell, James I. "Bud" Robertson, Richard Rollins, and John E. Talbott.

I did most of the research and writing of this book during three sabbatical leaves from Princeton University, two of them in residence as a Fellow at the Huntington Library. For financial support during those leaves and during an additional summer I am indebted to the Seaver Institute and the R. Stanton Avery Fund, administered through the Huntington Library; the Rollins and Davis Funds, administered through the Department of History at Princeton University; and the Princeton University Committee on Research in the Humanities and the Social Sciences. Martin Ridge and Robert C. Ritchie, directors of research respectively at the Huntington Library during my two fellowship years at that wonderful institution, provided a congenial atmosphere for research and writing. They were ably seconded by the Department of Readers' Services and the respective heads of the Huntington in 1987 and 1995–96, Robert Middlekauff and Robert Skotheim.

Many collections of soldiers' letters or diaries remain in private hands, usually in the possession of descendants. Other collections were in respositories that I did not visit personally. I am indebted to the generosity of the following individuals who have shared with me copies of materials in these collections (in a few cases these collections were subsequently published): Samuel Abernethy, Michael Allard, Don Allison, Wyndham Anderson, Joanie Betley, Kermit Bird, Louis Bross, Betty Burchell, Lauren Cook Burgess, O. Vernon Burton, Charles A. Coit, David G. Colwell, Janet Coryell, Mrs. John D'Arcy, Georges Denzene, J. M. "Mac" Dobie, Mary Marvin Dunlop, Robert F. Engs, John Campbell Farmer, James B. Futrell, Rusty Gaillard, Joseph G. Glatthaar, Richard Gottlieb, Robert N. Grant, Norman Halliday, J. Roderick Heller, David Holquist, Robert W. Ikard, James W. Johnston, Kent D. Koons, Charles LaRocca, Connie Leitnaker, Henry C. Lind, Francis MacNutt, Louis Mahan, Don Melvin, Gerald J. Miller, Stanley Robert Miller, Morton R. Milsner, John A. Morrow, Jeanne E. Murray, Mary Obert Norris, Bernard A. Olsen, Edward O. Parry, Sanford Pentecost, Lewis Perry, Victor Petreshene, Mary June Platten, Steven Poling, Warren V. Randall, Susan E. Richter, Allan W. Robbins, Hal Saffell, Christian G. Samito, Frances Saunders, Jeffry Scheuer, John Wellington Hope Simpson, Ann and David Thomas, Leland W. Thornton, Sally and James Tomlinson, Jerry Van Hoosier, Richard W. Walling, Barbara Wampole, Thomas Waterman, Zack Waters, the late Warren Wilkinson, Ruth and Guy Woodward, and Earl M. Wright.

For the past twenty years I have enjoyed a creative partnership with Sheldon Meyer, history editor at Oxford University Press, who has shepherded five of my books, including this one, through the publication process. The person most instrumental in helping me produce this volume has also been the most important person in my life for the past forty years, my wife Patricia. In addition to enriching my life every day, she has been a superb research assistant, having read almost as many soldiers' letters and diaries as I have. Along with those soldiers, she deserves to be named a co-author of *For Cause and Comrades*.

Princeton, New Jersey   James M. McPherson
July 1996

CONTENTS

FOR CAUSE
and COMRADES

CHAPTER 1

THIS WAR IS A CRUSADE

THE ORIGINS OF this book go back many years. In the spring
of 1976 I took several Princeton students to Gettysburg for the
first of what became many tours of that memorable battlefield.
On this occasion, as on subsequent visits, we finished the day by
walking the ground over which "Pickett's charge" took place at the
climax of the battle. As we strolled across the open fields in peaceful
twilight, knowing that those 13,000 Confederate soldiers had come
under artillery and then rifle fire almost every step of the way, students
asked in awe: What made these men do it? What motivated them to
advance into that wall of fire? What caused them to go forward despite
the high odds against coming out safely? I found that I could not give
my students a satisfactory answer. But the question planted the seed
of a book.

Another experience later that same bicentennial year of 1976 wa-
tered the seed. The day after Thanksgiving my cousin and I visited
the four Civil War battlefields near Fredericksburg, Virginia. As we
stood at the Bloody Angle of Spotsylvania on that crisp fall afternoon,
with no other living creature in sight except a hawk soaring high over-
head, the contrast between this pastoral scene and what happened on
the same spot 112 years earlier struck me with a painful intensity.

Wave after wave of Union attacks against entrenched Confederates during eighteen hours of ferocious fighting in the rain on May 12, 1864, had left thousands of killed and wounded men trampled into the mud and muck. Soldiers on both sides had leaped on the parapets and fired down at the enemy with bayoneted rifles handed up from comrades below, hurling each empty gun like a spear before firing the next one until they were shot down or bayoneted themselves. "I never expect to be fully believed when I tell what I saw of the horrors of Spotsylvania," wrote a Union officer, "because I should be loath to believe it myself" had he not been there.[1] As I recounted this story to my cousin, he asked in wonder: What possessed those men? How could they sacrifice themselves in that way? Again I was not satisfied with my reply. My determination to find an answer deepened.

With that cousin I share a great-great-grandfather who fought in the Civil War. This man, Jesse Beecher, emigrated from England in 1857 and became a prosperous wheelwright in an upstate New York village. In 1862, at the age of thirty-seven and with eight children, he enlisted in the 112th New York. What moved him to do so? His obituary and family tradition testify to a sense of duty and gratitude to the country that had given him opportunity. Another clue is provided by the name he bestowed on his first child born in the United States: Henry Ward Beecher, after the famous antislavery clergyman. Jesse Beecher fought in South Carolina, Virginia, and North Carolina. After his regiment broke through Confederate defenses in the successful attack at Fort Fisher on January 15, 1865, he died in Wilmington, North Carolina, and is buried there in the national military cemetery. What motivated him to give the last full measure of devotion for his adopted country? Unfortunately, none of his letters has survived to help resolve this question. But many letters from other soldiers like him suggest possible answers.

My initial grappling with the question of Civil War soldiers' motivation occurred during the aftermath of the Vietnam War. Others also probed this puzzle at the time. A veteran who became a student of the Civil War after his tour in Vietnam was awestruck by the dedication of soldiers in that earlier conflict. In all his Vietnam experience he had met only one American "who had the same 'belief structure' as the Civil War soldiers." In Vietnam "the soldier fought for his own survival, not a cause. The prevailing attitude was: do your time . . . keep your head down, stay out of trouble, get out alive." How different was the willingness of Civil War soldiers to court death in a conflict whose casualty rate was several times greater than for American soldiers in Vietnam. "I find that kind of devotion . . . mystifying." When General John A. Wickham, who commanded the famous 101st Airborne Division in the 1970s and subsequently rose to Army Chief of Staff, visited Antietam battlefield in the 1980s he gazed at Bloody Lane where several Union assaults had been repulsed before finally breaking through. "You couldn't get American soldiers today to make an attack like that," he marveled.[2]

Why not? That is probably the wrong question. The right question is: Why did Civil War soldiers do it? It was not because their lives were somehow less precious to them than ours to us. Nor was it because they lived in a more violent culture that took fighting and dying for granted more than we do. And it was not because they were professional soldiers or coerced conscripts; most Union and Confederate soldiers were neither long-term regulars nor draftees, but wartime volunteers from civilian life whose values remained rooted in the homes and communities from which they sprang to arms and to which they longed to return. They did not fight for money. The pay was poor and unreliable; the large enlistment bounties received by some Union soldiers late in the war were exceptional; most volunteers and their families made economic sacrifices when they enlisted. What prompted them to give up several of the best years of their lives—indeed, to give up life itself in this war that killed almost as many American soldiers as all the rest of the wars this country has fought combined? What enabled them to overcome that most basic of human instincts—self-preservation?

This is a vital question in all wars, for without such sacrificial behavior by soldiers, armies could not fight. Two psychiatrists who studied American G.I.s in World War II put it this way: "What is the force that compels a man to risk his life day after day, to endure the constant tension, the fear of death . . . the steady loss of friends? . . . What can possess a rational man to make him act so irrationally?" Eighty years earlier the novelist and Civil War veteran John W. De Forest asked the same question and offered an implicit answer. "Self-preservation is the first law of nature," he wrote in summing up his combat experience. "The man who does not dread to die or to be mutilated is a lunatic. The man who, dreading these things, still faces them *for the sake of duty and honor* is a hero."[3]

Duty and honor were indeed powerful motivating forces. They had to be, for some other traditional reasons that have caused men to fight in organized armies had little relevance in the Civil War. Religious fanaticism and ethnic hatreds played almost no role. Discipline was notoriously lax in Civil War volunteer regiments. Training was minimal by modern standards. The coercive power of the state was flaccid. Subordination and unquestioning obedience to orders were alien to this most democratic and individualistic of nineteenth-century societies. Yet the Union and Confederate armies mobilized three million men. How did they do it? What made these men fight?

In the middle of the war none other than Abraham Lincoln enumerated several motives that might induce a man to enlist: "patriotism, political bias [i.e., political or ideological conviction], ambition, personal courage, love of adventure, want of employment." In 1864 a Union soldier less literate but no less lucid than Lincoln compiled his list of motives in a letter to his father: "A soldier has but one thing in view, and that is two fight the Battles of his country with oner [honor], halve a likeing for all his Brothers in arms, and the Blessings of God and the prayers of his friends at home." Nearly half a century later one of the Civil War's genuine heroes, Joshua Lawrence Chamberlain, who won the medal of honor for his defense of Little Round Top and earned immortality in Michael Shaara's novel *The Killer Angels* and Ted Turner's movie *Gettysburg*, tried to explain the willingness of men to face bullets: "Simple manhood, force of discipline, pride, love, or bond of comradeship—'Here is Bill; I will go or stay where he does.' And the officer is so absorbed by the sense of responsibility for his men, for his cause, or for the fight that the . . . instinct to seek safety is overcome by the instinct of honor."[4]

Lincoln, Chamberlain, De Forest, and the soldier son of a dirt farmer each in his own way outlined the themes that will be analyzed in this book. Many soldiers did indeed fight bravely for country, duty, honor, and the right. In retrospect almost all soldiers on both sides believed that they had done so. But in practice, many had found ways to avoid fighting when bullets began coming too close. During the war a consensus existed that in many regiments about half of the men did most of the real fighting. The rest were known, in Civil War slang, as skulkers, sneaks, beats, stragglers, or coffee-coolers. They "played off" (shirked) or played sick when battle loomed. They seemed to melt away when the lead started flying, to reappear next day with tight smiles and stories about having been separated from the regiment in the confusion. Some deserted for good. Some really were sick much of the time. Others got what combat soldiers called "bombproof" jobs a safe distance behind the lines—headquarters clerk, quartermaster sergeant, wagon-train guard, teamster, hospital attendant, and the like.

Even the best regiments contained their quota of sneaks. "Strange how many men we have on the rolls and how few we can get into a fight," wrote a captain in the 1st Connecticut Cavalry. "Twenty or thirty men in my company" were "miserable excuses . . . for men" who "shirk all duty if they can." According to a corporal in the 33rd New York, by the end of the Seven Days battles "in our company of 60 men 11 were in line. . . . The rest of the brigade was nearly as bad as ours. . . . I tell you these things to let you know what a large number of miserable beings there is in the army. In case of a battle these stragglers are the very ones to start a panic." After the battle of Fredericksburg, a disgusted private in the 9th New York (who was later killed in action) wrote his brother that "the *sneaks* in the army are named *Legion*. . . . When you read of the number of men engaged on our side, strike out at least one third as never having struck a blow."[5]

The Confederate army had the same problem. A private in the crack 21st Mississippi thought that in such a regiment "there should be *no* sloth nor sluggard, no whimperer nor complainer," but regrettably the regiment contained "an absolutely fearful number of these creatures." The fighting was done by the truly dedicated soldiers (including himself of course) who had endured "privations and suffering like men without murmur or complaint . . . & this class is sufficiently strong to carry this war through to a glorious end but this good conduct can not efface the shameless acts of the other class."[6]

Some soldiers admitted to seeking a bombproof position or to skulking. A quartermaster sergeant in the 149th New York told his sister that he could have been promoted to orderly sergeant (a combat post) "but I prefer staying where I am, besides you know, those Rebel bullets don't exactly suit my fancy." After his regiment distinguished itself at Lookout Mountain on November 24, 1863, he wrote home that "while the battle was going on I wished myself in the company" but "when the wounded began to come in, I congratulated myself that I was not compelled to be where the bullets flew so thick." The diary entries of a private in the 101st New York candidly described his behavior at the second battle of Bull Run. *August 29, 1862:* "Marched about three miles and fought all day they marched us up to Reb battery and we skidadled then I fell out and kept out all day Laid in the wood all night with 5 or 6 others." *August 30:* "Laid in the woods all day while the rest were fighting."[7]

Helping a wounded comrade to the rear was a favorite device to escape further fighting. A private in the 53rd Virginia narrated his actions during the battle of Malvern Hill on July 1, 1862: "It is an awful thing to be in a battle where the balls is flying as thick as hail," he wrote to his wife. "I saw dudley on the battlefield soon after he was wounded and I started with him out we got to a place where they did not have such a good chance to hit us and dudley stayed there   I went a little further on and come to a ditch and it was crouded with men under the banks." Two months later the same soldier confessed that he was one of the thousands of Confederate stragglers who fell out of the ranks before the Army of Northern Virginia fought at Sharpsburg. "I was not up with them the day of the battle thank god I have escaped so far & I hope and trust I may come out safe in the end." Not to be outdone by the Virginians, a North Carolina private with Lee's army assured his wife in 1864 that "there is as good a chance to keep out of the War here as there is there for if it Gets too hot here We can cross the branch and keep out of it."[8]

Many of the derogatory comments about sneaks and stragglers came from officers and men of upper- and middle-class background. They had enlisted early in the war from motives—in their own eyes at least—of duty, honor, and patriotism. They looked down on the conscripts, substitutes, and bounty men who had been drafted or had enlisted for money. The soldier in the 21st Mississippi who denounced the sluggards and complainers in his regiment as "creatures raised a little above the brutes" was a planter's son who had attended Princeton. The captain in the 1st Connecticut Cavalry who deplored the "miserable excuses . . . for men" who "shirk all duty" was a prosperous farmer's son who had left Yale to enlist. With remarkable unanimity, fighting soldiers of middle-class origins commented in their letters home that "it isn't the brawling, fighting man at home that stands the bullets whistle the best." "Roughs that are always ready for street fighting are cowards on the open battle field." "I don't know of a single fist fighting bulley but what he makes a *cowardly* soldier." "As a general thing those at home that are naturally timid are the ones here that have the least fear. [Patrick Cronan] was a sort of street bully as they term it at home. . . . He skulked out of the fight and afterwards was court marshaled and sentenced to wear . . . a wide board on the back with the word *coward*. . . . Others that it was thought would not fight at all fought the best."[9]

The harvest of draftees, substitutes, and bounty men who came into the Union army after mid-1863 had a particularly poor reputation among the volunteers of 1861 and 1862. "The big bounty men are no men at all," wrote a Massachusetts private. "Most of them came out just to get the bounty, & play out as soon as they are able." The twice-wounded colonel of the 61st New York, who won the medal of honor for his performance at Chancellorsville, was shocked by the quality of men he received after the first draft in 1863. "Nearly all that have been sent here are *substitutes* and are miserable surly rough fellows and are without patriotism or honor," he wrote in August 1863. "They seem to have no interest in the cause and you would be surprised to notice the difference between them and the old veterans who have endured the hardships and borne the brunt of the battles for the last two years."[10]

Perhaps these comments should be discounted because of class or ethnic bias. The fighting reputation of the Irish Brigade in the Army of the Potomac and the Louisiana Tigers in the Army of Northern Virginia—both composed mainly of working-class Irish-Americans—should give one pause. At the same time, however, it is true that a disproportionate number of conscripts, substitutes, and (in the Union army) bounty men came from the ranks of small farmers and unskilled laborers. So did a disproportionate number of deserters in both armies. And studies of American soldiers in World War II and Korea found combat performance to correlate positively with social class and education.[11] So perhaps the similar observations of Civil War soldiers should not be entirely discounted.

The grumbling and grousing of many soldiers should not be confused with skulking. Soldiers' letters and diaries are filled with complaints about the hardships and suffering of life in the army. A sergeant in the 89th New York sarcastically described to his wife the glory of soldiering: "Laying around in the dirt and mud, living on hardtack, facing death in bullets and shells, eat up by wood-ticks and body-lice, cant hear from my Love and loved ones once a month, cant go where or do as I am a mind ter." Yet most of these complainers were determined and effective soldiers; many reenlisted when their terms expired. Griping has been the privilege of American soldiers in all wars; the biggest war of all was no exception. An Illinois soldier who complained of acute homesickness and almost died of diarrhea wrote to his fiancée that "a soldiers life is a dogs life at best. . . . I have a decided preference for the quiet pursuits of a citizens life to that of the excitement hardship and danger of a soldiers life." Yet he

reenlisted in 1864, married his fiancée during his reenlistment furlough, lost an arm at the battle of Jonesboro, and returned to his
regiment as a lieutenant after recovery to finish out the war. A corporal
in the 4th Louisiana wrote in his diary in 1863 that he was "weary, so
weary with this soldier's life" and "heartily sick and tired of the war,
but I suppose that I must make up my mind to go through with it
all"—which he did, to the bitter end.[12] After a forced march of fifty
miles in two and one-half days, a soldier in the 72nd Pennsylvania
wrote to his father: "O what deep heartfelt curses did I repeatedly
hear heaped upon the generals, the war, the country, the rebels, and
everything else." Yet this was one of the regiments that broke the back
of Pickett's charge at Gettysburg and broke through the Confederate
mule-shoe salient at Spotsylvania. A Massachusetts officer warned the
folks at home not to take such grousing at face value, "for these same
soldiers will fight like bull dogs when it comes to the scratch, and it
is a soldiers privilege to grumble."[13]

Why did so many of them fight like bulldogs? That is the question
this book seeks to answer. It does so by going to the writings of the
men who did the fighting. A great abundance of such sources exists.
One could start with the hundreds of memoirs by soldiers who survived the war, including such classics as "Co. Aytch" by Confederate
infantryman Sam Watkins and Hard Tack and Coffee by Union artilleryman John Billings. Most of these accounts were written in the last
quarter of the nineteenth century by old soldiers looking back on the
most intense experience of their lives. The memoirs shaded into another genre, regimental histories, most of which also appeared during
those same decades and were usually written by a veteran of the regiment who drew freely on the reminiscences and letters of his comrades. Another category of first-hand accounts consists of letters that
many soldiers wrote for publication in their hometown newspapers
during the war. Some of these have been reprinted in modern editions;
two fine examples are Hard Marching Every Day by Wilbur Fisk of the
2nd Vermont and On the Altar of Freedom by James Gooding, a black
soldier in the 54th Massachusetts. Still another genre is the wartime
diaries or journals that soldiers rewrote and "improved" for publication
after the war; two well-known examples are William Heartsill's Fourteen Hundred and 91 Days in the Confederate Army and John Haley's
The Rebel Yell and the Yankee Hurrah: The Civil War Journal of a
Maine Volunteer.

Such sources offer valuable insights into the minds and experiences of Civil War soldiers. Numerous scholars have drawn on them for penetrating accounts of the war from the perspective of the ranks. But these memoirs, regimental histories, newspaper letters, and re-written diaries are not the sources for this book. They suffer from a critical defect: they were written for publication. Their authors con-sciously or subconsciously constructed their narratives with a public audience in mind. Accounts written after the war present an addi-tional problem of potential distortion by faulty memory or hindsight. In all such writings the temptation is powerful to put the best face on one's motives and behavior, to highlight noble and courageous actions and to gloss over the ignoble and cowardly. That does not make these sources worthless; if they were all we had we could subject them to critical standards to filter out some of the distortion and construct a partly credible interpretation of soldiers' motivations.

But these sources are not all we have. Indeed, we have a great wealth of evidence that enables us to get closer to what Civil War soldiers really thought and experienced than for almost any other war. This evidence consists of the personal letters written by soldiers dur-ing the war to family members, sweethearts, and friends, and the un-revised diaries that some of them kept during their service. Literally thousands of collections of soldiers' letters or diaries are accessible in state and local historical societies, in university and research libraries, and in the possession of descendants who are willing to make them available. Hundreds of letter collections or diaries have been pub-lished in books or state historical journals edited according to (more or less) critical standards.

These are rich and in some ways almost unique sources. Civil War armies were the most literate in history to that time. More than 90 percent of white Union soldiers and more than 80 percent of Confed-erate soldiers were literate, and most of them wrote frequent letters to families and friends. Many of them were away from home for the first time; their letters were the only way to describe thoughts, feel-ings, and experiences to loved ones. Of course, letters to a wife or parent or sibling were written for an "audience." Even a diary was often intended to be read by others. Although the soldier may there-fore have been tempted to put the best face on his own motives and actions or to avoid mentioning unpleasant and awkward facts, these letters and diaries were nevertheless more candid and far closer to the immediacy of experience than anything the soldiers wrote for publica-tion then or later. Having read at least 25,000 personal letters from soldiers and 249 diaries, I am convinced that these documents bring us closer to the real thoughts and emotions of those men than any other kind of surviving evidence.

I stated that these letters and diaries were almost unique. Not only are there vastly more of them than for any previous war, but in contrast with twentieth-century wars, Civil War armies did not subject soldiers' letters to censorship or discourage the keeping of diaries. Soldiers' letters were therefore uniquely blunt and detailed about important matters that probably would not pass a censor: morale, relations between officers and men, details of marches and battles, politics and ideology and war aims, and other matters. This candor enables the historian to peer farther into the minds and souls of Civil War soldiers than of those in any other war.

One caveat is in order, however. As in other wars, Civil War soldiers found it difficult if not impossible to depict their combat experience to those who had not shared it. "I can't describe a battle to you," wrote a young officer in the 35th North Carolina to his mother after Antietam. "No one can imagine anything like it unless he has been in one."[14] Union soldiers echoed this sentiment: "A battle is a horrid thing. You can have no conception of its horrors." "Those who have not had the experience of battle cannot imagin what a sensation it does produce." "Of course I saw a great many hard sights the day of the fight but I will not tell them ever."[15]

But despite the difficulty of describing "my feelings while in battle," as a Massachusetts private put it after his first battle, some soldiers tried anyway.[16] And even more of them discussed a range of attitudes and emotions to explain what motivated them to enlist, to stay in the army, and to fight. These are the themes explored in the chapters that follow. I have borrowed part of my conceptual framework from John A. Lynn, an historian of the armies of the French Revolution. Lynn posited three categories: *initial* motivation; *sustaining* motivation; and *combat* motivation. The first consists of the reasons why men enlisted; the second concerns the factors that kept them in the army and kept the army in existence over time; and the third focuses on what nerved them to face extreme danger in battle.[17]

These categories are separate but interrelated. There may be a wide gulf between motives for enlistment in the first place and feelings when the bullets start flying, but an army could not fight if it did not exist, and it could not exist if it had not come into being in the first place. This book will argue for a closer relationship among these three categories for Civil War soldiers than some scholarship on combat motivation posits for that and other wars. The exhaustive studies by social scientists of American soldiers in World War II, for example, found little relationship between the rather vague patriotism of many men when they enlisted (or were drafted) and the "primary group cohesion" that was their main sustenance in battle. (See Chapter 7.) Yet for Civil War soldiers the group cohesion and peer pressure that were powerful factors in combat motivation were not unrelated to the complex mixture of patriotism, ideology, concepts of duty, honor, manhood, and community or peer pressure that prompted them to enlist in the first place. And while the coercive structures of army and state were key factors in sustaining the existence of the Union and Confederate armies by 1864, these factors could not have operated without the consensual support of the soldiers themselves and the communities from which they came.

"I am sick of war," wrote a Confederate officer to his wife in 1863, and of "the separation from the dearest objects of life"—his family. But "were the contest again just commenced I would willingly undergo it again for the sake of . . . our country's independence and [our children's] liberty." At about the same time a Pennsylvania officer wrote to *his* wife that he had to fight it out to the end because, "sick as I am of this war and bloodshed [and] as much oh how much I want to be home with my dear wife and children . . . every day I have a more religious feeling, that this war is a crusade for the good of mankind. . . . I [cannot] bear to think of what my children would be if we were to permit this hell-begotten conspiracy to destroy this country."[18] These convictions had caused the two men, and thousands of others, to volunteer and fight against each other in 1861. They remained more powerful than coercion and discipline as the glue that held the armies together in 1864.

CHAPTER 2

WE WERE IN EARNEST

O NE OF THE phrases often used to describe the American
Civil War is The Brothers' War. This imagery has both sym-
bolic and literal meanings. The Union was a marriage con-
summated in 1776, but by 1858 it had become, in Lincoln's words, a
house divided. One part of this troubled family decided to set up for
themselves in 1861 because they feared that Father Abraham might
deprive them of their most treasured possessions.

This breakup sometimes forced members of the same biological
family to choose opposite sides. James and John Welsh grew up as
brothers in Virginia's Shenandoah Valley. In 1853 James moved to Illinois, where he became a Republican and voted for Lincoln in 1860.
When Southern states in response to Lincoln's election formed an
independent nation and fired on the American flag, James Welsh
wrote to John back in Virginia that "Jeff Davis and his crew of pirates"
had committed "treason and nothing more nor less." John replied angrily that he was "very much pained to find . . . that I have a brother
who would advocate sending men here to butcher his own friends and
relations. . . . I have always opposed secession but I shall vote for it
today because I don't intend to submit to black Republican rule." John
also told James that by becoming a Republican he had forsworn

"home, mother, father, and brothers and are willing to sacrifice all for the dear nigger." Stung by this charge, James responded that he never dreamed a brother of his would "raise a hand to tear down the glorious Stars and Stripes, a flag that we have been taught from our cradle to look on with pride. . . . I would strike down my own brother if he dare to raise a hand to destroy that flag. We have to rise in our might as a free independent nation and demand that law must and shall be respected or we shall find ourselves wiped from the face of the earth and our name become a byword and the principles of free government will be dashed to the ground forever." The two brothers never wrote or spoke to each other again. John enlisted in the 27th Virginia and was killed at Gettysburg; James fought in the 78th Illinois, marched through Georgia with Sherman, and survived the war.[1]

As South Carolina seceded on December 20, 1860, Commander Charles Steedman of the United States navy returned to American shores with his ship and publicly affirmed his loyalty to the Union. His statement would have attracted little attention had Steedman not been a native of South Carolina. His brother James, a low-country planter, wrote Charles an icy letter: "I felt that my blood was cold in my veins . . . my Brother a Traitor to his Mother County . . . where lie the bones of his Father, Mother, & many dear relatives." How could "a Brother in whose veins flows the same blood, Southern, *true* Southern . . . ever allow Northern principles to contaminate his pure soul"? The answer, James thought, must lie in Charles's six months' absence at sea which had left him ignorant of the determination of "those fanatics to interfere with our domestic affairs" and deny us the right "to keep our slaves in peace & quietness." Once Charles learned what was really going on, "we all expect you to do your duty to your God, your State, and Truth." But Charles had a different view of his duty. He expressed his intention to fight for God and Truth—but not for his state. "I am as I have always been," he wrote, "a Union man—I know no North or South . . . all that I know is my duty to flag & country under which I have served for the last 30 years." Charles was as good as his word, rising to the rank of captain and commanding Union warships on blockade duty and in the attacks on Charleston and Fort Fisher.[2]

Steedman could have resigned his commission and joined the Confederate armed forces. Hundreds of his fellow officers in the U.S. navy and army did just that. Their actions underlined a vital truth about the American Civil War: during its first year all of those who enlisted and fought on one side or the other *chose to do so*. The same was true of most soldiers and sailors during the war's second year. Together these volunteers of 1861 and 1862 constituted the overwhelming majority of genuine fighting men during the war. Without their willing consent there would have been no Union and Confederate armies, no Civil War. The powerful convictions that propelled the Welsh and Steedman brothers toward fratricide motivated many of those volunteers as well.

The initial impulse came from what the French call *rage militaire*— a patriotic furor that swept North and South alike in the weeks after the attack on Fort Sumter. Northern cities and towns erupted overnight into volcanoes of oratory and recruiting rallies. "The heather is on fire," wrote a Harvard professor who had been born during George Washington's presidency. "I never knew what a popular excitement can be. . . . The whole population, men, women, and children, seem to be in the streets with Union favors and flags." In New York City, wrote a young man who enlisted on April 15, 1861, "the feeling runs mountains high, and thousands of men are offering their services where hundreds only are required."[3] Diarists recorded the *rage militaire* in Philadelphia. April 20: "A wild state of excitement." April 22: "Everyone I saw, with the exception of two or three Democrats, is filled with rage and resentment." April 30: "The city seems to be full of soldiers, most every other man in the street is in some kind of uniform."[4]

From Oberlin College on April 20 a student wrote to his brother that "WAR! and volunteers are only topics of conversation or thought. The lessons today have been a mere form. I cannot study. I cannot sleep, I cannot work." In Wooster, Ohio, a twenty-one-year-old carpenter wrote in his diary on April 16: "The president's war proclamation has been issued which causes no little excitement throughout the village. I went to work . . . in the morning but became so much excited by the war news that I was unable to resume my labors in the afternoon. Hearing that Spink & Shelby had opened a recruiting office I . . . put down my name." Two days later he reported "war fever 80 percent above par, still raising, received a dispatch from Col. that our company was accepted. Hurrah."[5]

Little wonder that Ohio's governor wired the War Department, which had given his state a quota of thirteen regiments under Lincoln's April 15 call for troops, that "without seriously repressing the ardor of the people, I can hardly stop short of twenty." The same was true of other Northern states, for the sentiments expressed by an Illinois farmer in a letter to his fiancée were widely shared: "My heart burns with indignation" against "armed *rebels* and *traitors* to their country and their country's flag." My hope "has always been for a peaceful, *quiet* home of my own, with you as a companion," but "I have concluded to volunteer in the service of my country. . . . This step will caus you pain and sorrow I know. . . . I love you still and always shall," but "I cant stay behind, no, no." They never married; he was killed in action in 1863.[6]

In the seven cotton states that seceded before April 1861 the fires of martial enthusiasm had spread for months without benefit of the spark of Fort Sumter that kindled the flame of Northern patriotism. Fort Sumter and Lincoln's call for troops ignited the crucial upper South states of Virginia, North Carolina, and Tennessee (along with Arkansas) to the same white-hot incandescence. In Richmond a huge crowd marched to the state capitol, lowered the American flag, and ran up the Confederate stars and bars. Everyone "seemed to be perfectly frantic with delight," wrote a participant. "I never in my life witnessed such excitement." In Goldsboro, North Carolina, a correspondent of the *Times* of London watched "an excited mob" with "flushed faces, wild eyes, screaming mouths, hurrahing for 'Jeff Davis' and 'the Southern Confederacy.'"[7] In Charlottesville an eighteen-year-old student at the University of Virginia wrote in his diary on April 17: "No studying today. The news of Va.'s secession reached here about 10 oc'lk amid huzzas and shouts. . . . 'War!' 'War!' 'War!' was on placards all about. My company was called at 4:45. All was excitement and 'go.'" From Nashville a new recruit wrote that "nothing else is talked of anywhere but War War." He did not expect the fighting to last long, for "the scum of the North *cannot* face the chivalric spirit of the South."[8]

The *rage militaire* of April and May 1861 eventually cooled. But it flared up again at later points of crisis in the war. Enlistments also rose and fell, often in inverse proportion to the fortunes of war. Additional Northern volunteers flocked to the colors after the humiliating rout at Bull Run in July 1861 and after the setback of the Seven Days in June and July 1862. Another wave of Southerners enlisted in response to Union invasions and Confederate defeats in the early months of 1862.

Most of these volunteers professed patriotic motives for enlisting. A young clerk in the lumber business in Massachusetts sought his parents' consent before he joined up, but whether they consented or not "I *am going*. . . . I am not laboring under any 'sea fit,' as I once was, but a duty which everyone ought to perform,—love of country." Although "decidedly homesick," a nineteen-year-old Indiana farm boy who enlisted in July 1861 was determined to stick it out "to aid my country in her desperate struggle against oppression and slavery, against Rebels and Traitors."[9] A twenty-four-year-old clerk in a small Michigan town defied the wishes of both his wife and parents to enlist in August 1861, trying to explain that "the state of the country" required "all true patriots to sustain her government. . . . They admitted that our country needed men but their plea was that thare was anuff without me but I had made up my mind to enlist so thare was no stoping me." An unmarried farmer from Michigan had no such complications. "The Government must be sustained," he wrote to his sister after enlisting in August 1861, for "if the union is split up the goverment is distroid and we will be a Rewind [ruined] nation. . . . Do not borrow eny trouble about me if I dy in the batle feild I [do so] with plasure."[10] In August 1862 he was killed at the battle of Baton Rouge.

Many Union soldiers explained in more depth the ideological convictions that moved them to enlist. Lincoln had said in his inaugural address that secession was "the essence of anarchy" for it defied the Constitution and the rule of law. Union volunteers echoed these words. "This contest is not the North against South," wrote a young Philadelphia printer six days before he enlisted. "It is government against anarchy, law against disorder." An Indiana lawyer who rose to brigadier general during the war and secretary of state after it told his pacifist wife in April 1861 that "it is better to have war for one year than anarchy & revolution for fifty years—If the government should suffer rebels to go on with their work with impunity there would be no end to it & in a short time we would be without any law or order." An immigrant working in a Philadelphia textile mill explained to his father back in England why he had enlisted in the 3rd New Jersey. "If the Unionists let the South secede," he wrote, "the West might want to seperate next Presidential Election . . . others might want to follow and this country would be as bad as the German states. . . . There would have to be another form of a constitution wrote and after it was written who would obey it?"[11]

Union volunteers invoked the legacy of the Founding Fathers. They had inherited a nation sanctified by the blood and sacrifice of that heroic generation of 1776. If disunion destroyed this nation, the generation of 1861 would prove unworthy of the heritage of republican liberty. "Our fathers made this country, we their children are to save it," wrote a young lawyer to his wife who had opposed his enlistment in the 12th Ohio, leaving her and two small children behind. If "our institutions prove a failure and our Country be numbered among the things that were but are not . . . of what value will be house, family, and friends?" Civil war "is a calamity to any country," wrote a recruit in the 10th Wisconsin, but "this second war I consider equally as holy as the first . . . by which we gained those liberties and privileges" now threatened by "this monstrous rebellion."[12]

Relatively few Union volunteers mentioned the slavery issue when they enlisted. But those who did were outspoken in their determination to destroy the "slave power" and to cleanse the restored Union of an evil they considered a mockery of American ideals of liberty. The main purpose of "this wicked rebellion," wrote an Iowa volunteer, was "to secure the extension of that blighting curse—slavery—o'er our fair land." An Ohio artillery officer believed in June 1861 that the war "will not be ended until the subject of slavery is finally and forever settled. It has been a great curse to this country." A Massachusetts infantry captain, a Harvard graduate, wrote to his mother in November 1861 that "Slavery has brought death into our own households already in its wicked rebellion. . . . There is but one way [to win the war] and that is emancipation. . . . I want to sing 'John Brown' in the streets of Charleston, and ram red-hot abolitionism down their unwilling throats at the point of the bayonet."[13]

Some Confederate volunteers did indeed avow the defense of slavery as a motive for enlisting. A young Virginia schoolteacher who joined the cavalry could not understand why his father, a substantial farmer and slaveowner, held out so long for preservation of the Union when reports in Southern newspapers made it clear that the Lincoln administration would "use its utmost endeavors for the abolition of slavery." After all, Lincoln himself "has declared that one of the peculiar institutions of the South, which involves the value of four billions . . . is 'a moral evil.'" No true Southerner could hesitate. "Better, far better! endure all the horrors of civil war than to see the dusky sons of Ham leading the fair daughters of the South to the altar." A slave-owning farmer enlisted in the 13th Georgia because "our homes our firesides our land and negroes and even the virtue of our fair ones is at stake," while a young Kentucky physician told his slaveholding relatives that he would join the Confederate forces "who are battling for *their* rights and for an institution in which Kentucky, Virginia, and Tennessee are [as] interested" as the lower South. "The vandals of the North . . . are determined to destroy slavery. . . . We must all fight, and I choose to fight for southern rights and southern liberty."[14]

This pairing of slavery and liberty as the twin goals for which Confederates fought appeared in many volunteers' letters. As Lincoln sarcastically put it, "the *perfect* liberty they sigh for" is "the liberty of making slaves of other people." Lincoln was not the first to make this point. Referring to the leaders of the American Revolution, most of whom owned slaves, Samuel Johnson had asked in 1775: "How is it that we hear the loudest yelps for liberty among the drivers of negroes?"[15] That question had struck an exposed nerve among many Americans of Thomas Jefferson's generation, who felt embarrassed by the paradox of fighting for liberty while holding other people in slavery.

Little of such feeling seems to have troubled Confederates in 1861. Some dealt with the paradox by denying that it existed. A lowcountry planter's son of aristocratic bearing who enlisted in a South Carolina regiment dismissed the rhetoric about the rights of man as "simple nonsense; I for one am fighting for the maintenance of no such absurdity. . . . We are appealing to chartered rights. . . . It is insulting to the English common sense of race [to say that we] are battling for an abstract right common to all humanity. Every reflecting child will glance at the darkey who waits on him & laugh at the idea of such an 'abstract right.' "[16]

But most Southern volunteers believed they were fighting for liberty as well as slavery. "Our cause," wrote one in words repeated almost verbatim by many, "is the sacred one of Liberty, and God is on our side." A farmer who enlisted in the 26th Tennessee insisted that "life liberty and property [i.e., slaves] are at stake" and therefore "any man in the South would rather die battling for civil and political liberty, than submit to the base usurpations of a northern tyrant."[17] One of three brothers who enlisted in a South Carolina artillery battery believed that "a stand must be made for African slavery or it is forever lost." The Confederate states were united by the institution of "slavery[,] a bond of union stronger than any which holds the north together," wrote the second brother. Therefore, added the third, the South's "glorious cause of Liberty" was sure to triumph. A wealthy planter who married one of Mary Todd Lincoln's sisters became an officer in the 4th Alabama to fight for "Liberty and Independence." "What would we be," he asked his wife, "without our liberty? . . .

[We] would prefer Death a thousand times to recognizing once a Black Republican ruler . . . altho' he is my brother in law."[18]

Southern recruits waxed more eloquent about their intention to fight *against* slavery than *for* it—that is, against their own enslavement by the North. "Sooner than submit to Northern slavery, I prefer death," wrote a slaveowning officer in the 20th South Carolina. The son of a Mississippi planter dashed off a letter to his father as he rushed to enlist: "No alternative is left but war or slavery." *Subjugation* was the favorite word of Confederate recruits to describe their fate if the South remained in the Union or was forced back into it. "If we should suffer ourselves to be subjugated by the tyrannical government of the North," wrote a private in the 56th Virginia to his wife, "our property would all be confuscated . . . & our people reduced to the most abject bondage & utter degradation." Thus "every Southern heart" must "respond to the language of the great Patrick Henry in the days of '76 & say give me Liberty or give me death." He met death at Gettysburg.[19]

This invocation of the Founding Fathers was as common among Confederate volunteers as among their Union counterparts—for an opposite purpose. Just as the American Patriots of 1776 had seceded from the tyrannical British empire, so the Southern Patriots of 1861 seceded from the tyrannical Yankee empire. Our Fathers "severed the bonds of oppression once," wrote a twenty-year-old South Carolina recruit, "now [we] for the second time throw off the yoke and be freemen still." The American Revolution established "Liberty and freedom in this western world," wrote a Texas cavalryman in 1861, and we are "now enlisted in 'The Holy Cause of Liberty and Independence' again."[20]

For Union and Confederate volunteers alike, abstract symbols or concepts such as country, flag, Constitution, liberty, and legacy of the Revolution figured prominently in their explanations of why they enlisted. For Confederate soldiers a more concrete, visceral, and perhaps more powerful motive also came into play: defense of home and hearth against an invading enemy. The territorial instinct is a potent drive in humans as well as in other animals. Studies of the will of armies to fight have found defense of the homeland to be one of the strongest of combat motivations.[21] "When a Southron's home is threatened," wrote a lawyer who organized an Alabama infantry company, "the spirit of resistance is irrepressible." We are "fighting for our firesides and property," reiterated many Confederate volunteers, to defend our homes against "vandal enemies" and "drive them from the soil polluted by their footsteps. . . . I am determined to dispute every inch of soil with the Hessians e'er they shall invade the sunny south   I will die in defending the country where all doth dwell that I hold dear and sacred."[22]

Several Confederate enlistees echoed Southern propaganda about the rapacious designs of Yankee invaders. A Georgia planter wrote to his wife from the camp of the 6th Georgia in June 1861 that it would be "glorious" to die "in defence of innocent girls & women from the fangs of the lecherous Northern hirelings, who from the accounts here stated, are indeed engaging in this strife, for 'beauty & booty.' " Fifteen months later he was killed far from Georgia, at Sharpsburg, Maryland.[23]

As residents of the first state to experience invasion, Virginians tended to express the strongest convictions about this matter. Unionism had persisted longer in the state of James Madison and John Marshall than in the lower South. Like Robert E. Lee, a good many Virginians such as a twenty-year-old graduate of the University of Virginia had vowed not to fight "unless it be in defence of Virginia." He enlisted when his state seceded because it became clear that Virginia would become a battleground. A native of the commonwealth who had moved west and had enlisted in the 9th Mississippi could scarcely wait for his unit to be sent to Virginia: "I would give all I have got just to be in the front rank of the first brigade that marches against the invading foe who now pollute the sacred soil of my native state with their unholy tread."[24]

THE CONSCIOUSNESS OF *duty* was pervasive in Victorian America. Union volunteers filled their letters and diaries with such phrases as "I went from a sense of duty"; if my three-months regiment reenlists for three years "it would be my duty to go"; I must sacrifice "personal feelings and inclinations to . . . my duty in the hour of danger"; in enlisting "I performed but a *simple* duty—a duty to my country and myself . . . to give up *life* if need be . . . in this battle for freedom & right, opposed to slavery & wrong."[25]

Many Northern men found the language of duty essential to persuade reluctant parents or wives to sanction their decision to enlist. The English-born son of a farmer in upstate New York was sorry that his father "was so much opposed to my going to do my duty towards putting down this awful rebellion," but "I ought to and I must" fight

for the "rights & Freedom" of "our adopted Country." The son of a
Boston Brahmin, having completed his junior year at Harvard, insisted
to his father that "it is every one's duty to enlist, if he possibly can,
and why is it not mine as much as other people's? . . . If you are not
willing to send your sons why should others be willing to send theirs?"
A recruit in the 11th Michigan wrote to his fiancée, who had pleaded
with him not to enlist: "No Jenny . . . while your happiness is as dear
to me as life duty prompts me to go my country first home and
friends next Jenny what would friends be to me if I had no
country?"[26]

Victorians understood duty to be a binding moral obligation involving reciprocity: one had a duty to defend the flag under whose protection one had lived. "My country had a demand on me which made all
my plans, calculations, hopes and expectations of minor conse-
quence," wrote a schoolteacher two weeks after mustering into the
64th Ohio. A Kentucky physician explained to his sister why he joined
the Union army: "I know no reason why I should not be as subject to
duty as any man, as I have had the protection of government all my
life. . . . My absence from home is, of course, a source of grief to
Lida and the children . . . but an all-absorbing, all-engrossing sense
of duty, alike to country and family, impelled me." A lieutenant in a
three-months Pennsylvania regiment wrote in May 1861 that "I will
not enlist for a longer period than three months unless my country
needs me, in which event I would enlist for life." That is precisely
what he did, fighting for two years until captured at Gettysburg and
dying in Libby prison.[27]

A good many Confederate soldiers also cited the obligations of
duty. But they were more likely to speak of *honor*: one's public reputation, one's image in the eyes of his peers. To shirk duty is a violation
of conscience; to suffer dishonor is to be disgraced by public shame.
"Life is sweet but I would alwas prefer a honorable death to a disgraceful and shameful life," a sergeant in the 24th Mississippi told his
sister. "I much reather be numbered amongst the slain than those that
stay at home for it will be a brand upon their name as long as a
southren lives."[28]

Honor was primarily a masculine concept, not always appreciated
by wives who sometimes felt that a man's duty to his family was more
important than pride in his reputation. Several married Confederate
volunteers therefore found it necessary to lecture their wives and
daughters on the finer points of the male code of honor. Even though

he was thirty-nine years old and father of several daughters, a South Carolina planter felt compelled to enlist after the Union capture of the South Carolina sea islands in November 1861. "I would be disgraced if I staid at home, and unworthy of my revolutionary ancestors," he explained to one daughter. "I stand alone in my family. There is no one bearing my name left to fight for our freedom. The honor of our family is involved. . . . A man who will not offer up his life . . . does dishonor to his wife and children." An Arkansas planter, also in his late thirties, told his wife that "on your account & that of my children I could not bear the idea of not being in this war. I would feel that my children would be ashamed of me when in after times this war is spoken of & I should not have figured in it."[29]

Honor and duty were not incompatible; indeed some Confederate volunteers mentioned both in the same breath. "No man now has a right to stay at home," a forty-two-year-old planter admonished his wife, who had opposed his enlistment in the 45th Tennessee. "Duty, patriotism and, aye, honour calls him to the field." Another planter who joined an Alabama cavalry regiment rebuked his wife for urging him to back out. "How can you ask me to remain at home an idle spectator? . . . My honor, my duty, your reputation & that of my darling little boy" call me forth "when our bleeding country needs the services of every man."[30]

A substratum of truth underlies the stereotype of the antebellum South as a society with a profound sense of honor (public reputation) while Yankees were driven by conscience (a private compact with God). Like all stereotypes, however, it oversimplifies a complex reality. The letters of Union soldiers also bristled with references to honor and its opposite, shame: "I should be ashamed of myself if I didnt do something." "I whould sooner loose my life then have my chrildren ashemed of their Father." "If I should come home alive, and live to be old, I want to be able to say that I fought willingly for my country and not have my name branded as coward." "We all of us have a duty to perform in this life. . . . My honor is now bound up with the Army. . . . God grant that my children may never blush for their father's memory."[31]

Among Confederates the emphasis on honor occurred most often in the letters of upper-class soldiers and officers. In the Union army such sentiments ranged more broadly across the social scale. But public prominence did intensify the potential for shame and dishonor if one stayed out of the army. Charles Francis Adams, Jr., the great-grandson and grandson of America's second and sixth presidents, rejected the wishes of his father that he stay at home to manage family affairs while Charles Sr. went to London as American Minister to the Court of St. James and took his son Henry with him as secretary. "For years our family has talked of slavery and of the South, and been most prominent in the contest of words," wrote Charles Jr. to his father, who had run for vice president on the Free Soil ticket in 1848, "and now that it has come to blows . . . it seems to me almost disgraceful that in after years we should have it to say that of them all not one [of your sons] stood in arms for that government with which our family history is so closely connected." With or without his father's blessing, Charles intended to enlist "in this great struggle . . . to sustain the government and to show that in this matter our family means what it says." He went in as a lieutenant in the 1st Massachusetts Cavalry and emerged as colonel of the 5th Massachusetts Cavalry, a black regiment that was the first to enter Richmond when it fell in April 1865. The Ohio Republican leader Rutherford B. Hayes declared that "I would prefer to go into it [even] if I knew I was to die or be killed in the course of it, than to live through and after it without taking part." He went in as a major, was twice wounded and breveted major general, and later became president of the United States.[32]

At the other end of the social scale, adoptive Americans also felt the pull of honor. A Swedish immigrant explained to his wife why he must enlist in the 3rd Minnesota. Only five of nearly two hundred men who had thus far enlisted from the Red Wing area were Scandinavians, he noted. "People began to ask, Why don't you do anything for the defense of your country. . . . You have often spoken of how your people were loyal to their new country and to the party of freedom. . . . Are you too cowardly or too indifferent to defend yourselves and us?" He enlisted (and eventually rose to the rank of colonel) because "the honor of our nation [i.e., Swedish-Americans] was at stake."[33]

Duty and honor were closely linked to concepts of masculinity in Victorian America. Boyhood was a time of preparation for the tests and responsibilities of manhood. And there could be no sterner test than war. It quite literally separated men from boys. The letters and diaries of Union and Confederate volunteers alike—those in their thirties as well as those in their teens—are full of references to the need to prove one's self a man: "I determined to stand up to duty and preserve my manhood and honor let come what may" (20th Illinois).

"I would be less than a man if in any way I fell short of the discharge of duty at my country's call" (8th Missouri Confederate). "I really inwardly feel that I want to go and do my part—as a Man" (16th Pennsylvania Cavalry). Anyone who stays home "is no part of a man" (4th North Carolina).[34] "It ought to be a consolation to know that you have a Husband that is man enough to fight for his Country" (62nd Pennsylvania). "I have acted the part of a man" (3rd Virginia Cavalry). Anyone who cannot stand the hardships and dangers "had better pack his knapsack and gow home to his mother" (2nd Michigan, killed at Williamsburg).[35]

Two versions of manhood competed in the Victorian era: the hard-drinking, gambling, whoring two-fisted man among men, and the sober, responsible, dutiful son or husband. Some soldiers found that the army transformed them from one kind of man to the other, better kind. The wild habits of a Baltimore youth, son of a respectable baker, had driven his mother to a sickbed. In a sudden fit of remorse "I determined to enlist in the hope that I should at some time be engaged in a battle, and there have an end put to my worthless and disgraceful career." To his surprise the army sobered him up, inculcated a sense of responsibility, taught him self-respect, promoted him to sergeant, and "made a man of me."[36]

Southern soldiers affected a more boastful style of masculinity than Northerners, who tended to worry about whether they would pass the test of manhood. "There is not a man in the Southern army," wrote a lieutenant in the 4th Virginia, "who does not in his heart believe that he can whip three Yankees, he would consider it beneath his manhood to count on whipping a less number." This assertion hints at another motive for enlistment in both South and North: the quest for adventure, for excitement, for the glory to be won by "whipping" the enemy and returning home as heroes to an adoring populace. This romantic vision has existed at the outset of many wars. It marched to the Marne with the youth of France, Germany, and Britain in 1914. Americans sailed off to the "splendid little war" with Spain in 1898 in search of adventure and glory. The foremost student of soldiers in the American Civil War, Bell Irvin Wiley, maintained that "the dominant urge of many volunteers was the desire for adventure . . . the prevailing excitement, the lure of far places . . . the glory and excitement of battle."[37]

There is indeed evidence in soldiers' letters for these motives. Several volunteers linked the themes of adventure and glory to concepts of manhood and honor. A Pennsylvania cavalry recruit declared: "How often in boyhood's young days when reading the account of soldiers' lives have I longed to be a man, and now the opportunity has offered." The son of a South Carolina planter really did fit the stereotype of a "Southron" inspired by Sir Walter Scott. "I am blessing old Sir Walter Scott daily," he wrote soon after enlisting, "for teaching me, when young, how to rate knightly honour, & our noble ancestry for giving me such a State to fight for." A wound at the first battle of Manassas did not dim his romantic ardor. "I am like a knight in a beleagured fortress," he wrote a month later, "& must not pass out with the women & the sick, when the castle is to be stormed, so long as I can put on my harness & wield my blade." Heroic tales passed down by oral tradition and song also inspired visions of glory. A farmer's son from New York state reminded his father in 1862 of the time "when I was quite young, and listened with pleasure to hear you sing Old Kentucky Boys, and other war songs; and thought how I would like to become a soldier: that childish wish has now come to pass." Two years later this soldier died at Andersonville after being captured at Spotsylvania.[38]

Many others also discovered that the romance and glory of war had been exaggerated. A twenty-year-old planter's son who left college to enlist in the 12th North Carolina wrote his mother from training camp that "the excitement, the activity, and the novelty are perfectly captivating. I have a glorious time." The novelty wore off, however, and in February 1863 he wrote home: "I am sick and tired of the service and I would give almost anything to have this abominable war ended." He almost saw its end—but was killed in one of the last battles, at Five Forks on April 1, 1865. A Georgia soldier who had told his wife when he enlisted that he intended to "*immortalise* myself before I come home" never came home—he was killed at Fishers Hill. A lawyer impelled by patriotic rather than romantic motives helped recruit the 14th New Jersey and went into the service as its major. He wrote to his mother in 1862 to discourage his eighteen-year-old brother from enlisting. "If he expects fun and excitement (which between us is at the bottom of all his patriotism) he will be most emphatically mistaken. It is too preposterous to think of." The younger brother stayed home; the older brother was killed two years later in the third battle of Winchester.[39]

In explaining to family members and friends their motives for enlisting, far more volunteers mentioned patriotism and ideology than adventure and excitement. Should we take them at face value? An historian of the American army in the Mexican War maintains that in soldiers' letters from that war "a desire for personal glory and adventure" was "sometimes masked in the rhetoric of patriotism."[40] It is not clear how he knows this. In any event, perhaps the same was true for Civil War volunteers. And perhaps also the many references to duty, honor, and manhood were only a glorified way of describing community and peer pressure that made a young man a demasculinized pariah if he failed to enlist.

Some soldiers admitted as much. On the first anniversary of his enlistment a private in the 72nd Indiana confessed to his parents that "I enlisted for what I couldent tell. I did it without reflecting what the life of a Volunteer was. . . . In fact I done it just to be doing." A captain in another Indiana regiment, disgusted with the large number of "beats" in his company, wrote sourly that "they all pretend to be ill whenever there is anything to do. . . . Nine tenths of them enlisted just because somebody else was going, and the other tenth was ashamed to stay at home."[41]

But the historian must be careful not to read too much between the lines of soldiers' letters. We cannot know that those who spoke of duty, honor, country, and liberty were merely "masking" other motives. For that matter, the motives of many volunteers were mixed in a way that was impossible for them to disentangle in their own minds. A young bank clerk in Massachusetts enlisted in the fall of 1861 because "we must all make sacrifices for the sake of the government that has protected us for so long" but also because "the fact has long been coming over me that I am living an aimless life" and that to fight for his country would make him "a good useful man in this world."[42] One kind of motive did not necessarily mask the other. It is impossible to understand how the huge volunteer armies of the Civil War could have come into existence and sustained such heavy casualties over four years unless many of these volunteers really meant what they said about a willingness to die for the cause.

Genuinely committed soldiers viewed that commitment with a clear and resolute eye. An abolitionist farmer in his late thirties who enlisted in the 20th New York, and whose son later joined the 120th New York and was killed in action, wrote in December 1861: "If any one enlists to be a soldier with any less motive than a pure sense of duty my humble opinion is that he will be disapointed   any dream he may have indulged in will melt away like a frost under the influence of the June sun. . . . Let all come in welcome but let them know what is before them." A year after he went to war, a homesick soldier in the 24th Mississippi posed a rhetorical question to his fiancée: "Why am I here   was it merely that I might be an actor in Seenes noval and exciting that I turned my back on all the delights of home and subjected myself to the untold trials and privations of camp life and the fearful dangers of the battle field?" No, he answered, "I am here because a numerous and powerful enemy has invaded our country and threatened our subjugation." On the first anniversary of his enlistment a soldier in the 36th Pennsylvania wrote of himself and his messmates: "When we enlisted in this war, we did no idle thing, *we were in earnest*. One year has passed away, and all the fancied romance of campaign life has proved itself to be stern reality to us, yet we are still *in* earnest, ready for another year of harder, bloodier work, if such is necessary to crush this wicked rebellion."[43]

These soldiers and hundreds of thousands like them soon enough encountered bloody work. How did they stand up to the fear and stress of combat?

CHAPTER 3

ANXIOUS FOR THE
FRAY

To JUDGE FROM their correspondence early in the war, most soldiers were "spoiling for a fight." Rebel and Yankee alike, they clamored for a chance to "see the elephant"—a contemporary expression denoting any awesome but exciting experience. "Our boys are dieing for a fight," wrote a recruit in the 8th Georgia. An officer in the 37th North Carolina told his wife that "our Men are allmost Crazy to Meet the Enemy," while a lowly private in the 13th North Carolina wrote to his father that "the Company is all anxious to get in to a battle and they cannot go home with out a fite."[1]

Union soldiers were no less eager. "We are all impatient to get into Virginia and have a brush with the rebels," wrote a lieutenant in the 2nd Rhode Island in June 1861. A private in the 10th Wisconsin criticized "our *donothing* Generals" for "not leading us forward. . . . We came not for *the paltry pay* but to *Fight*. All we want is to be led on to *Battle*." Orders to move toward the enemy "filled me with an exciting feeling, & I took off my cap & gave one loud yell," wrote an Indiana private. "We pushed on anxious for the fray."[2]

In 1861 many soldiers on both sides shared with a recruit in the 2nd Michigan "a general fear that it will all be over before we have a chance to do anything." When the 36th Pennsylvania finally got its chance to fight, "the men cheered most lustily and appeared to be almost besides themselves with enthusiasm." A private in the 25th Mississippi reported similar zeal when action at last appeared imminent: "For almost an hour there was the most deafening yells that ever was made by one regiment   it seemed as if they was wild and mad for the fight   I never felt so much like facing the canons."[3]

This eagerness of green recruits for combat grew in part from their notions of manliness. A Tennessee Confederate explained that "we are all anxious for a chance to let the Enemy know what kind of men they have to fight." As if in reply, a soldier in the 72nd Illinois wrote that the "men want to be tried to see what they are made of."[4] Officers especially felt that their manhood was on trial before the rank and file. A Wisconsin captain was eager to "have a chance to lead them into danger to see what they are made of & if *I* would run." A lieutenant in the 20th Massachusetts, a Harvard graduate who had some initial doubts about his manhood, "wanted to have a speedy engagement in order to try myself." He turned out to be a superb officer who rose to the rank of major and was killed leading his regiment at the Wilderness.[5]

The concern for honor also stimulated a desire to see the elephant. A unit that was kept to the rear while others were fighting lost face; it was *dishonored.* A South Carolina cavalry officer whose company had been on picket far from the scene of First Manassas felt shame when he encountered those who had fought there. "I am heartily tired of hearing men say what they did in the fight—and I have no showing," he wrote sourly to his wife. A private in the 23rd Ohio wrote home that "the boys are anxious to meet the Rebels at the point of the bayonet" so that we can "have a name as well as other regiments." A sergeant in the 70th Indiana, which spent the first twenty months of its service guarding railroad bridges far to the rear, wrote in disgust that "we are not gaining much honor here. . . . The boys are very anxious to see a little of the *elephant,* and would jump for a chance to have the name of at least *one* battle inscribed on the flag."[6]

The sheer boredom of inactivity caused some men to crave the alternative of action. "We are dying with monotony and *ennui,*" wrote a New York soldier stationed in the Washington defenses where no enemy had come within miles since his enlistment nine months earlier. "Camp life is so monotonous," wrote a South Carolina officer, which "accounts for the fact that Soldiers grow extremely eager for a fight." Although serving as occupation troops in the endlessly fascinating city of New Orleans, "nearly every officer and the majority of the men" in the 12th Connecticut "would prefer to go up the river . . . with a fair chance of being killed or wounded, rather than stay here drilling and guard mounting in peace," wrote an officer of that regiment in June 1862. "When the long roll beat for the Seventh Vermont to start forward, they hurrahed for ten minutes while we sulked over their luck."[7]

Morale was generally higher among front-line troops than those stationed in the rear. When part of the Union 16th Corps garrisoned Corinth, Mississippi, in 1863 while Grant's campaign against Vicksburg went forward two hundred miles to the south, the men "lie in camp all the time with nothing to do but stand a dreary guard at certain intervals," wrote a staff officer, so "they get greatly discontented which frequently amounts to insubordination and turbulence, and such fellows to complain and whine and find fault with everything I never saw." But the next year, when these same soldiers fought in the front lines of Sherman's Atlanta campaign, where if "the sun dont beat down in red-hot rays . . . it rains in fearful torrents, and the ditches [trenches] in which they lie fill with water . . . covered with mud, ticks, body lice . . . and if they lift their heads six inches from the ground a sharp shooter sends a ball whizzing through their brains . . . the men are in better spirits, there is less grumbling, less swearing, less cussing officers, less wishing old Abe and the whole government was in 'hell,' and every conceivable blasphemy, such as soldiers practice, than I ever heard in the army before."[8]

THE ZEAL OF unbloodied troops for trial by combat was scarcely unique to the Civil War. Even in World War II, which Americans entered with less enthusiasm than most previous wars, soldiers seemed anxious for the fray. "The anticipation of . . . getting into a fight stimulates a powerful excitement, which the men habitually refer to as 'eagerness,'" wrote two army psychiatrists during the war. "They become very restless for combat and impatient of delay. . . . The men seldom have any real, concrete notions of what combat is like. Their minds are full of romanticized, Hollywood versions of their future activity in combat, colored with vague ideas of being a hero. . . . They are not at all prepared for the nightmare experiences in store for them. . . . Combat is always a surprise and a shock, because there is no way of preparing for the emotional impact short of actual experience."[9]

Substitute Currier and Ives for Hollywood in this passage, and it

would serve as an accurate description of Civil War soldiers. Many of
them found their first experience of combat indeed a surprise and a
shock. An Ohio soldier who had written home before his first battle
that "Wee ar all big for a fight" told his wife afterwards: "Mary I went
into the fight in good hart but I never want to get in another it was
offal [awful] mary you cant form any idy how it was   the bulets and
cannon ball and shells flew thick as hail." A private in the 6th North
Carolina wrote his father after the first battle of Manassas: "Sutch a
day the booming of the cannon the ratling of the muskets you have
no idea how it was   I have turned threw that old Book of yours and
looked at the pictures and read a little about war but I did not no any
thing what it was."[10] A Texan penciled breathless diary entries during
and immediately after his first battle: "We are lying down in the dark,
actually scared nearly to death. . . . We hear amid all the roar of the
artillery zip-zip-zip bullets from the enemy. . . . *Whoopee* now comes
the business. . . . Oh what *is* the matter—is this the end of the
world?" A shell exploded nearby "killing one man and cutting off both
legs of his brother. The one that had his legs shot off turned his body
about half way to speak to his brother, not knowing that he was dead.
As soon as he saw his brother was dead, he takes his pistol (a 6
Shooter) puts it to his head and killed himself." Little wonder that a
Virginia private could write, after similar experiences, that "I have seen
enough of the glory of war. . . . I am sick of seeing dead men and
men's limbs torn from their bodies."[11]

Once they had seen the elephant, few Civil War soldiers were eager to see it again. Whether or not they had passed this test of "manhood" with "honor," their curiosity about the nature of battle was fulfilled, their ardor for a brush with the enemy sated. Rebel and Yankee
alike, a great many soldiers wrote home after their first battle in similar words: "I hope I will never be in another . . . no man can tell me
any thing about war I have got a plenty." "I am satisfied with fighting.
I wish the War was over." "You can never realize the severity of battle
and I hope it may never be my lot to go into another one."[12] A teen-
ager who enlisted in the 9th Indiana Cavalry in 1864 with visions of
glory in his head wrote after his first fight, against Nathan Bedford
Forrest's troopers, that he "got to see the Elephant at last and to tell
you the honest truth I dont care about seeing him very often any
more, for if there was eny fun in such work I couldent see it. . . . It
is not the thing it is braged up to be."[13]

When the romance and glory of war dissolved in the soldier's first battle, a veteran's solemnity replaced the recruit's eagerness. No outfit had been "more anxious . . . to get into a battle" than the 4th Alabama, wrote a captain in that regiment, but 190 casualties at First Manassas "has produced a visible change in the regiment. You hear much less hilarity and joyous songs. My own company has lost some of its best men." After the 26th Virginia's baptism of blood at Seven Pines, a lieutenant told his mother that " 'the boys' are not the same romping fellows they were at Glo[ucester] Pt. but a seriousness seems to have come over them all. They say they all wanted 'to get into a fight,' but they have had enough of it, until necessity compels them again to it."[14] A veteran captain in the 1st Maryland (Confederate) noted in 1863, a few months before he was killed at Gettysburg, that new recruits to the regiment "think it would be a disgrace never to have been in an engagement. I can appreciate their feeling and could once have expressed myself the same desire but now all such romance has vanished from my mind." When the 7th New York Heavy Artillery, which had spent almost two years in the Washington defenses without firing a shot in anger, received orders in May 1864 to move to the front as an infantry regiment, a sergeant "was awakened by the hilarious cheering of the men." Nine brutal months later, after losing an astounding 291 men killed and more than 500 wounded in action, the shattered remnant of the regiment indulged in "general noisy hilarity" when ordered to dull garrison duty in Baltimore.[15]

Long after reality had replaced romance in the soldiers' view of combat, the image conveyed by the press seemed unchanged. The "reports of newspaper correspondents that the troops are all 'eager for the fray,' " wrote a Minnesota sergeant to his wife in July 1862, are "simply all 'bosh.' I don't know any individual soldier who is at all anxious to be led, or *driven,* for that matter to another battle." The journalist who reported that "soldiers *are clamorous to be led against the enemy,*" commented a Massachusetts sergeant in November 1862, "is either a numb-skull, or else he has . . . never seen a 'grey back' and don't know how shells sound when they are bursting around a fellow." Confederate veterans made the same point. "There are very few men really eager for battle, and 'spoiling for a fight,' at this stage of the war," wrote a private in the 3rd Georgia to his sweetheart in 1863. "Perhaps you will think this a rather unchivalrous sentiment for a Southern soldier . . . but let me explain that we do not fear the foe with a cowardly fear, that would make us shrink from our duty to our country, but we have that undefinable dread which the knowledge of an unplesant task before us always occasions."[16]

The experiences of G.I.s in World War II paralleled those of Civil War soldiers. Before their drop behind German lines on D-Day, men in the elite 101st Airborne Division were "gung-ho." When the survivors returned to England to prepare for their next mission, "the boys aren't as enthusiastic or anxious to get it over with as they were before Normandy. Nobody wants to fight any more."[17] Yet fight they did, again and again, sustained by grim determination and unit pride. The same was true of many Civil War soldiers who said after their first battle that they never wanted to see another, but who nevertheless fought many more, sustained by that sense of "duty to our country" which the soldier in the 3rd Georgia expressed.

One finds repeatedly in soldiers' letters the sentiment that "I have no desire to get into another fight, but if duty calls I am ready to go." "All the money in the world would not *hire me* to go into another battle but I shall go cheerfully when I am ordered to." "I can tell you I don't care about being in another battle . . . but I have got to stand my chance with all the rest and I can do it with as much grace as any man in our company."[18] A soldier in the 2nd Iowa who had fought at Fort Donelson and Shiloh was "heartily sick of War & Battles and I look forward to the time with longing when *peace* will once more be restored," but so long as the war continued "I do not wish to be elsewhere than here for it is for My Countries Flag that I am fighting." Likewise a captain in the 46th North Carolina wrote after fighting in the Seven Days battles and at Antietam that "I would be willing for the war to close properly now without acquiring any more glory—but still am perfectly willing to keep on until the war is properly ended"— that is, with Confederate independence.[19]

Of course not all soldiers felt this way. The initial combat experience produced a winnowing effect in many regiments, with the chaff drifting to the rear or finding their ways into bombproof noncombatant duties. Among them were some who had expressed the greatest eagerness to fight. "I find that men who talk the most are not always the bravest," wrote a sixteen-year-old farm boy who passed for eighteen and enlisted in the 25th Wisconsin. "Maybe they are more anxious to die for their country than I am but from what I know of them I am doubtful." In that regiment's first action "all at once there came the ring of rifles on every side. The ranks were broken and men supposed to be brave as lions dodged right and left, while others fired their guns out of pure fright with no enemy in sight." This young soldier and the hard core of his regiment settled down and became effective fighting men. But in this and other regiments some shook themselves loose, agreeing with the sentiments of a Missouri Confederate officer that "visionaries may talk of dying gloriously on the battle field . . . but I am old fogie enough to admit that it will require some very vivid sketches of fancy to make me prefer it to living." A good many men pulled strings to get assigned to the quartermaster service or some other rear-echelon position. "I want to get somewhere where I can get out of this hard fighting," wrote a North Carolina lieutenant in 1863. "Some men have to fill easy positions why shouldn't I be one of them."[20]

EVEN AFTER THEY had seen the elephant and found it ugly, however, most of the 1861–62 volunteers remained determined to fight. The belief in duty, honor, and country that had caused them to enlist in the first place held them to the firing line. But the fighters, no less than the skulkers, had to cope with the battlefield's most pervasive presence: fear. Because the conventions of masculinity equated admission of fear with cowardice, however, many soldiers were reluctant to confess what surely all felt. Some Civil War soldiers grasped intuitively, and more acquired by experience, the modern understanding that courage is not the absence of fear but the mastery of it. Nevertheless, to admit fear openly, even to family or close friends, came hard for them.

Some resorted to denial. "I never feel fear at all," wrote a rough-hewn farmer in the 10th Virginia Cavalry to his wife. "I am getting so used to the cannon balls flying over my head that I don't mind them." A New York captain boasted after his first battle that "I have yet to feel the sickening anxiety so often spoken of as affecting men going into battle."[21] A private in the 22nd Wisconsin wrote home after his initial combat experience: "Strange as it may appear to you who know me . . . I never once felt the sensation of fear." A New Jersey soldier claimed that he "felt just as cool and no more excited than if i had been shooting birds in the woods," while an Ohio corporal assured his parents that "I have been scared worse many a time when I was at home working on the farm."[22]

Such bravado arouses suspicion that these soldiers did protest too

much. Others who feigned a nonchalant attitude toward combat unwittingly betrayed something quite different. Lieut. Col. Rutherford
B. Hayes of the 23rd Ohio recorded in his diary that he had felt no
more anxiety upon going into his first battle than when rising to address the court as a trial lawyer. Indeed, "as we waited to form, we
joked a good deal. . . . [Officers] and privates—all were jolly and
excited by turns." A Virginia officer noted that "the nearer we are to
the enemy the greater seems the inclination to jest and merriment."
A private in the 39th Ohio told his wife that "as for fear there seemed
to be very little on the battlefield, men joke and laugh just the same
as they do in other places."[23] This joking and laughing, of course, was
a way of discharging the buildup of nervous tension. Whether these
soldiers recognized this cathartic function is unclear; in their writings
they gave no sign of doing so. Much of the bantering was gallows
humor. A New York private quoted a messmate who had become company cook: "He says his business now as cook is 'to fat up you lean
buggers for the next killen' time.' These solemn jokes are very common
in camp."[24]

Some soldiers who were loath to admit fear came up with a variety
of euphemisms instead. "The feeling of *fear* did not enter my breast,"
wrote an Alabama private; rather "it was a painful nervous anxiety." A
young lieutenant in the 2nd North Carolina described "the musketry
and booming of artillery" as "fearful" but claimed that "I had no fear
at all but was perfectly carried away by the excitement." George Whitman, Walt Whitman's brother and a sergeant in the 51st New York,
refused to use the F word but acknowledged that "it was mighty trying
to a fellows nerves as the balls was flying around pretty thick."[25]

But as time went on, soldiers who had proved their courage under
fire grew more candid in admitting fear. A captain in the 39th North
Carolina, a veteran of several battles, conceded that he was always
"*badly scared*. . . . I am not as brave as I thought I was. I never
wanted out of a place as bad in my life." A young planter from Louisiana who enlisted as a private in the elite Washington Artillery wrote
to his wife after Shiloh: "I tell you May! I have never had such feelings
in my life and would have given a great deal several times, if I could
have been away."[26] During the battle of Antietam, wrote a captain in
the 108th New York, "I don't pretend to say I wasn't afraid, and I must
say that I did not see a face but that turned pale or hear a voice that
did not tremble." A corporal in the 26th Virginia wrote to his hero-

FOR CAUSE AND COMRADES

worshipping younger brother: "You may say what you please about not being scared & all that, but . . . I don't believe there is any man who is not a little agitated when he hears the roar of the cannon."[27]

Nearly all soldiers agreed that the time of utmost anxiety occurred *before* the actual fighting, as the tension mounted while they waited to go into action. "It is worse for a soldier to wait for a battle to begin than it is to do the fighting," wrote a Rhode Island veteran of several battles. "A man's heart is put in a FLUTTER by the suspense," admitted a Georgia corporal. The strain was greatest when soldiers were compelled to endure enemy fire without a chance of shooting back. "Oh how my heart palpitated!" wrote a sergeant in the 33rd Illinois describing the waiting under heavy fire for orders to go forward in the assault on Confederate trenches at Vicksburg on May 22, 1863. "The sweat from off my face run in a stream from the tip ends of my whiskers. God only knows all that passed through my mind. Twice I exclaimed aloud . . . 'My God, why don't they order us to charge.' "[28]

Action broke the unbearable tension of waiting. "As soon as we got orders to advance fear was gone," marveled a soldier in the 39th Pennsylvania in words that were echoed by a corporal in the 89th New York: "[When we] started all dread as far as I was concerned left and it seemed as though I didnt care a d—n." Describing his first battle, a Massachusetts sergeant told his mother that "before we went into it, I could not help feeling a little afraid of those bullets. But once I had discharged my rifle, I did not mind the bullets buzzing around my ears in the least. . . . All our men felt the same I afterward found."[29]

Another way that soldiers relieved tension once they went into action was to yell at the top of their voices. Such was probably the origin of the famous Rebel Yell. For many soldiers, yelling came unbidden, perhaps an instinctive throwback to their cavemen ancestors. "I always said, if I ever went into a charge, I wouldn't holler," declared a soldier in the 46th Mississippi. "But the very first time I fired off my gun, I hollered as loud as I could, and I hollered every breath till we stopped!" Yankees yelled just as loudly, though in a deeper pitch. "Such a yell as ascended from our Regt. as we rushed up the hill," wrote a Rhode Island lieutenant after the first battle of Manassas, "has seldom been heard since the Indian war whoop has become extinct." On at least one occasion Union soldiers even sang while fighting. A brigade commander in the Army of the Potomac rode along his lines during the battle of Hatcher's Run in February 1865 and found that "our boys were singing at the top of their lungs 'Rally Round the Flag, Boys,' and in the finest spirits imagenable. At the same time they were loading and firing away." [30]

Many soldiers expressed surprise at their own coolness once the fighting began. "I did not feel afraid as I thought I should," wrote a twenty-year-old farmer's son in the 81st New York. "I was surprised at myself I expected to be excited and trembling but instead I took everything as a matter of course," explained a young Vermont cavalryman to his sister.[31] A captain in the 108th New York admitted to shaky knees before the attack on Bloody Lane at Antietam, but "once over the fence at the top of the hill I was never more cool in my life. I don't know how it was, but I was perfectly indifferent, and had no more fear than I should have in your bathtub at home." Similarly a Massachusetts captain wrote home after his first two battles: "I was astonished that I felt so little fear while in battle. My mind was wholly absorbed in controlling my men & directing their fire . . . & it was only when some one near me fell wounded or dead that I fully realized the terrible reality of the scene." [32]

My mind was wholly absorbed. Several soldiers tried to explain insensibility to danger by their keyed-up concentration on the task at hand. The chaos of combat "quickened all your ideas to their highest pitch," wrote one Union officer. "At such times," added a Massachusetts infantryman, "we have so much to do that we hardly have time to be scared." [33] A New Hampshire private admitted "a dread of [combat] at first when I know I have to go in, but . . . it isn't long before you won't think or care whether you are in it or not . . . for a man in the heat of battle thinks nor cares for nothing but to make the enemy run." The most thoughtful analysis of this phenomenon came from a New York artillery officer who repeatedly found himself the target of enemy sharpshooters as well as enemy cannons. "Whatever may have been the cause, whether it was having so much to do, or whether it was the excitement, or both together, I know not, but I cannot recall having felt the least personal fear while under fire," he wrote in his diary. "Could there be a stronger proof that courage is merely a nonrealization of the danger one is in owing to excitement, responsibility, or something of the sort?" [34]

That "something of the sort" was undoubtedly a jolt of adrenalin released into the bloodstream by fear or rage. This physiological response to emotional trauma vastly increases the body's capacity for "flight or fight." The more extreme the stress the greater the amount of adrenalin and norepinephrine secreted by the adrenal glands, giving an individual almost superhuman strength and agility. The most stressful situation imaginable is combat. The first impulse of men under fire is an overwhelming desire to flee the danger. Many soldiers do run away, or cower into frozen immobility. But if discipline or willpower or some other factor nerves them to overcome the impulse to flight, when they go into action the flood of adrenalin turns many soldiers into preternatural killing machines oblivious to danger and fear. This hyped-up behavior has been variously described by psychologists or by soldiers themselves as combat frenzy, fighting madness, or battle rage.[35]

Civil War soldiers knew nothing of the chemical changes in their bodies during combat—adrenalin was not identified and named until 1901. But their descriptions of feelings and behavior in battle provide fascinating insights into the consequences of those chemical changes. Yankee and Rebel alike, they spoke of "behaving like wild men." "No tongue, or pen can express the excitement." "Our men became insane, howled and rushed forward."[36] Despite much previous combat experience, the major of the 47th Ohio wrote his wife after the battle of Atlanta in 1864: "I had no idea that I had such determination, such stubborness or strength. I was almost frantic, yet perfectly sane—directed the entire line. . . . I saw men perform prodigies, display the most unparalleled valor—One man Joseph Bedol Co 'D' was surrounded & knocked down by rebels, he came to, jumped up, killed and wounded three & knocked a fourth down with his fist." A sergeant in the 7th Indiana explained to his fiancée that "a man may & will become so infuriated by the din & dangers of a bloody fight, that if he ever had a tender heart it will [be] turned to stone & his evry desire [be] for blood." Describing his feelings at the battle of Malvern Hill, a Massachusetts lieutenant told his mother that "during that terrible 4 or 5 hours that we were there I had not a thought of fear or anything like fear, on the contrary I wanted to rush them hand to hand . . . and yet will you believe it? all day before the battle I dreaded it . . . and yet it seemed as the moment came all fear and all excitement passed away and I cared no more than I would in a common hail storm. How curious it is."[37]

The rush of adrenalin could overcome illness or debility. A Confederate brigade commander was sick in an ambulance as he approached the Antietam battlefield, but when he heard the firing and saw his men going in, "I got well again—mounted my horse & overtook my brigade just before it came up with the enemy. I never felt better or stronger than during the whole time the battle lasted [but] when it was over I found myself completely prostrated, and lay in a stupor all the next day." An anemic Yale graduate who somehow passed the physical exam (he died of Bright's disease after the war at age twenty-six) wrote his mother in wonder after his first battle that they had charged the rebels "yelling like a pack of demons [and] so much excited that the double-quick was altogether too slow a pace for us so on we went every man for himself and each striving to get into the [enemy] breastwork before the others. . . . How I crossed that ditch is something I cannot explain."[38]

Even wounds failed to slow some men in the grip of combat frenzy. A private in the crack 83rd Pennsylvania, which lost an extraordinary sixty-one men killed or mortally wounded at Gaines Mill and another forty-one at Malvern Hill four days later, described in letters home his actions in these battles. At Gaines Mill his two tentmates were wounded next to him and the colonel was killed nearby. "After that, they tell me, I acted like a madman. . . . I was stronger than I had been for a month [he had been sick] and a kind of desperation seized me. Scenes that would have unnerved me at other times had no effect. I snatched a gun from a man who was shot through the head, as he staggered and fell. . . . I was blazing away at the rascals not ten rods [55 yards] off when a ball struck my gun," splintered it and drove some of the splinters into his shoulder. He grabbed another rifle but a bullet clipped part of the stock and another one glanced off his canteen and went partway into his thigh. "I pulled it out, and, more maddened than ever, I rushed in again. . . . A buckshot struck me in the left eyebrow," but he kept firing because "the feeling that was uppermost in my mind was a desire to kill as many rebels as I could."

Somehow this soldier stayed in the ranks during the weary retreat to the James River. By the time the remnant of his regiment reached Malvern Hill, "we were so worn out by excitement, fatigue, and want of sleep" that they were zombies. But when the rebels attacked, the men woke up and "we poured it into them as fast as we could load and fire. . . . I felt exultant. . . . It was more the work of fiends than of human beings."[39]

Another term for this state of super-adrenalized fury is "combat narcosis," because its effect "acts almost like a hallucinogenic drug." An historian who is a World War II veteran described it as the "glaze of war" that enabled men in combat "to separate themselves psychologically from what was going on" and to "advance not in defiance of death but rather because the battlefield and therefore the danger of death, seemed somehow distant. After battle, most people returned to normal . . . but at the time the glaze of war was, for those lucky enough to experience it, a powerful narcotic."[40]

Several Civil War soldiers noted with awe this phenomenon in their own experience. "There is one thing in the human mind almost inexplicable," wrote a fifty-year-old captain in the 85th New York, "and that is the almost entirely dreamlike state [in battle]—without any realization of fear." A Texas artillery captain referred to "that wild hallucination which none but those in the brunt of battle can feel." At the battle of Iuka, wrote a sergeant in the 5th Iowa which suffered 40 percent casualties in that engagement, "there was a strange unaccountable lack of *feeling* with me. . . . Out of battle and in a battle, I find myself two different beings."[41]

One's reservoirs of adrenalin are not unlimited, however. The end of a battle, or even a brief lull, causes a profound reaction of lassitude, exhaustion, even illness as the body tries to restore its chemical balance. "I stood it remarkably well as long as there was any marching or fighting going on," wrote a captain in the 33rd North Carolina after the battle of Seven Pines, "but after all the excitement and every thing was over my whole system seemed to have given way I was right sick for a few days." A Connecticut captain told his mother that "I never felt so perfectly above all fear as during the heavy fighting in the morning" at Drewry's Bluff in 1864, but afterward, "I was so thoroughly worn out that I doubt whether I could have reached camp if I had not begged a ride in our Ambulance." After a repulse and a fallback to their own lines at the battle of New Hope Church in 1864, a private in the 28th Mississippi "vomited 'like a very dog' & . . . threw myself [down], completely prostrated, upon the ground, panting with the white slime running from my mouth."[42]

Such a physical reaction usually occurred after the fighting was over. But it could also happen in the middle of a battle, especially if the momentum turned from an advance to a retreat. The psychological shock produced by such a reversal could cause a sudden relapse from fearlessness to abject terror. This phenomenon helps explain how a retreat could turn into a rout. A Pennsylvania corporal described one such experience. After holding firm against Confederate attacks for hours at Gaines Mill on June 27, 1862, the Union line began to leak stragglers like a small breach in a dam that grew larger until it suddenly gave way with a rush. "When the break was made, a perfect confusion ensued," and the terrified men began running. "To attempt to rally them at this point was folly; a sort of panic appeared to have taken hold of them" and "one could call it none other than a perfect rout." The same adrenalin that had sustained their fight now hastened their flight.[43]

During the post-battle letdown, fears banished during the heat of combat often returned with redoubled intensity. "A battle seems more dangerous in thinking it over afterwards than it does right in the midst of it," wrote an Illinois officer to his wife after Perryville. "The mind can discover dangers while thinking back over it that were not apparent while the fight was on." Describing the "fever and excitement of the action" that kept him going through the Seven Days battles, a Massachusetts captain began "to feel a sickness at the stomach" after the fighting ended. Then the "groans and gasping and more horrors" in the field hospital and the "poor fallen bodies" waiting for burial in a mass grave "haunts me like a nightmare." A New York officer likewise reported after the Gettysburg campaign that "the glorious excitement" had borne him up for several days, but "after the fight is over, then one realizes what has been going on. Then he sees the wounded, hears their groans. . . . Such scenes completely unman me. I can stand up and fight, but cannot endure the sight of suffering, particularly of our own men."[44]

Many soldiers fought battles over again in nightmares, which "frighten me more than ever the fight did when I was wide awake," in the words of a captain in the 21st Alabama who led his company at Shiloh. For two weeks after that battle another Alabamian, an artillery lieutenant, dreamed every night "that I was in the midst of the fight, and the bullets would whistle by me and the cannon roar just as they had" during the battle.[45] A Louisiana veteran of several battles was unnerved by his experience at Stones River; for two weeks afterward "in my sleep I see nightly the gastly upturned faces of the dead, and here the groans of the mangled and dying, the hissing of the shot and shell." Yankees experienced similar nightmares. "Even when I sleep," wrote a soldier in the 10th Massachusetts which lost a quarter of its men at Fair Oaks, "I hear the whistling of the shells and the shouts and groans, and to sum it up in two words it is *horrible*."[46]

The soldiers quoted here were not incapacitated for further combat. Although they exhibited some of the symptoms of what was called shell shock in World War I, combat exhaustion or battle fatigue in

World War II, and post-traumatic stress disorder today, all of them continued to function as combat soldiers. But they were changed forever by their experiences. No longer were they anxious for the fray. Most were men in their late teens or twenties. Although some of them had known the death of a parent or sibling, like most young people they had not previously confronted the prospect of their own mortality. Even if the "excitement" of battle had made them oblivious of danger during the fighting, the sober contemplation afterward of what they had narrowly escaped—and of what some of their comrades had *not* escaped—gave them serious pause. Next time they might not be so lucky.

In August 1861 a young sergeant in the 14th Virginia told his mother (as if it were news to her) that "this thing called dying is an awful thing to think of. I never had such a feeling on me before as I did when Sam Pierce & that other fellow was hollering & dying both at the same time." A soldier in the 6th Georgia wrote his wife after the Seven Days battles describing "the scenes of anguish & of pain, the dead & the dying . . . the stiffened bodies lie grasping in death the arms they bravely bore, with glazed eyes, and features blackened by rapid decay. . . . Who trods a battle ground, but shrinks at the thought, that he too may find a resting place there."[47]

When illusions of glory and eagerness to see the elephant were gone, would the motives of duty, honor, and patriotism be sufficient to prod the soldier forward in his next battle now that he knew from experience the potential consequences? "I have spent much time in analyzing my feelings and those of others befor going into battles," wrote a twenty-two-year-old Connecticut veteran wise beyond his years in 1864. "It is the fear of Death that makes men cowards." After the battle of Fredericksburg in which the 10th New York suffered 36 percent casualties, including most of its officers, the junior captain left in command of the regiment wrote home that "it was a perfect slaughter house . . . you would have been astonished to see the men come up & face death line after line but it was no use, I am glad it is over & thank God I am out of that one safely and dont want to go in another like that. . . . I dont think I could get twenty-five to the front again."[48]

This regiment had fought in six battles during the past six months and had been bled down to 130 men. Modern studies of combat effectiveness have found that soldiers' skills and efficiency improve with experience through their first three or four battles or their first twenty or twenty-five days of continuous combat, or through six to eight months of intermittent combat. "Beyond that, however, their skills continue but their enthusiasm and energy fade away. They get to know too much about the terrible risks which combat entails, and they take deliberate measures to keep out of it whenever they can."[49] A Confederate veteran of four battles and several skirmishes in the 1st Virginia of Pickett's division anticipated these conclusions when he wrote after his capture at Gettysburg that he had felt increasing anxiety in each of his battles, "and I believe that soldiers generally do not fear death less because of their repeated escape from its jaws. For, in every battle they see so many new forms of death, see so many frightful and novel kinds of mutilation . . . and appreciate so highly their deliverance from destruction, that their dread of incurring the like fearful perils unnerves them for each succeeding conflict."[50]

Yet somehow most of these men did nerve themselves for succeeding conflicts. The armies would have collapsed had they not done so. What kind of external, institutional means and—more important—internal resources motivated them to risk their lives, not only the first time, but again and again?

CHAPTER 4

IF I FLINCHED I
WAS RUINED

THE TRADITIONAL MEANS of motivating soldiers to fight are
training, discipline, and leadership. Civil War volunteer regiments were notoriously deficient in the first, weak in the second, and initially shaky in the third. The 16,000-man peacetime army
at the beginning of 1861 mushroomed into Union and Confederate
armies totaling nearly a million men a year later by do-it-yourself mo-
bilizations centered in communities and states. The volunteers considered themselves civilians temporarily in uniform to do a necessary job
as quickly as possible so they could return to their homes and families.
In most volunteer regiments the men elected their company officers,
few of whom had combat experience. Many regiments went into action scarcely a month or two after they had been organized.

Under these circumstances training was minimal and haphazard,
especially in the early regiments. They were lucky if they had any
officers who knew something about drill and tactics. Most officers had
to burn the midnight oil trying to master William Hardee's or Silas
Casey's *Tactics*. Infantry training consisted mainly of the manual of
arms and close-order drill, with a little bayonet exercise and target
practice thrown in when time and equipment were available.

Drill taught the basic evolutions of column and line that had not changed much for a century or more. Soldiers' letters are full of references to drilling several hours a day—not always complimentary references. "A soldier is not his own man," complained a young Indiana private to his sister. Take drill, for example. "You fall in and start. You here feel your inferiority, even the Sargeants is hollering at you to close up, Ketch step, dress to the right, and sutch like, the man in youre reer is complaining of youre gun not being held up. Perhaps you will let this [cause you to] make some remark when you will be imediately tolde by a Lietenant to be silent in ranks or you will be put in the guard house."[1]

Officers, especially those from the old regular army, saw drill as an essential means to inculcate the habit of unquestioning obedience. "*Drill and discipline* will make good soldiers of any man," wrote a captain in the 85th New York. "In order to get men to fight well they must be well fed and then discipline and drill will do the rest." This was easier said than done, however, in an army of independent-minded citizen volunteers who had elected many of their officers. American white males were the most individualistic, democratic people on the face of the earth in 1861. They did not take kindly to authority, discipline, obedience. "I like to see discipline," wrote a Pennsylvania artillery sergeant, "and there can be discipline in the volunteers & still be a good feeling between officers & men. The Regulars are different their officers follow the army for a Business and the men for a living . . . while in the volunteers we are . . . actuated by certain motives with a view to the successful termination of the principles at stake therefore I dont think it necessary to be so strick or exact . . . in the volunteers." A lieutenant in the 43rd North Carolina tried to strike a balance. "Napoleon the first said 'a man to be a good Soldier must first be converted into a machine,' & I am inclined after some experience to concur with him," he wrote in 1863. "I do think however that there is a degree of manly, personal independence which, if properly restrained & properly respected, adds greatly to the virtues & essentials of a Soldier. For if this be destroyed, & ignored, & we can come to the servile belief that we are slaves, then our duties would have to be dragged out of us."[2]

The comparison of a private's lot to that of a slave was a common one—especially among privates. "We are just like Negroes," wrote an Ohio soldier in 1861, a sentiment echoed by a Mississippi private who had first-hand experience with slavery, for his father was a planter. The major of his regiment ordered the men around "as if they were a lot of negroes. I am in favor of discipline but not of tyranny."[3] Many privates vowed not to accept such treatment. "I like a soldiers duty well enough," wrote an enlisted man in the 27th Massachusetts, "but I do not like to have a master [and] to be drove like a niggar. . . . I think I am just as good as enny boddy." A yeoman farmer who enlisted in a North Carolina artillery battery declared angrily that "I valenteard in this bloddy ware for to fight for my cuntery [and] for my rights . . . and I am determind to have my rights in the company or I will fight every bloddy officer in the company . . . they never was a man born yet that cold shit on me for I think I am just as good as they make them."[4]

Throughout the war, officers continued to complain about the deficiencies of discipline in their volunteer regiments. Robert Gould Shaw, a captain in the 2nd Massachusetts, wrote in 1862 that because of a "want of discipline . . . a part of the men skulk . . . in every battle. . . . Their behavior depends almost entirely on the discipline." Two years later Sydney S. Champion, a captain in the 28th Mississippi and owner of the plantation on which the battle of Champion's Hill was fought in 1863, declared that "the great want in our army is thorough discipline. Too many officers do not exercise that authority relative to the discipline of the soldiers—because they are looking forward to *civil promotion* [after the war] hence are afraid of offending their men by adopting rigid rules . . . hence as a body—in the hour of danger—they are inefficient—because straggling *is the rule.*"[5]

These assessments are too negative. Civil War armies could not have inflicted and endured such carnage had they remained undisciplined mobs. Good volunteer regiments—and there were many—learned from experience the value of discipline. Soldiers even came to see the benefit of the much-derided drill, which instilled a sense of cohesion and order, enabling them to maneuver as a unit in battle. The war furnished numerous examples of officers who put their panicky men through a drill routine while waiting under fire to go into action in order to steady their nerves. "In the midst of this tempest of bullets . . . while men were falling all around us," wrote a New York corporal in 1864, "Lieut. Col. Bates put our regiment through the 'Manual of Arms.' . . . It was a good thing for our men, and kept them cool and collected."[6]

The most extreme form of discipline was coercion: the use or threat of deadly force to compel a soldier into the firing line against his will. This was the preferred method of eighteenth-century profes-

sional armies, whose officers often came from the aristocracy and enlisted men from the lowest classes. Soldiers in the Prussian army of
Frederick the Great stood firm under fire because they feared their
officers more than they feared the enemy. The same was true of the
British redcoats. Americans during the Revolution had expressed hor-
rified contempt of this coercion, so alien to the republican society of
freemen they were fighting to achieve. Yet George Washington found
it necessary to use some of the same compulsion in the Continental
Army, and echoes of it survived in the volunteer armies of the Civil
War.

After the battle of Bull Run in July 1861 a Union lieutenant wrote
home that "when we first went into action, our men . . . seemed
inclined to back out, but we stationed ourselves behind them and
threatened to shoot the first man that turned." This occurred in a
battalion of regulars, but officers in volunteer regiments reported similar methods. Even the crack 20th Massachusetts had its share of
skulkers; at the battle of Fair Oaks Captain Oliver Wendell Holmes,
Jr., found it necessary to give one soldier "a smart rap over the back-
sides with the edge of my sword—and stood with my revolver & swore
I'd shoot the first who ran." At the battle of Third Winchester Confederate General Bryan Grimes kept his brigade of North Carolinians in
line while other units were breaking by "threatening to blow the brains
out of the first man who left ranks."[7]

As the war went on, the armies implemented coercion with heavier
firepower than an officer's revolver. A soldier in the 15th Indiana related one anecdote that would have been funny had it not been deadly
serious. At the battle of Shiloh many green regiments on both sides
broke and ran, sometimes led by their officers. On the Union side,
Ohio regiments were reputed to have been the worst. After the battle
this Indiana soldier happened to be camped next to the 53rd Ohio
and overheard General William T. Sherman dress them down, officers
and men alike, for nearly an hour. "Of all the rebukes that I ever heard
men get he gave them, calling them cowards, dastards and evry low
name he could think of, telling them they were a disgrace to the nation and finally wound up by promising them that at the next battle
they should be put in the foremost rank with a battery of Artillery
immediately behind them and then if they attempted to run they
would open on them with grape and canister."[8]

Whether Sherman carried out his threat is unknown; in any event
cavalry rather than artillery became the preferred arm for this service.

In big set-piece battles like Gaines Mill, Second Manassas, Antietam, Fredericksburg, and others, cavalry were of limited value except for patrolling flanks or fighting dismounted, but their mobility and the intimidating effect of horses made them useful for stopping skulkers and forcing them back into line. At the battle of Kinston in North Carolina in December 1862, a trooper in the 3rd New York Cavalry reported that his company patrolled the rear of the Union line. "It was our duty to keep Stragglers back or men that would fall out of ranks for fear of getting shot there were from 4 to 6 of us behind each brigade." The 3rd Virginia Cavalry performed the same function for the Confederate army at Seven Pines, "doing the most disagreeable of all work, catching stragglers from the army and sending them back," according to a lieutenant in that regiment. In the Army of the Potomac, reported a New Hampshire private in August 1862, "I have been into battle when the lines of cavalry were drawn up in our rear, so that if a man attempted to run, they would stop him or take his head off and it has been done to my knowledge."[9]

Despite this observation, cavalrymen proved reluctant to shoot soldiers wearing the same uniform. A half-dozen troopers stationed behind a brigade were a leaky sieve. Alarmed by the large number of stragglers in the Antietam campaign, Robert E. Lee ordered the formation of provost guards in the Army of Northern Virginia, usually consisting of a sharpshooter infantry company for each brigade. A lieutenant in the 2nd North Carolina commanded such a company in Stonewall Jackson's corps at Chancellorsville. Describing Jackson's famous flank attack on May 2, this lieutenant wrote home that "at 5 p.m. we . . . commenced our advance upon the enemy. The sharpshooters were deployed about a hundred yards in the rear of the brigade, with orders to shoot every one who fell to the rear, unless wounded."[10] This policy seemed to work, if a Northern soldier's letter to his father is reliable evidence. "I will tell you how the Rebels fight so well," he wrote in January 1863 at a low point in Union fortunes. "They have File Closers behind the Regts. of Infantry, & if a man falls out of the ranks they shoot him on the spot. . . . Now if our men did the same we should not meet with so many defeats."[11]

By 1863, however, Union and Confederate armies alike had designated units of provost guards to drive stragglers into line. These units functioned with varying effectiveness. It was not easy to get them to shoot fellow soldiers. But a New York lieutenant commented that when some Union regiments proved reluctant to obey orders to attack at Cold Harbor on June 3, 1864, "one Regt. was driven out of our intrenchments by the Provost Gd. at the point of the Bayonett." Some veteran Union regiments that were filled out with conscripts, substitutes, and bounty men in 1864 had their own way of dealing with the high quotient of sneaks among such recruits. "They will be under a hot fire from front and rear," commented a sergeant in the 9th New Jersey, "because the old Volunteers shoot cowards from their own ranks as well as the rebels. This is done in our army every day, but we do not see no account of it in the papers, every man that is killed is not killed by the rebels, so a coward is in a rather bad position."[12]

A slightly more subtle way to compel unwilling soldiers to fight was to court-martial "cowards" and shame them publicly. Both armies applied this method to officers and enlisted men alike. A soldier in the 147th Pennsylvania wrote home after Chancellorsville (the regiment's first battle) that "2 Captains have resigned, also a Lieut on the strength of charges being preferred against them for cowardice." A private in the veteran 2nd Minnesota boasted that "there are few cowards here and those that are, are drummed Before the Regt on dress Parade." There were several variants of this process. A corporal in the 1st Minnesota noted in his diary that "the provost guard of our Div. passes through the different camps 'drumming out' a man said to belong to the 20th Mass. Vols. The prisoner had a board tied to his back labeled 'Coward.' " Another soldier, this one in the 1st Minnesota itself, was sentenced to a year at hard labor for "misbehavior before the enemy."[13]

The Confederates seemed to devise harsher punishments. "This evening our Brigade is ordered out to witness a horrible sight," wrote a private in the 1st Virginia, part of Pickett's division. "One of the 24th Va. Infantry being tried by court martial for cowardice at the battle of Sharpsburg is condemned to be whipped publicly and then dishonorably dismissed." The whole brigade stood at attention to watch the "wretched creature" get thirty-nine lashes on his bare back. It was not lost on these Southern soldiers that thirty-nine lashes was a typical punishment for slaves. In the eyes of many Confederate commanders, skulking out of battle was as bad as desertion. As a deterrent they sometimes executed skulkers. "Several men have been sentenced to be shot for running out of the Fredericksburg fight," wrote a lieutenant in the 12th Georgia of Jackson's corps. "It will have a good effect. . . . The evil of straggling is almost entirely cured."[14]

Some officers tried a carrot and stick approach to motivating their men, not only threatening punishment but also promising rewards for good behavior. The colonel of the 1st Massachusetts made a brief speech to his regiment before going into action on the Yorktown lines in April 1862. "He told every Capt. to shoot the first man who showed any cowardice, and to watch those who were *brave* and tell him, for, said he, 'many who are now privates in the Mass. 1st will have commissions in a few months, if they behave well,' " wrote a private to his parents. "I am going to try for one, so look out." Eight days later he was killed.[15]

Throughout the war, however, ambition for promotion and reputation stimulated many soldiers. "I didn't come to remain and return a common soldier," wrote a banker's son who enlisted as a private in the 5th Louisiana. "Give me a chance & I'll bet I come home an officer."[16] Again and again in soldiers' letters occur such phrases as: "I am so anxious to have some opportunity of distinguishing myself." "I am agoing to endeavor to make a reputation for myself." "I am a little ambitious and want them at home to know that I am conducting myself in the army with credit to myself and the family of little boys and girls at home. . . . Tell the chilren about my promotion and teach them that they have gained something by it."[17]

The Civil War had its share of glory hunters whose aspirations for promotion did not endear them to men under their command. A soldier in the 95th Illinois censured his colonel, who "is looking for Stars and is willing to sacrifice every man in his Regt to accomplish his aims." This colonel did not win his stars; he was killed leading the regiment at Brices Crossroads.[18]

THE PHRASE "FIGHTING drunk" suggests another kind of incentive to combat. Throughout history, soldiers have fortified themselves with liquid courage before going into battle. Many soldiers at Agincourt were "less than sober"; British regiments at Waterloo fought in squares with a barrel of gin or whisky in the center; the Soviets often gave soldiers a generous shot of vodka before attacks in World War II.[19]

Did Civil War soldiers nerve themselves with spirits before going into combat? Some unquestionably did—especially officers, who had more access to liquor than did enlisted men. There were several egregious examples of high-ranking officers so drunk during a battle that they could scarcely stand up. Soldiers' letters also refer occasionally to an issue of whisky rations—but usually before they were to perform heavy fatigue duty in adverse conditions, like building a bridge while standing waist-deep in cold water.

References to a liquor ration before combat are extremely rare. More common—but highly suspect—are references to *enemy* soldiers drunk on whisky or, even more implausibly, a concoction of whisky and gunpowder. A Union sergeant who marveled at the repeated Confederate attacks on his position at Malvern Hill wrote to a friend: "It was not moral courage that made the rebels fight so but it was the whiskey and gunpowder administered by their *demon like* leaders. I saw men delerious with it and picked up canteens that were filled with it." At the battle of Atlanta, according to a private in the 25th Wisconsin, "the rebel soldiers it seems were crazed with gunpowder and whiskey given them to make them brave." Not to be outdone, a Confederate officer attributed the "unwonted impetuosity and dash" of Union attacks at Spotsylvania and Cold Harbor to "the strongest whisky. . . . Some of the Yankees were so drunk when they charged that they could hardly stand on their legs"—a curious example of impetuosity and dash.[20]

And so it went. Such stories are a good example of how soldiers live by rumor. The sober fact was that liquid courage was marginal and exceptional in Civil War armies—with the notorious exception of some high-ranking officers, most of whom proved to be abject failures. The lieutenant colonel of the 122nd Illinois was on the mark when he wrote to his wife in 1864: "I would like to correct the idea that prevails in the North in regard to the use of whisky in the army. In the field the rule is so far as my experience goes that there is none used." Some soldiers and more officers drank too much in camp or garrison, "but it ceases with marching orders and consequently no very great Eavil grows out of it."[21]

STUDIES OF COMBAT motivation focus on leadership as a key factor in the fighting effectiveness of a unit. Perhaps this emphasis is not surprising, since many of these studies are intended for the training of officers. Nevertheless, most Civil War soldiers would have agreed that the quality of their officers had a great deal to do with their willingness and ability to fight. They would also have agreed that the two most important criteria for a good officer were concern for the welfare of his men and leadership by example—that is, personal courage and a willingness to do anything he asked his men to do.[22]

Although combat leadership by example was probably the foremost single attribute of a good officer in the Civil War, the soldiers' first official contacts with their officers came in training camp. The trust and liking between officers and men that developed or failed to develop in their time together before combat had a great deal to do with how well the unit performed in battle. In their uncensored letters both enlisted men and officers wrote candidly about that relationship.

Company officers generally came from the same community or county as their men. They were several years older than enlisted men on the average, with more education and a higher social status. They often promised parents to take care of their "boys" in the army. The best of these officers took an almost paternal interest in the men. "The colonel of a Regiment in camp is compelled to be a father to a large family who call on him for every thing," wrote the colonel of the 54th Ohio. Many company officers felt the same way. A popular thirty-four-year-old captain in the 27th Massachusetts who was later killed in action told his brother in 1861 that a captain "must not only attend to their drill & obedience to orders, but he must look after their personal habits, their cleanliness, must listen to their little complaints, settle personal disputes & take as much care of them as of the same number of little children."[23]

Like most paternal relationships, this one had a hard edge of authority. The captain of a Virginia cavalry company explained to his wife that "to keep 60 or 70 raw, undisciplined troops in proper subjection—to instruct them, attend to all their wants—to gratify and deny them—to keep up their spirits—to punish and reward and all the while retain their respect and regard is no easy task." Sometimes there was an element of calculation in the officer's concern for his men. The major of the 78th Illinois visited the sick and wounded of his regiment every day "because I thought it my duty. The sick soldiers like to have their comrads visit them and especialy their officers, for [then] they think that the officers care something for them."[24] But the paternal affection was usually genuine. A captain in the 46th Pennsylvania who returned from leave to his regiment in 1864 really meant it when he wrote that he was back "in the bosom of my family—my soldiers." When a captain in the 1st North Carolina rejoined his company after recovering from a wound and typhoid fever, some of his men "told me that children never wanted to see their father as much as they have wanted to see me."[25]

Enlisted men appreciated and reciprocated considerate treatment

by their officers. "The Capt. is the most generous hearted and naturally kind man in the world," wrote a private in the 6th New York
Cavalry. "He will bear more from the men than the sergeant will. He
lends money and forgets all about it; if he hears men coughing in the
night he gives them medicine from his own chest." Many soldiers felt
a profound sense of loss when officers were killed or promoted. "I lost
my best friend in the army," wrote a private in the 124th New York
after his first lieutenant was killed at Chancellorsville. "Every man that
knowde him loved him . . . he never spoke a cross word to any of us
. . . I allways went to him when I wanted any thing money or aney
thing else he never refused me." When a captain in the 14th North
Carolina was promoted to the colonelcy of another regiment, his men
were happy for his promotion but "very sorry we had to part with him
for he treated us so kindly I would rather be under him than any man
in my knowing."[26]

Enlisted men were particularly impressed by officers who were
willing to share their burdens on the march. "Everybody likes Maj.
Dan Kent," wrote a private in the 19th Iowa. "While on the march he
will walk half the time and let boys who are unwell or tired ride his
horse." In the 15th New Jersey "our Major is the best and kindest
high officer in the regiment," wrote a nineteen-year-old private. When
one of the men gave out on a march the major "dismounted and let
him ride, and carried his gun in the bargain." In the 97th New York
"our colonel is as good a man as ever came on the field   he is a
regular old N.Y. farmer   he is a father to his men   if you were here
you would see him with 2 men on his horse & him a foot carrying a
knapsack and a gun." It is worth noting that the 97th New York was
one of the best regiments in the Army of the Potomac.[27]

The affection of enlisted men for officers who would lend them a
horse or carry their gun suggests an important truth: in these democratic citizen armies "the men think themselves as good as their officers," wrote a lieutenant recently promoted from the ranks in the 1st
Connecticut Cavalry, "and I suppose they are." When officers flaunted
their rank and acted like they were better than privates, the latter
resented it and made their dislike of such officers abundantly clear.
"There is too much difference made between privates & officers,"
complained an Ohio private who believed that "a great many privates
know more than their officers."[28] A lieutenant in the 14th New
Hampshire "is rather unpopular among the boys, and all on account
of this matter of feeling above the privates." A private in a Wisconsin

artillery battery at Nashville in November 1864 was angered by the officers' appropriation of comfortable houses while enlisted men froze in their tents. "I trust that my patriotism is now as bright as ever," he wrote bitterly, "but this is unnecessary and too much." The officers "toast their feet and drink their wines without ever a thought of us, who are engaged in a common cause with them."[29]

Even after he had risen from the ranks to become a captain in the 8th Alabama Cavalry, a University of Virginia graduate continued to deplore "the unwarrantable distinction so often and invidiously drawn between officer and private." An enlisted man in the 30th Georgia put it more colorfully. "A private Solger is looked upon by the big officers as no more than dogs," he wrote to his wife in 1863. "Sum times I would not care a slap of my finger if the confederacy sunk into oblivion just to see the difference between privates and officers." The large number of "gentleman privates" (sons of planters or professional men who did not seek a commission but proudly enlisted in the ranks) complicated this matter in the Confederate army. They often considered themselves better than the rough-mannered parvenues who commanded them. "It is very disagreeable to a *gentleman*," wrote a private in the 6th Virginia, "to have to mind and be on his 'p's & q's' to those who are officers, and not gentlemen."[30]

Soldiers were also quick to condemn incompetent officers. If the number of such complaints in soldiers' diaries and letters is an accurate indication, the problem was worse in Union than in Confederate regiments early in the war. "Much dissatisfaction exists in the Regiment in regard to some of our field officers," wrote a sergeant in the 15th Iowa two months after it was organized. "Some of them are notoriously incompetent   the Col does not know the difference between file right and file left." A private in the 2nd Ohio Cavalry was disgusted by petty rivalries and squabbling among his officers. "It seems that *Position and pay* is all our Officers are after. What can we expect from the men but discontent and utter disregard of their duty toward *Superiors* (Inferiors)." A lieutenant in the 1st Rhode Island Cavalry (who later won a congressional medal of honor) vented his spleen in letters to a friend in 1862 denouncing his colonel as a "lunk headed old fool . . . the old puke . . . a God damned fussy old pisspot utterly incompetent for the position he holds."[31]

Drunken officers seem to have been a serious problem in some units. A sergeant in one Illinois regiment branded most of the captains "a set of rum suckers," while a corporal in another regiment from the same state described a captain who was "always so drunk he knows not which end his head is on."[32] At a low point in the Union cause, an enlisted man in the 18th Pennsylvania Cavalry attributed the army's "inglorious defeats" to "whiskey and incompitent officers." After the humiliating repulse at First Bull Run, which many Northerners blamed on inept officers, the Union army established boards to examine officers and remove those found unfit. The Confederates did the same in October 1862. Many officers resigned rather than face the boards; others failed the test and were removed. The improvement wrought by these proceedings was reflected in a letter from a private in the 36th Massachusetts, who praised his new captain whom "we all love and respect   i never liked a man so well in my life   the Compeny was never in better discaplin than at present." As for the previous captain, "thare was not a man that respected [him] for he was drunk half of the time."[33]

More than anything else, enlisted men resented the petty authoritarianism of some officers, the harsh punishments meted out for minor infractions, the repressive enforcement of senseless regulations—all the things that World War II veteran Paul Fussell eloquently described as "chickenshit." Civil War soldiers did not use that term, at least not in their letters home, but they used others almost as pungent. "The officers in this Regiment is the God damndest meanest lots of curs, this side of Hell," wrote a soldier in the 33rd New Jersey. "The Blood boils in my veins with maddness to know that I am to be ordered around by the scraping of the lowest Whore Houses, Mary, You have no idea what an Enlisted man has to put up with." A private in the 125th Illinois considered his captain "worse than a niger driver . . . he will punish us for the least little thing." According to a private in the 4th Massachusetts, the "squirts of officers" in several companies were nothing more than "a few upstarts of shoulder-strapped snobs who never were anything at home but neighbors to these poor boys and very poor ones at that," while the colonel was "very unpopular on account of his assuming such unbecoming airs, arbitrary conduct, and tyrannical behavior."[34]

Part of the problem stemmed from efforts by old-army regulars, or officers who imitated them, to impose regular-army discipline on volunteers. One captain's "meanness," according to a private in the 29th Indiana, stemmed from his attempts to "make regulars of vol[unteers]. He meets with any amount of opposition." A Wisconsin artilleryman predicted that despite his "tyrannical" methods, his commanding officer "never can make mere human machines of the intelligent, strong-minded volunteers."[35]

As in other wars, resentful enlisted men muttered about shooting unpopular officers when they got into battle.[36] Officers who heard rumors of such threats tended to dismiss them as "*bosh,* all *bosh,* every whit of it."[37] There is no way of knowing whether such "fragging" of officers (to use a term from the Vietnam War) ever occurred in the Civil War. Probably it did, on a few occasions at least, but while several letters or diary entries mentioned *threats* to shoot officers, not a single account of it actually *happening* turned up in the research for this book.

Relations between officers and men usually improved, sometimes dramatically, when they moved from camp or garrison into active campaigning. The common danger they faced drew them together emotionally, while the conditions of march and bivouac brought them together physically. Captains and lieutenants marched in the same dust or mud, slept on the same hard ground, suffered from the same hot sun or freezing rain, and faced the same bullets as enlisted men. And the men suddenly discovered that orders, obedience, and discipline had a useful function.

A survey of American soldiers in World War II concluded that "officers in inactive theatres were invariably held in lower esteem by their men, whilst in active theatres the best relations were found in front-line units." The same was true in Civil War armies. On their first campaign, wrote a Massachusetts sergeant, "we didn't find any fault for the officers, from the Col. down camped out with us" because they said "they wouldn't sleep in a house without the whole regt. could." During the Chancellorsville campaign a sergeant in the 155th Pennsylvania wrote home that "I am beginning to like the business better and better. The men are more on an equality with the officers here than in camp."[38]

The ultimate test of leadership was combat. No officer could pass this test unless he demonstrated a willingness to do everything he asked his men to do. When Robert Graves joined his company on the Western Front in 1915 he found that "the only thing respected in young officers was personal courage." In the Civil War it was not the only thing, but it was the most important thing. Officers were well aware of this. At the first battle of Bull Run, wrote a Massachusetts lieutenant, "I knew if I flinched I was ruined." During a skirmish in western Virginia, wrote a captain in the 47th Ohio, "the boys besought me to take cover but I knew what must be done & I had told them on former occasions that I would not ask them to do anything which I would not do myself, therefore I set the example by taking the most exposed place."[39]

Confederate officers dwelt even more on the importance of leadership by example. The young daughter of a captain in the 1st North Carolina had urged her father to keep himself safe behind a tree when the bullets started flying. "Tell Annie she must not wish me to be a tree dodger," her father wrote to his wife. "I would rather be hung on a tree than dodge behind it, if my men cannot dodge as safely as I." A lieutenant in the 28th Mississippi admonished his wife, who had urged him not to take risks, that "an officer has to be very careful of his reputation for courage. . . . When once the troops lose confidence in the bravery of their Commander, they necessarily have an utter contempt for him." Despite pain from two wounds and heartache because of his brother's death in battle, a South Carolina lieutenant in the Richmond trenches in 1864 felt he could not let down. "Was up all night," he wrote in his diary. "Men so worn out could scarcely keep them awake although so near the enemy. . . . Am very unwell with cold and dysentery, but must not give way to feeling. Must keep up for sake of example. Too much shirking is going on."[40]

The example of courage in combat could go a long way toward redeeming the reputation of an unpopular officer. The "bravery on the field of battle" of two previously disliked officers in a brigade of the Union 14th Corps "gained the respect of the troops," wrote a corporal in the 64th Ohio. "One reason why they were unpopular was that they used to belong to the regulars, but they have totally disarmed their men of the jealousy they used to entertain toward them on that account." A private in the 23rd Massachusetts had commented on the company's hostility toward the captain and second lieutenant before the unit's first battle, at Roanoke Island, "but every one of us are now willing to confess our mistake. Capt. Whipple was just the man in action I never saw him when he was more cool and pleasant—and Emmetson ditto. Our praises and boasts of them after the battle were even extravagant."[41]

By the same token, cowardice could harm the reputation of a formerly popular officer. A surprising example concerned General Lewis Armistead. The image of Armistead holding his hat aloft at swordpoint as he led his men over the stone wall at Gettysburg to die at the Confederacy's high-water mark is familiar to every student of the Civil

War. A year earlier, however, after the battle of Malvern Hill a private in the 9th Virginia of Armistead's brigade wrote home: "We are in a miserable brigade, regt. and everything else. Armistead cares nothing at all for the men. He is full enough of saying 'go on boys' but he has never said 'come on' when we are going into a fight." Another surprising case was Colonel Willis Gorman of the famed 1st Minnesota, who "is no longer popular with the boys" after First Manassas because "his conduct on the field did not characterize him as a *very* brave man. . . . There is a good deal of feeling against him all through camp." But at the regiment's next major engagement, "Gorman, by his conduct at the Battle of Fair Oaks, has retrieved his character, & it stands high in the estimation of the boys; he is now *liked*. He showed himself a brave man."[42]

The personal courage of officers was unquestionably a powerful factor in motivating men to follow them. "I will go as whare and stay as long as eney of my offersers will," wrote a sergeant in the 2nd Rhode Island. The men in the 42nd Illinois "think everything" of their colonel, wrote a soldier in that regiment. "When we go to meet the enemy he does not get in the rear and say Boys go and do this or that, but he goes in 'front' and says, 'Boys Come' and there is but few in the Regt but that delights in going where he says." "By his acts under fire," wrote a 2nd lieutenant of his captain in the 56th Massachusetts, "he would encourage the greatest coward living to pluck up spirit."[43]

Not all leaders were officers; every company had noncoms, even privates, who in a crisis might seize the mantle of leadership. A corporal in the 74th New York described an incident in the battle of Gettysburg when Confederates overran a nearby artillery battery, capturing all of the guns and most of the men. One of those who escaped capture was a sergeant who then "dashed along the line like an infuriated tiger and halted about the centre [of the 74th] and cried 'Boys! you said you'd stick to us. . . . There's the Guns! . . . If you're men, com on!' . . . With one impulse the whole line yelled 'Charge,' and Hi . . . hi . . . hi . . . away we dashed after him. . . . We were standing beside the guns mad with success before we were scarce aware we had started to do it."[44]

Actions like these earned thousands of enlisted men promotion from the ranks during the war, while officers who "showed the white feather" were shamed into resigning. The experience of a sergeant in the 29th Georgia was replicated in many regiments. "I have been in command of our company 3 days," he wrote to his wife in 1864. "Lieut

Tomlinson stays along but pretends to be so sick he can not go in a fight but so long as I Keepe the right side up Co 'K' will be all right. The most of the boys have lost confident in Lt. Tomlinson," and he was soon gone.[45] This sifting process brought tested leaders to the fore and shunted incompetent or fainthearted officers into obscurity. But the high casualty rate of courageous officers who led from the front meant that Civil War armies, like most combat-hardened armed forces, never had enough good officers.

THE OLD ADAGE, "You can lead a horse to water but you can't make him drink," has some relevance to Civil War soldiers. The institutional structure of the army could train and discipline them (after a fashion), could station cavalry or a provost guard in their rear, and could (sometimes) furnish courageous leaders. But these were not British redcoats or the professional soldiers of Frederick the Great. Neither the flaccid coercive mechanisms of Civil War armies nor charismatic leadership could alone or together have kept these armies in existence or made them fight. Like the horse that would not drink, these citizens in uniform would not fight unless they wanted to. They came from a society that prized individualism, self-reliance, and freedom from coercive authority. The army broke down some of this individualism, or tried to, but could never turn these volunteer soldiers into automatons.

The cultural values of Victorian America held each individual rather than society mainly responsible for that individual's achievements or failures. What really counted were not social institutions, but one's own virtue, will, convictions of duty and honor, religious faith—in a word, one's *character*. God controlled human destiny, but God helped those who helped themselves. These were the beliefs and values that most soldiers brought with them into the army. Training, discipline, and leadership could teach them *how* to fight and might help them overcome fear and the instinct of self-preservation. But the deeper sources of their combat motivation had to come from inside themselves.

CHAPTER 5

RELIGION IS WHAT MAKES BRAVE SOLDIERS

A BATTLEFIELD OFFERS THE extreme challenge to the belief that man can control his fate. Like rain, shells and bullets fall on the just and unjust alike. Soldiers quickly become fatalists. "It is true that we are liable to get killed or wounded in any engagement we may have," wrote one of two brothers in the 5th Tennessee to their mother, "but that is only what may be expected. . . . The battles must be fought & we must take our chances in them." If this letter was meant to comfort her, it probably did not accomplish its purpose. Nor did a similar letter from a nineteen-year-old farmer's son in the 29th Georgia, who tried to reassure his mother in 1864: "Dont grieve a bout me. It does no good. If I get killed I will only be dead. I hav but one time and one way [to die] and when that time comes I will have to go shore." Six months later he was killed in action.[1]

Confronted with seemingly inexorable fate—another word for chance—soldiers in many societies have sought the aid or comfort of superstition. One might carry a rabbit's foot or the lock of a lover's hair or some other good-luck charm; another may go to a fortune teller. A private in the 10th Wisconsin told his younger brother and sister in 1863 not to worry about him, "for if I was born to be shot thats all if I wasnt I shant   if there is any thing in fortune telling the ball [bullet] wasnt made yet thats to hit me." The fortune teller was right; he was not shot, but unfortunately he was captured at Chickamauga and died in Andersonville prison.[2]

This fatalism, and the superstitious means of coping with it, have helped nerve soldiers in many wars to face the dangers of combat without giving way to fear: there is no use worrying or running away, for if fate decrees one's death there is nothing one can do about it; but if the good-luck charm works, one will go through safely. I have encountered no evidence of Civil War soldiers carrying rabbits' feet or anything else that they might have considered a talisman. But many of them did carry pocket Bibles or New Testaments, and numerous are the Civil War stories of a Bible in a breast pocket stopping a bullet. Union and Confederate soldiers were products of the Second Great Awakening, that wave of evangelical revivals which swept the United States in the first half of the nineteenth century. Civil War armies were, arguably, the most religious in American history.

Wars usually intensify religious convictions. The possibility of sudden death increases concern for the state of one's soul. It was a World War II chaplain who said that "there are no atheists in the foxholes."[3] This saying acquired an edge of cynicism, for it seems akin to a deathbed conversion. A British army doctor who specialized in psychiatric casualties during World War II perhaps unwittingly reinforced such cynicism when he wrote: "Since history undoubtedly proves that sound religious faith is a strong component in high morale . . . it is clearly the duty of every officer, whatever his private beliefs, to be seen as a Christian, even if he can only be what I call 'an Army Christian.' "[4]

Whether expedient or genuine, however, religious faith has unquestionably been important for soldiers in many wars. A survey of American enlisted men in World War II found that the foremost factor enabling them to keep going when the going got tough was prayer. The same was true of Civil War soldiers. There were few atheists in the rifle-pits of 1861–65. "If a man ever needed God's help it is in time of battle," wrote a private in the 24th Georgia, a sentiment echoed across the lines by a private in the 25th Massachusetts: "I felt the need of religion then if I ever did."[5]

Many men who were at best nominal Christians before they enlisted experienced conversion to the genuine article by their baptism of fire. "I am not the Same Man, Spiritually, that I was" before fighting at Fort Donelson and Shiloh, wrote a corporal in the 2nd Iowa. "My only fear is that I am almost too late . . . but with Gods help I will come through all right—at least I will try." A private in the 114th Ohio assured his father that "I am trying to live a better man than I was at home   I see the necessity of living a christain here where thy ar droping all around you." Men dropped all around a soldier in the 4th Delaware at Cold Harbor. "In that dreadful place," he wrote a week after the battle, "I resolved to forsake my evil ways and to serve god. I have done so and I pray the allmighty to forgive me and make me pure from sin."[6]

Soldiers who were deeply religious when they enlisted became more so on the battlefield. A devout private in the 38th Tennessee who fought at Shiloh "continually raised my heart to him, in prayer, and in the thickest of the fight, I envoked His protection," he assured his wife three days after the battle. "I have struggled and prayed to God until I am altogether another person. . . . Oh, I feel as I have not felt in years." A private in the 100th Pennsylvania, who carried a well-thumbed Bible while under fire nearly every day for a month in the Wilderness campaign, wrote to his sister that, despite his Christian upbringing, "I never knew the comfort there is in religion so well as during the past month. Nothing sustains me so much in danger as to know that there is one who ever watches over us. . . . I shall be a better Christian if I get home for having served in the army."[7]

He did not get home; in July 1864 he was killed at Petersburg. He would have regarded this fate as God's will. The faith of Christian soldiers gave a special edge to their fatalism. God ruled the world; not even a sparrow could fall without His knowledge. "I know He watches over all," wrote a lieutenant in the 5th New Jersey, one of a good many Quakers whose patriotism and antislavery beliefs overcame their pacifism. "Our fate is in His hands."[8]

This Christian fatalism had both pessimistic and optimistic overtones. The differences between the two were subtle. Both helped soldiers overcome the fear of death and thereby strengthened their will to fight. The "pessimists" were resigned to their fate. If it was God's will for them to die in battle, there was nothing they could do about it. Everyone died sometime and the Lord could take them as readily from their own fireside as from the field of battle. An officer in the 6th South Carolina told his wife in 1862 that "I used to feel a great dread" of death in battle, but he now believed that "the Almighty does what is best for those that love him. . . . You have no idea what a tower of strength this reflection is to me." A private in the 11th Georgia who had been wounded three times expressed himself in 1864 "joust as willing to go in" as ever because, as he had put it earlier, "i trust in god to Protect me in the Battle field if he sees Proper that i should get kild no living man can help it and if it is not his will that i should get kild i dont Care for the Balls."[9]

God willed their survival. But other pessimists met their expected fate. An eighteen-year-old soldier in the 35th Pennsylvania tried to console his family after his older brother in the same regiment had been killed at the battle of Dranesville in 1861: "His time was set by the Almighty Man. He was due to die, and if he hadn't been killed in the battlefield he might have died in the hospital or some other place. I think our time is all set when we shall die and before we want to die, and it makes no difference where we are." The writer of these words was killed at Antietam less than a year later. A captain in the 4th Alabama told his wife that "I might as well die at home as in battle," for "we are feeble instruments in the hands of the Supreme Power" and "no man can die before the day appointed, or live after that hour." His appointed hour came at Port Gibson on May 1, 1863.[10]

At least one of the several hundred women who managed to enlist as soldiers in the Civil War expressed similar sentiments. Having passed as Lyons Wakeman to join the 153rd New York in 1862, Sarah Rosetta Wakeman wrote to her parents the following year when she expected to go into battle: "I don't dread it at all. . . . If it is God will for me to be killed here, it is my will to die." She survived the only battle in which she fought, Pleasant Hill in April 1864, but died two months later of chronic diarrhea.[11]

While accepting the possibility that God might call them home at any time, the "optimists" tended to look on the positive side. "Do you not know that the path of every ball is directed by our kind father," a Confederate navy lieutenant wrote his fiancée before going into action against the Union fleet below New Orleans, "and that no harm can come near me except by His special permission?" One of the Civil War's most famous soldiers, Joshua Lawrence Chamberlain, tried to reassure his wife in the same manner. "Most likely I shall be hit somewhere at sometime," he wrote her in 1862, "but all 'my times are in His hand' . . . & no harm can come to me unless it is wisely & kindly ordered so." God did not order it so, for though wounded six times, twice thought fatally, he survived them all and lived out his years to four score and six.[12]

Southern or Northern, Protestant or Catholic, soldiers across the class and ethnic spectrum echoed this positive religious fatalism. "The God who protects me in the peaceful walks of every day life, can . . . as well preserve us in the battle's front as in the shade of our own fig tree," wrote an officer in the 28th Mississippi, a lawyer by profession. "This is a sustaining thought to me." During his first months in the army, wrote a captain in the 47th Ohio, also a lawyer, "I thought of death on the battle field so often" that he was almost unnerved until he realized that "I am under the same protecting aegis of the Almighty here as elsewhere. . . . It matters not, then, where I may be the God of nature extends his protecting wing over me."[13] During the Mine Run campaign in 1863, a sergeant in the 20th Indiana, a farmer's son who had left medical school to enlist, wrote in his diary: "At one P.M. we were told we would have to charge on the Rebel rifle pits, and works, this evening.—Felt very much downcast, but putting my trust in God felt more composed." His trust was not misplaced; both he and his brother survived the assault, and also survived the war, even though the 20th Indiana had one of the highest combat mortality rates of all Union regiments. The same was true of an Irish-American corporal in another high-casualty regiment, the 74th New York, who wrote his sister after coming out of the Seven Days battles unscathed that "all our lives are in the hands of God and . . . he can save from danger those who put their trust in him, tho' encompassed by hosts of enemies."[14]

Some religious fatalists felt no reluctance to take the most dangerous job in the infantry, color bearer. "I think that one place is as dangerous as another," wrote the color bearer of the 4th Virginia, a farmer's son, "for God has appointed our day and we are perfectly safe until that day comes." That day did not come for him during the war. But another Irish-American soldier, a carpenter by trade, in the 28th Massachusetts of the famed Irish Brigade was not so lucky. In defiance of his wife's wishes he accepted the honor of carrying the green regimental flag: "i will carry it as God gives me strength for i know that he can as easily protect me there as if i was in the strongest tower that ever was built by the hands of man." The tower was not strong enough; he was killed at Spotsylvania.[15]

The Christian fatalism of so many Civil War soldiers seemed to bear a close resemblance to predestinarianism. Some confessed such a theological conviction. "I believe in Predestination," wrote a lieutenant in the Union marine corps, "and if my reasoning is correct I am bound to live pleasantly to a ripe old age and if otherwise it is just the same." A South Carolina lieutenant agreed. "God rules all things," he told his fiancée, and it "would be very unsoldierly in me to beg that my life be preserved. So I trust all to him having little to say in the matter." A lieutenant in the 8th Kansas also subscribed to this doctrine. "What little Presbyterianism I have left," he wrote to *his* fiancée in 1862, "makes me something of a fatalist. I am in the hollow of Gods hand whether on the Field, in my Tent, or in your Parlor." But unlike the South Carolinian, the Kansan admitted that "I do pray occasionally . . . even on the battlefield" for God's protection, and after doing so "I felt calmer & clearer in mind [and] lost sight of danger altogether."[16]

It is quite clear that in the matter of their fate on the battlefield, more soldiers were practical Arminians than strict Calvinists. By the mid-nineteenth century most American Protestants believed in their free will to choose the path of salvation by voluntarily placing themselves in a position to receive God's grace. The Calvinist doctrine of predestined election of a select few appealed to a declining number of Americans in this age of evangelical revivals, democratic egalitarianism, and the ambitious quest for upward social mobility. And just as most American Christians by 1860 believed they could achieve salvation by faith and an attempt to abjure sin, so most Civil War soldiers believed they could improve the chances of God's protection on the battlefield by faith and prayer.

A sergeant in the high-casualty 61st Pennsylvania who had survived a half-dozen battles wrote in January 1863 that "I have prayed to God to forgive me my sins & keep me from danger. I do in my heart beleave he has heard them as I am satisfied after the fight at Fredericksburgh that by faith and prayer you can accomplish many things." A captain in the 8th Connecticut wrote after his first battle that "I should make but a poor soldier if I had not faith in God's answer to fervent prayer." After his third fight he told his mother that "I do not think I could indure the battle fields or the thought of one if I was denied the priviledge of prayer." After his fourth battle, Fredericksburg, he reflected that "every battle makes us the more dread another. I do not know that I could endure it if I could not pray."[17]

Soldiers also asked their families to pray for them—a request that was readily fulfilled. "I know your prayers were going up to God the very day" of Shiloh, wrote a lieutenant colonel in the 54th Ohio, and thus "the God of Battles . . . stretch[ed] forth his protecting arm." Roman Catholic soldiers had the additional support of special masses arranged for them by relatives. "I am ever so thankful to Aunt for using the money as she did," wrote the beneficiary of one such mass, for it was only through "the goodness of God that I came out safe" in the carnage of Antietam.[18]

Some soldiers, however, were wary of theological unsoundness if they implored God for protection. That was up to Him. The purpose of prayer was to cleanse the soul, not to shield the body. "I do not think that I have any right to pray for exemption from physical harm in the discharge of my duty as a soldier," wrote a Maryland Confederate, "but only [for] protection from moral wrong and that I may always be prepared to die, come what may." A Massachusetts private, a stonemason before he enlisted, daily prayed for grace through "my faith in the Lord Jesus Christ" not to save himself from death but so "if I fall I shall rise again." A soldier in the 5th Iowa informed his wife that several men in the regiment had formed a prayer group—a common occurrence. They prayed for grace and forgiveness of sins, he wrote five months before he was killed at the battle of Iuka, because death could come at any time "and therefore I realize the importance of being 'always ready.'"[19]

Ready for what? In the answer to this question lies the explanation for the conviction of a Pennsylvania soldier that "religion is what makes brave soldiers." Many Civil War soldiers believed literally in heaven, in salvation of the soul and a life after death. Bodily death held no terrors for the true believer because it meant entry of the soul into a better world where it would live in peace and happiness with loved ones for eternity. "Christians make the best soldiers," wrote a private in the 33rd Mississippi to his wife, "as they would not fear the consequences after death as others would."[20]

Skeptics and nonbelievers confirmed this observation. A South Carolina artillery officer confessed that the prospect of death terrified him because "I am not a christian—a christian can afford to be a philosopher because he believes in a certain reunion hereafter but a poor devil who cant believe it hasn't that support." And a profane Michigan private wrote simply that "I hope I will never get killed in battle for I am a fraid my chance for heaven would be slim."[21]

In contrast, devout Christians professed to be unafraid of death. Few went quite so far as an Illinois cavalryman who wrote that because death was merely "the destruction of a gross, material body . . . a soldier's death is not a fate to be avoided, but rather almost to be gloried in," or a Georgia naval officer who found "something solemn, mysterious, sublime at the thought of entering into eternity."[22] But many shared the sentiments of a private in the 33rd Massachusetts, who indicated that because "our cause is just I am willing to risk my life in its defence, believing that if I shall fall . . . it is but going home to my *savior* whom I love." A private in the 96th Pennsylvania and a lieutenant in the 43rd Mississippi found common ground in the belief that "if we keep faithful dying is merely changeing worlds for a better home." "If I live faithful here on earth I shall live again in Heaven."[23]

More than one soldier tried his hand at poetry to express this conviction. A private in the 32nd Ohio, who wrote in one of his diary entries that "I have a hope of getting to heaven, which is the only hope that strengthens me," penned the following lines while lying under fire in the Vicksburg trenches:

> *The Christian soldier has a friend*
> *Who once for him did bleed. . . .*
>
> *No matter how the cannons roar*
> *Or thick the bullets come*
> *He feels that if he falls*
> *That Christ will take his spirit home.*[24]

Another Union soldier, a printer by trade, kept a journal of religious thoughts while in the army, in which he wrote a poem, "Facing Death," after he had fought in three battles:

> *Why should we not, when'er the fear of death*
> *Takes hold of us, look upward and believe. . . .*
>
> *And fit ourselves for heaven: for only there*
> *Will glorious visions of eternity*
> *Possess our souls with rapturous delight.*
> *Where, then, O cruel Death, will be thy sting?*
> *And where, O yawning tomb, thy victory.*

The yawning tomb awaited him after a wound at Gettysburg weakened him to the point that he succumbed to pneumonia.[25]

For some soldiers, salvation was more a hope than a certainty. They *wanted* to believe, but were not quite sure. This uncertainty was reflected in the tortuous phrases of a letter from a Virginia lieutenant to his sister on the eve of the battle of the Wilderness: "I would like to survive the conflict. . . . I must say that to me life is sweet and death has some terrors, but the love of Christ is able to remove all this. . . . There is something awful in stepping off this world, even with the hope and faith in the gospel." Other soldiers also used the language of optimism rather than that of conviction. "If I fall on the field of battle I hope I will fall into the arms of a blessed sweetness . . . where there will be no sorrowing or crying but a continual happiness," wrote another Virginia officer. A private in the 38th North Carolina, whose small daughter had died, wrote to his wife in 1862 that "if I fall in the battel field I hope my sole will be wafted in heavin by Angels thare to meet little Mary."[26]

When writing to family members, however, devout Christian soldiers usually reassured them of the *certainty* of reunion in heaven. Wives who expressed anxiety to their husbands in the army were the most likely to get such letters. "After all," wrote a private in the 18th Missouri (Union) to his wife in 1862, "what are the few short years we might have lived in the enjoyment of each others friendship compared to that Eternity we shall spend together beyond the grave?" "We will be unspeakably happy in that next world," a soldier in the 3rd Virginia Cavalry comforted his wife, "where we shall be free from pain and from sin and from all anxiety and be separated no more forever." Similar solace came from sons to mothers. "Dont make yourself uneasy about me," wrote a sergeant in the 14th Tennessee to his mother, for "if I never see you any more on this side of the grave I will try and meet you in heven." One hopes that he succeeded, for he was killed at Fredericksburg.[27]

Death and dying were favorite topics of sentimental Victorian fiction as well as of religious tracts. Premonitions of death and tearful deathbed scenes run rampant through the literature. In Civil War armies, life—and death—sometimes imitated art. Stories of death premonitions have always been common in wartime; sometimes they came true. After living through the enormous casualties suffered by his regiment in the campaign from the Wilderness to Petersburg, a captain in the 126th Ohio felt sure he would be killed in the next battle after his regiment went to the Shenandoah Valley with General Philip Sheridan. Nevertheless "I am comfortable and happy," he wrote his wife. "There is a reality in Religion. . . . I am able to look death in the face without fear. . . . Sometimes when I think how you will miss me at home it is hard to be entirely willing to never see you and the boys again, but . . . we will meet again in the better land. . . . Kiss the boys for me. Goodbye, my dearest, best earthly friend. God bless you." Nineteen days later he was killed in the Third Battle of Winchester.[28]

The most poignant true deathbed scene I have encountered occurred at a Washington army hospital in October 1863. There died a sergeant in the renowned 8th Illinois Cavalry, a farmer who in 1861 had postponed his wedding to enlist in the army. He wrote frequent letters to his fiancée urging her to remain cheerful, for "if I go first I will wait for you there, on the other side of the dark waters" in "that better world, where we can live free from sin, and wickedness." This soldier survived all the campaigns and battles during 1862–63, including Gettysburg, where his regiment opened the battle, only to be mortally wounded in a minor skirmish near Culpeper. His fiancée, Augusta Hallock, rushed to his bedside, where she was able to write down his last words: "We'll meet in Heaven. I'll wait for you there. . . . It looks light. O Lord take my spirit. . . . Gusta kiss me,—kiss me closer. You will love me always *wont* you Gusta."[29]

RELIGIOUS BELIEF HELPED many soldiers overcome the fear of death. But what of the commandment "Thou shalt not kill"? Jesus advised His followers to turn the other cheek. The message of his ministry was peace, not war. How could a true Christian take up arms to kill his fellow man? "I think it is a hard job to learn to fight, and to be a Christian at the same time," wrote an Illinois recruit in 1861. A Pennsylvanian who enlisted in the cavalry to help put down "this unholy rebellion" nevertheless hoped that "the war will end without me having to kill anybody." Even after two years of combat experience, the lieutenant colonel of the 57th Indiana continued to agonize about the question: "How can a soldier be a Christian? Read all Christ's teaching, and then tell me whether *one engaged in maiming and butchering men*—men made in the express image of God himself—*can be saved* under the Gospel." He had still not resolved the question when he was killed at Resaca in May 1864.[30]

The reluctance to kill a fellow human being is embedded in many cultures, including Western societies shaped by the Judeo-Christian ethic. Yet those same societies have fought the most savage and destructive wars in history. The concept of a just war has enabled millions to overcome such scruples—but not without trauma. In both world wars a common cause of psychiatric breakdown among front-line soldiers was an inability to reconcile their duty to kill and their identification with the fellow humans they were ordered to kill.[31] In his famous book *Men Against Fire,* the military historian S. L. A. Marshall maintained that the cultural inhibition against killing was one reason why fewer than one-fourth of American infantrymen in World War II fired their rifles in any given action (the other reason was that they were frozen by fear). Marshall's critics claim that he invented a nonexistent problem; even his defenders concede that he exaggerated the problem and plucked the figure of one-fourth out of thin air.[32]

Whatever the truth in the Marshall controversy, it is clear that the injunction "Thou shalt not kill" bothered a good many Civil War soldiers. There is little if any evidence for psychiatric breakdown of soldiers on such grounds. And in the close-order ranks of most infantry tactical formations in the Civil War, with soldiers under the eyes of company officers whether firing by command or at will, the problem of inadequate firing that Marshall claimed to have identified in World War II was scarcely relevant in the Civil War. If anything, the problem was too much wild shooting and a lack of fire discipline among nervous troops for whom firing their muskets was one way to relieve tension.

But when they deliberately shot *at* somebody, they had to find a way to justify it. In the 1st Minnesota a soldier confessed that "I cant feel right to try to kill my brother man *although I see no other way to settle this matter.*" A private in the 77th New York wrote after his first skirmish that "I never thought I would like to shoot at a man, *but I do like to shoot a secesch* . . . and I either killed or wounded one of them." A lieutenant in the 8th Kansas who subsequently saw plenty of action wrote his fiancée in January 1863 that "I have killed no one yet" and "God grant it may be so ordered I never may," yet *"I am heart & soul in the war & its success"* and will thus be *"duty bound"* to kill "if such Cup is however presented to me" (emphasis added).[33]

The italicized phrases explain how these soldiers overcame their inhibitions: it was a just war, a holy cause against an evil enemy. Both sides believed that God was on their side and that they were doing their duty to God and country by trying to kill the godless enemy. The letters and diaries of Confederate soldiers contained many such expressions. "We look to God & trust in him to sustain us in this our just cause," wrote a Florida cavalry captain in 1863. "Surely the God of battles is on our side," thought a soldier in the 37th Mississippi as he read the 91st Psalm before going into action at Vicksburg on May

19, 1863. An Alabama artillery lieutenant wrote in February 1863 that "I have always believed that God was with us—if I had not my arm would long since have been palsied." A year and a half later, discouraged by the fall of Atlanta and other defeats, he still could not "believe that our Father in Heaven intends that we shall be subjugated by such a race of people as the Yankees."[34]

But that was precisely what God did intend, according to those very same Yankees. A Pennsylvania private was sure "that God will prosper us in the movements about to be made against this cursed rebellion." A religious lieutenant in the 16th New York, who would be twice wounded and win the congressional medal of honor, wrote in 1862 that "the cause for which we battle is one in which we can in righteousness claim the protection of heaven. Humanity is largely interested in the issues of this monstrous rebellion hence He who is the embodiment of humanity will bestow in great abundance His blessings upon his and our cause." A devout Indiana private, who became a clergyman after the war, described his actions during the battle of the Wilderness on May 6, 1864: "I think I must have fired at least two hundred rounds. Several in the rear loaded for me. I was up and firing almost incessantly until the enemy was repulsed. . . . Thank God, that in his strength we drove back the enemy. . . . To God our blessed Father in Heaven be all the glory."[35]

These words offer another clue to the capacity of Christian soldiers to overcome the sanctions against killing: in the hot blood of combat it was a question of self-defense, of kill or be killed. "You would think it was a cruel thing to [shoot] a man at ten rods distance," an Illinois corporal wrote to his brother and sister, "but just think that your life is at stake if you don't and it will incurige you in this cruel business." A lieutenant in the 13th Georgia wrote home after his first skirmish, referring to a dead enemy soldier: "I was and am certain that I killed him & when I . . . saw his pale face I felt strange but cannot say that I am sorry any. When I know he would have killed me if he could."[36] At the battle of Shiloh a private in the 61st Illinois who fought in the desperate defense at the hornet's nest rationalized his action on the grounds that "fore every secesh that we killed there would be one less to shoot at us. I thought of that several times during the day." Meanwhile, across the way in the 26th Alabama at Shiloh, a thirty-seven-year-old farmer with the imposing name of Liberty Independence Nixon reflected gloomily that "here I am ready to take the life of my fellow man when the Scriptures of eternal truth positively declare

'Thou shalt not kill.'" But then the enemy opened up, and "we were ordered to fire   I became resigned to my fate let it be what it might. My nerve seemed to be as steady as if I was shooting at a beast."[37]

To ease their consciences further, many Civil War soldiers made a distinction between combat and murder. Pickets on opposing sides often agreed not to shoot each other—that would be murder. "It has no effect upon the results of the war," wrote a Union officer in 1864, and was therefore "a miserable and useless kind of murder." Sharp-shooters (snipers) who took deliberate aim at an unsuspecting enemy when not in active combat were much hated by most soldiers, because that too was murder. Early in the war an officer in the 24th New York with a brother in the same regiment described in a letter home an incident during a skirmish: "Your Uncle Levi had a rifle and took delib-erate aim at one of the rebels at a distance so short that he could have sent him to eternity in a second, but says he could not fire on a man in that murderous fashion, and he dropped his gun, letting the rascal go. I think he did right. . . . In battle it would be different and I would be killing as many of them as possible."[38]

Considerable hardening of attitudes occurred as the war escalated in scope, and such nice distinctions became less common. During the furious artillery duels around Charleston in 1863, the commander of a section of Confederate guns wrote his fiancée that "in peace times it made me sick to see a man injure himself badly but I can see one torn to pieces by a shell & not a muscle move now—so far from it I feel a perfect delight when I see my shell crash in among them." A sergeant in the 2nd U.S. Sharpshooters wrote that the chaplain was "a fine man, and one of the best shots in the regt., and doesn't hesitate to show his skill in shooting rebels."[39]

But old ideas about the sanctity of human life did not die out altogether. At the battle of Bentonville on March 19, 1865, a crack shot in the 100th Indiana was ordered to pick off the artillerymen of a Confederate gun blocking the road. As he got in range the enemy limbered up to move to a new position. "The rider was on the rear mule," wrote the marksman in his diary. "I pulled up my rifle," but "just as I was going to fire something seemed to say to me: 'Dont kill the man; kill the mule,'" which he did. "He went down and that delayed them so much that we got the gun. . . . I am glad that I shot the mule instead of the man."[40]

*   *   *

MANY PEOPLE TURN to God in times of trouble and sorrow. By 1863 the trouble and sorrow in the dis-United States was almost beyond calculation. The war by then had killed at least 300,000 men. In the South, particularly, death and devastation touched almost every family. Nowhere, of course, was the presence of death more palpable than in the armies. And after Gettysburg, the fall of Vicksburg and Port Hudson, and the debacle at Missionary Ridge, the dark specter of defeat hovered over the Confederacy. The response was a remarkable wave of religious revivals, first in the Army of Northern Virginia during the months after Gettysburg and then spreading to the Army of Tennessee and other Confederate armies during the fall and winter of 1863–64. Scores of thousands of soldiers confessed their faith in Christ; many were baptized for the first time; prayer groups proliferated in almost every regiment.[41]

Although no such large-scale revivals occurred in Union armies, localized outpourings of the spirit took place in Northern camps from time to time. Union soldiers also became more religious as death grew ever more manifest. With the approach of spring in 1864, men on both sides recognized that the forthcoming military campaigns would be more terrible than anything that had gone before. The most frequent word in soldiers' letters as they anticipated this fighting was "dread." Without the comfort of God's hoped-for protection and the solace of salvation, many soldiers would not have been able to face the prospect. The Confederate revivals had gone a long way toward raising morale in Southern armies from its low point at the end of 1863. Heightened religiosity helped to prevent the collapse of both armies during the terrible carnage of 1864, but was a particularly potent force in the Confederacy. It may not be an exaggeration to say that the revivals of 1863–64 enabled Confederate armies to prolong the war into 1865.

"No better place in the world for serving God than in the army," wrote a captain in the 8th Alabama to his wife in October 1863, describing the prayer meetings going on in camp. "If you could have been with our company 4 months ago and could be with it now you would be highly pleased with the change." When this officer returned to the army in March 1864 after a furlough, he wrote that "citizens at home were more demoralized than are the soldiers. . . . We have more religion among soldiers as a mass than now exists among citizens," and the troops were consequently "in high spirits . . . sanguine of our success." Wherever one turned, a captain in the 13th Louisiana informed his wife in the spring of 1864, "you see soldiers holding prayer meetings." He found one whole regiment on their knees praying "for forgiveness for their sins, for strength and courage to resist the invader, and for success to the Confederate cause." From the trenches around Atlanta in the summer of 1864, a private in the 33rd Mississippi wrote home that three of his messmates including his best friend had been killed, "but when I took the last look at him I felt very happy to think that he had gone to a better world." Religion was the only thing that kept this soldier going; even in the trenches "we have prayer meetings every night when we don't have preaching."[42]

Many previously unregenerate Union soldiers also got religion during the final, grueling year of the war. A young corporal in the 103rd Ohio wrote home in May 1864 that for the first time "I feal confident that I have found grace in the sight of god   why then should we be afraid to die." A hard-bitten hell-raiser before he joined the army, the color bearer in the high-casualty 86th New York came to the Lord after he was twice wounded. On the eve of the final assault at Petersburg on April 2, 1865, he wrote in his diary: "Jesus owns me, O, how sweet to feel that if we fall on the field of strife, we only fall to rise to higher and more perfect bliss than this world can give. My object is to live for Heaven."[43]

The conclusion drawn by a study of G.I.s in World War II holds true for Civil War soldiers as well: religious faith "did not impel the individual toward combat but did serve the important function of increasing his resources for enduring the conflict-ridden situation of combat stress."[44] What then did impel Civil War soldiers to combat? Part of the answer lies in the same ideals of manhood and honor that had impelled many to enlist.

CHAPTER 6

A BAND OF BROTHERS

C IVIL WAR SOLDIERS wrote much about *courage, bravery, valor*—the three words meant the same thing. The quality they described was the mark of honor. But soldiers wrote even more about cowardice—the mark of dishonor. Many soldiers lacked confidence in their courage. But most of them wanted to avoid the shame of being known as a coward—and that is what gave them courage. Civil War soldiers went forward with their comrades into a hail of bullets because they were more afraid of "showing the white feather" than they were of death. The soldier who visibly skulked out of combat could never hold up his head again as a man among men. S. L. A. Marshall wrote of soldiers in World War II: "Personal honor is the one thing valued more than life itself by the majority of men."[1] Civil War soldiers would have agreed. "Death before dishonor" is a phrase that occurs in their letters and diaries more times than one can count. And they really seem to have meant it.

A postwar novel by a Civil War veteran included an episode depicting a visit by wives and mothers to soldiers in camp. The women praised their manly courage and contrasted it with the timorous nature of womanhood. The second lieutenant replied: "We are as much afraid as you are, only we are more afraid to show it." To show fear was to court contempt. A captain in the 14th New Hampshire expressed pride at having so few skulkers in his company "and the others shame those few so much that they must of necessity come up to scratch or be in disgrace." After a soldier in the 16th Mississippi had fallen to the rear at Malvern Hill, "he is irretrievably disgraced," reported his sergeant. "Not one of the Regt. deign to notice him at all."[2]

Few soldiers with "any pride of manhood in them" could bear the shame of such contempt. "I cannot boast of much pluck," wrote a private in the 39th Ohio after his first battle, "but I have got my full share of pride and could die before I could disgrace the name I bear." He was confident that his wife also "would sooner hear of my death than my disgrace."[3] It is by no means clear that wives and mothers shared this sentiment. But husbands and sons liked to think they did. A New York private wrote his wife in 1863: "I would not show myself [a coward] if I was ever so big a one, *would you?*" A sergeant in the 64th Ohio informed his mother that "it is better to die the deth of a brave Soldier than to liv a cowards life." The wife of a Texas infantry captain was probably not thrilled by a letter from her husband in 1863 declaring that if he ever showed "the white feather" in battle, "I hope that some friend will immediately shoot me so that the disgrace shall not attach either to my wife or children." He was later killed not by a friend but by the enemy, at the battle of Pleasant Hill.[4]

Before their first battle many soldiers were apprehensive that they would not pass this test of manhood. Those who did pass uttered a sigh of relief after it was over. "I am so afraid I shall prove a coward," an officer in the 8th Connecticut told his family. "I can hardly think of anything else." But after the battle of Newbern he wrote elatedly that he was "a little shaky at first but soon got used to the music. I know no one will say that I behaved cowardly in the least." While waiting to go into action for the first time, a private in the 36th Pennsylvania feared that he might "find myself acting the coward," but in fact "the opposite was the case; I was never more cool and self possessed than while in the hottest of the fight." Before attacking Confederate trenches at Fort Donelson, an Iowa corporal "did not know whether I had pluck enough to go through," but afterward, "I have no fear but I can do my duty. . . . I would rather be in a soldier's grave than to have acted as some of our boys did," especially the "fist-cuff rowdies" from the waterfront slums of Davenport, who were last seen "running away into the timber" while "all the Wolf Creek boys did their duty bravely."[5]

In Civil War argot, one of the favorite devices of men who wanted to skulk out of combat was to "play off"—to feign sickness—when their real ailment was "cannon fever." Letters from fighting soldiers are full of contempt for men in their companies who were "taken very suddenly ill" when action portended. A captain in the 63rd Ohio wrote in his diary after a fight that "the usual number of cowards got sick and asked to be excused."[6] A private in a Kentucky Confederate regiment damned the "infurnel cowards" in his company who "reported Sick when the fight was expected." But he was proud that all of his messmates "walk out like men" to meet the enemy. A soldier in the 38th Tennessee told his wife after Shiloh that "some of our Company disgraced themselves by falling back, pretending to be very lame. I would have gone in if I had to have gone in on one leg."[7]

To avoid the taint of cowardice, many genuinely sick soldiers did go into battle on one leg, so to speak. A corporal in the 24th Michigan wrote in his diary during the battle of Fredericksburg: "Feel quite sick. If it were not for being called a Sneak and a coward I would not be in the ranks today." A sergeant in the 155th Pennsylvania disobeyed the surgeon's order sending him to the hospital during the Bristoe campaign because "there are so many get off by pretending to be sick that a man is always looked upon with suspicion if he goes to a hospital, especially if there is a fight expected soon." A lieutenant in the renowned 15th Alabama was "quite sick" at the battle of Gaines Mill, he admitted to his wife afterward, "but I was determined to not have it said that our Comp. was in a fight and I not with them."[8]

Soldiers who went into action despite a real illness sometimes paid a steep price. A private in the 62nd Pennsylvania remained with his regiment despite the surgeon's orders to the contrary, for "if I had of Staid behind I would have been called a coward." He later regretted this decision, for he became seriously ill and did not recover for weeks just because "my foolish Pride kept me in the ranks." A corporal in the 1st Minnesota fought at First Bull Run despite sickness and afterward lost sixty pounds and almost died during three months in an army hospital. The 2nd Massachusetts was one of the war's elite regiments, with many of its officers from Boston's Brahmin class. One of them, Robert Gould Shaw, reported that four of his fellow officers refused to stay out of the battle of Cedar Mountain even though they were "quite ill." "It was splendid," Shaw wrote his mother, "to see those sick fellows walk straight up into the shower of bullets, as if it were so much rain." For that splendor three of the four paid with their lives.[9]

Most of the men in a volunteer company had enlisted from the same community or county. Many of them had known each other from childhood. They retained close ties to that community through letters home, articles in local newspapers, and occasional visits by family members to the regiment's camp. Because of this close relationship between community and company, the pressure of the peer group against cowardice was reinforced by the community. The absence of censorship meant that reports of cowardice would quickly find their way back to the community. The soldier who proved a sneak in battle could not hold up his head again in his company *or* at home.

Fighting soldiers did not hesitate to name skulkers in their letters home. "I am sorry to say that Norman Hart is a D——n coward," wrote a private in the 10th Wisconsin after Stones River. "He run away from the company just as we were going under fire the first day. . . . I tell you I do hate a coward   I am a big enough coward my self but never will desert in a trying time like Hart so help me God." A private in the 20th Indiana wrote home after a skirmish at Mine Run that "we did have A lot of skedadlers." He named nine of them, adding that "they should be published to the world." Likewise a private in the 18th Mississippi wrote an amusing letter describing the antics of men in his company who found excuses to disappear when the drums beat the long roll for action. One of these men was harried out of the regiment by the ridicule of his fellows. He could never go home again because "the boys have written so much about him." [10]

Officers did not escape this kind of censure; indeed, they were held to a higher standard. "Capt. Lucy of our company has resigned and gone home," wrote a lieutenant in the 17th Connecticut after Chancellorsville. "The company called him a coward and we told him that we hoped the folks at home would treat him as such." A captain in the 47th Ohio reported to his wife a rumor that another captain from their community "ran away and left his men" during a skirmish. "I hope not for the honor of our town." When the same officer "proved himself a coward" in another battle, it polluted forever "his family alter—what a stigma for men to transmit to their posterity—your father a coward!" [11]

That was why so many soldiers echoed the words of a private in the 20th Georgia: "I had rather dye on the battle field than to disgrace my self & the hole family." Or like a lieutenant in the 26th Tennessee they proudly wrote home after a battle that "I did not disgrace our name. . . . The Boys all know it & can tell of it." Two brothers in the

10th Connecticut who fought at Newbern informed their father after the battle that "shame need not settle on your face in behalf of your two sons."[12]

In some cases, soldiers who had been assigned to safe duty behind the lines pulled strings to return to their regiments at the front because folks back home might think they were playing off. As a private in the 21st Mississippi explained it, "I prefer the ranks" because his detachment as brigade clerk "is what is technically known as a 'Bomb proof' & that is something that I never want." Similarly a private in the 36th Massachusetts who had been detailed for two months as a teamster was "glad of the chanch to com back to the company" because "I should not lik to go home with the name of a couhard."[13]

Some studies of combat motivation have found that the felt need of a soldier to prove himself in the eyes of his comrades is strongest in his first battle or two. After that the veteran believes he has done enough to demonstrate his courage, and subsequently his fear of death or a crippling wound sometimes overmasters his fear of showing fear. One study finds the same to be true for the Civil War, in which the seemingly endless carnage by 1863 supposedly eroded the Victorian notions of manhood, courage, and honor that soldiers had carried into the army.[14]

Soldiers' letters offer some evidence for this interpretation. Reluctance to fight often characterized "short-timers" during their final weeks of enlistment—especially those Union soldiers whose three-year terms expired in 1864 and who had not reenlisted. "The 2nd RI has got but 4 days more and if they get into a fight I don't think they will last a minute," wrote a lieutenant in the 10th Massachuetts, another regiment in the same brigade, in June 1864. "It makes all the difference in the world with the mens courage. They do dread awfully to get hit just as thier time is out." A private in the 3rd New York Cavalry with a good combat record confessed when he had only three weeks left of his enlistment that "I am what the Boys call 'playing off' " by pretending not to have recovered from an illness. "I have been sent for half a dozen times but So far have got out of going. . . . I am in hopes that it may last until my time is out."[15] This psychology did not exist in the Confederate army because there was no such thing as a Confederate short-timer. The Richmond Congress required men whose enlistments expired to reenlist or be drafted.

A majority of Union soldiers served through the end of the war unless killed or badly wounded, however, because half of the three-year volunteers of 1861 reenlisted and the terms of the 1862 three-year volunteers did not expire before Appomattox. Among these men, and among most Confederate soldiers, little change in the values of honor and courage they brought into the war is reflected in their letters and diaries. "I do most earnestly hope that I may be enabled to meet my duties like a man when the breath of battles blows around me," wrote a corporal in the 64th Ohio in language that sounds like 1861 but was actually written in 1864 as he returned from his reenlistment furlough. Although he had fought in such bloody battles as Shiloh, Perryville, Stones River, Chickamauga, and Missionary Ridge, he expressed the same sentiments that had animated him three years earlier: "I do hope I may be brave and true for of all names most terrible and to be dreaded is *coward*." Another reenlisted veteran of many battles, a private in the 2nd Vermont of the Vermont brigade, which suffered more combat deaths than any other brigade in the Union army, wrote after his regiment lost 80 men killed and 254 wounded in the Wilderness that "I am sure if I had acted just as I felt I should have gone in the opposite direction [i.e. to the rear] but I wouldn't act the coward. . . . I clenched my musket and pushed ahead determined to die if I must, in my place and like a man."[16]

These were far from isolated examples. If anything, the motivating power of soldiers' ideals of manhood and honor seemed to increase rather than decrease during the last terrible year of the war. A veteran in the 122nd Ohio wrote in 1864 that "I would rather go into fifty battles and run the risk of getting killed than as to be . . . a coward in time of battle." The lieutenant colonel commanding the 70th Indiana in Sherman's Atlanta campaign broke down from stress in June 1864 after a month of almost continuous fighting. Although he was still sick and exhausted, he returned to his regiment after a week in the hospital because "those who keep up are full of ugly feelings toward those who fall [behind], intimating in every way possible that it is cowardice that is the cause. . . . By being with the rest [I] can prevent anyone feeling that I lack the pluck to face what others do." And on the eve of marching through South Carolina with Sherman in 1865, a veteran corporal in the 102nd Illinois wrote simply, in language he might have used three years earlier, of "the soldier's person—more valuable to him than all else in the army, save his honor."[17]

THE PRIDE AND honor of an individual soldier were bound up with the pride and honor of his regiment, his state, and the nation for which he fought, symbolized by the regimental and national flags. "None but soldiers can know how sensitive the men of a good Regiment are of its reputation," wrote a lieutenant in the 2nd Michigan. Unit pride created a sense of rivalry with other regiments that sometimes took the form of denigrating their courage. A soldier in the elite 5th Wisconsin wrote with contempt of the 26th New Jersey, which "ran like sheep" at Chancellorsville, leaving the 5th to fight the enemy front and flank. While the 26th "turned their backs to the Rebels . . . not a man in our Regiment was shot in the back and all our dead lay with their heads toward the enemy."[18]

This disparagement of a regiment from another state was typical. Regimental honor was associated with state pride. When several hundred men from New York regiments broke and ran at the battle of Kinston in December 1862, soldiers in the 23rd Massachusetts threatened to shoot them, according to a member of that regiment. "Our boys called them cowards, and told them to go back to their regiments but they did not know where their regiments were—though the bullitts were whistling around us we had to laugh at the excuses of these cowards."[19]

In the Confederacy, North Carolina regiments endured a great deal of disdain from those of other states, especially Virginia. Union victories over small armies composed mainly of North Carolina troops at Hatteras Inlet, Roanoke Island, and Newbern early in the war rubbed salt in the psychological wounds of North Carolinians. One general from the Tarheel State made the soldiers in his brigade pledge "not to visit wife, children, or business till we have done our full share in retrieving the reputation of our troops and our state." When North Carolinians fought courageously in later battles with the Army of Northern Virginia, particularly at Fredericksburg, a major in the 46th North Carolina was elated. The conceited Virginians had been put in their place. "It was the proudest day of my life," wrote the major after Fredericksburg. "It was a proud day for the old state."[20]

Individual soldiers whose courage nobody questioned nevertheless shared the humiliation of units with which they were identified—company, regiment, state. A lieutenant in the 75th New York, a veteran of many battles in which his regiment had performed well, was deeply ashamed when the regiment broke at Third Winchester. "This was the first time the 75th had ever run and I felt the disgrace," he wrote in his diary. "I never felt so bad in my life . . . and I cared little whether I was shot." Such a feeling of dishonor could become a powerful spur to courage in the next battle. When the 22nd Wisconsin fell apart in its first two battles and was subsequently assigned to rear-area guard duty in Tennessee, a private wrote with bitter shame that "the regiment is disgraced in the eyes of this army and its Commander." He hoped they would be sent to the front and get a chance to salvage their reputation, "for pride is what makes a soldier. It seems to me as if I could not bear the thought of the 22nd going back [home] as they are now." [21] The regiment did redeem itself as part of one of the best brigades in the 20th Corps during Sherman's Georgia campaign of 1864.

Unit pride and loyalty prompted many three-year veterans in Union regiments to reenlist in 1864. "I have studied on your advice," wrote a sergeant in the 12th Iowa to his parents, who had urged him not to reenlist. But he did, because more than three-quarters of the veterans in the 12th had reenlisted and the regiment would therefore retain its designation. The 12th had a proud history, and if this sergeant did not reenlist he feared he would be "put in another Regt to serve the remainder of my term, perhaps that Regt has disgraced itself in some previous engage[ment]." Anyway, what would he do after leaving the army if the war still raged? "Do you have the least idea that I could remain quiately at home and see those boys who have been with me constantly for over two years, who have endured the same hardships have been through the same dangers, and now leave them to bear my burden? *Not much.*" [22]

The most meaningful symbols of regimental pride were the colors—the regimental and national flags, which bonded the men's loyalty to unit, state, and nation. The flags acquired a special mystique for Civil War soldiers. Color bearers enjoyed a special pride of place—and also a special risk, since the enemy directed its heaviest fire against the colors. But "the post of danger is the post of honor," to quote a Civil War phrase used so often that it became a cliché. There was rarely any shortage of volunteers to carry the flags if the color bearers were shot down. One of the most honorable feats a regiment could accomplish was to capture enemy colors; the worst shame imaginable was to lose its own colors to the enemy.

Perhaps the best description of the powerful mystique associated with the colors comes from a noncombatant. In December 1862 Walt Whitman visited his brother George, a lieutenant in the 51st New York, after he had been wounded at Fredericksburg. Finding his wartime vocation, Walt Whitman stayed in Washington as a volunteer nurse, learning as much about soldiers as anyone outside that fraternity could learn. In April 1864 he described to his mother a regimental flag he had received from a wounded soldier he tended. "It was taken by the secesh in a cavalry fight, and rescued by our men in a bloody little skirmish. It cost three men's lives, just to get one little flag, four by three. Our men rescued it, and tore it from the breast of a dead Rebel—all that just for the name of getting their little banner back again. . . . There isn't a reg't . . . that wouldn't do the same."[23]

Perhaps the only achievement that could eclipse the honor of taking enemy colors or retaking one's own was to plant the national flag on a captured enemy position. Regimental rivalries to be the first to do so help explain the reckless courage of many Civil War assaults. In 1864 an officer in the 12th New York described a successful attack on Confederate lines defending the Weldon Railroad near Petersburg. When the American flag appeared above the battle smoke on the enemy works, "it is impossible to describe the feelings one experiences at such a moment. God, Country, Love, Home, pride, conscious strength & power, all crowd your swelling breast . . . proud, proud as a man can feel over this victory to our arms—if it were a man's privilege to die when he wished, he should die at such a moment."[24]

This identification with regiment, state, country, and flag is related to but not precisely the same as the "primary group cohesion" that has been the focus of most writings about combat motivation since World War II. The soldier's primary group consists of the men closest to him with whom he interacts every day in camp, on the march, in combat. For the Civil War soldier this group may have been as large as his company but was likely to be smaller: his messmates, the men from his town or township with whom he enlisted, the squad commanded by his sergeant. All other groups were "secondary": regiment, brigade, army, country, even community and family so long as he remained in the army.

Bonded by the common danger they face in battle, this primary group becomes a true band of brothers whose mutual dependence and mutual support create the cohesion necessary to function as a fighting unit. The survival of each member of the group depends on the others doing their jobs; the survival of the group depends on the steadiness of each individual. It is the primary group that enforces peer pressure against cowardice. If any member of the group "plays off" or succumbs to "cannon fever" during combat, he not only endangers his own and the others' survival but he also courts their contempt and ostracism; he loses self-respect as a man and may be exiled by the group. For many soldiers this could be quite literally a fate worse than death; it was a powerful incentive for fight rather than flight.

Primary group cohesion has presumably existed among combat soldiers from time immemorial and has been implicitly understood by those who experienced it. But it was the studies of German, American, and British soldiers in World War II by social scientists that gave the concept a hard analytical edge and a language to describe it. These studies have multiplied since the 1940s; most armies have incorporated the theory of primary group cohesion into their training and doctrine.[25]

"For the key to what makes men fight," wrote one modern student of combat motivation, "we must look hard at military groups and the bonds that link the men within them." The answer, according to another analysis, lies in "the intense loyalty stimulated by close identification with the group. The men are now fighting for each other and develop guilty feelings if they let each other down. . . . This spirit of self sacrifice, so characteristic of the combat personality, is at the heart of good morale."[26] In World War II the soldier "became increasingly bound up with his tiny fraternity of comrades. . . . In the last analysis, the soldier fought for them and them alone." Or as William Manchester put it in his memoirs of service in the American Marine Corps during World War II: "Those men on the line were my family, my home. They were closer to me than . . . my friends had ever been or ever would be. They had never let me down, and I couldn't do it to them. . . . Men, I now knew, do not fight for flag or country, for the Marine Corps or glory or any other abstraction. They fight for one another."[27]

Civil War armies presented no exception to the importance of primary groups. Indeed, the territorial basis of company recruitment reinforced this cohesion by bringing friends and relatives together in the same unit, thus linking primary groups at home with those in the army. In many cases, especially in Confederate regiments, two or more biological brothers enlisted in the same company. Soldiers' letters contain many references to the "band of brothers" theme—literal as well as metaphorical. "We feel like the kindest of brothers together" (10th Virginia Cavalry). "You would not believe that men could be so attached to each other we are all like brothers" (1st Ohio Heavy Artillery).[28] "We love each other like a band of brothers" (11th Georgia). We all "seem almost like brothers. We have suffered hardships and dangers together and are bound together by more than ordinary ties" (8th Texas Cavalry). A corporal in the 9th Alabama returned to his regiment in October 1862 after convalescence at home from a wound in the battle of Glendale. "A soldier is always nearly crazy to get away from the army on furloughs," he observed, "but as a general thing they are more anxious to get back. There is a feeling of love—a strong attachment for those with whom one has shared common dangers, that is never felt for any one else, or under any other circumstances."[29]

The significance of this bonding became clear in combat. A veteran in the 122nd New York tried to explain how it worked. His sister had asked what kept him going through the carnage of the Wilderness, Spotsylvania, Cold Harbor, and Petersburg. "You ask me if the thought of death does not alarm me," he replied. "I will say I do not wish to die. . . . I myself am as big a coward as eny could be," he admitted in July 1864, "but give me the ball [bullet] before the coward when all my friends and companions are going forward. Once and once only was I behind when the regt was under fire, and I cant discribe my feelings at that time none can tell them only a soldier. I was not able to walk . . . but as soon as the rattle of musketry was heard and I knew my Regt was engaged I hobbled on the field and went to them. . . . The untrained and old soldier are different in many respects. As to life the new one looks out for himself in or out of Battle the old one when away from his companions thinks of them and goes in and the danger to himself is forgotten."[30]

The experience of combat did more than strengthen existing bonds; it also dissolved the petty rivalries and factions that existed in some regiments and forged new bonds among men who saw the elephant together. "Those who had stood shoulder to shoulder during the two terrible days of that bloody battle," wrote an officer in the 54th Ohio after Shiloh, "were hooped with steel, with bands stronger than steel." After the 6th Missouri (Union) fought its first battle at Chickasaw Bluffs, a captain who had previously lamented the bickering and backbiting among its officers wrote that "we all feel proud of our men and there is a better feeling among the officers." After the 83rd Pennsylvania suffered 75 percent casualties in the Seven Days battles, a private commented that "it seems strange how much the rest of our company has become united since the battles. They are almost like brothers in one family now. We used to have the 'aristocratic tent' and 'tent of the upper ten,' and so on, but there is nothing of that kind now. We have all lost dear friends and common sorrow makes us all equal."[31]

The fire of battle could even fuse the breach that existed in many companies between the pious and the profane. Not only did some of the profane suddenly get religion, but also some of the pious found surprisingly admirable qualities in their blasphemous brethren. "I have now spent a whole year with my comrads in battle," wrote a teetotaling private in the 23rd Massachusetts. "Every one of them is as a brother to me. . . . The members of Company F have won from me a lasting love. It is true many of them are very profane and the demon whiskey is not refused by many of them but with all their faults I love them because they are brave, generous, intelligent, and noble-hearted." [32]

The ties of comradeship caused many a soldier to resist a soft assignment away from his company or even to refuse promotion if it meant transfer to another unit. An aristocratic South Carolinian turned down a chance to transfer from the infantry to an elite cavalry outfit because "I am very proud of this company . . . & I am too much attached to my intimate friends to seek an opportunity of parting with them." A lieutenant in the 20th Massachusetts refused promotion to captain in another company. "It is a pretty hard thing to throw away a chance of rising," he explained to his father, but "I can't make up my mind to leave my own company. I have got really attached to the fellows." A Quaker captain in the 5th New Jersey faced a different kind of decision. His wife and mother pressed him to resign; his Quaker brethren threatened to read him out of Meeting if he did not do so. "Yet I should leave with much regret the men who stood manfuly by me in the hours of dainger through which I have passed," he told his wife. In the end he could not bring himself to leave them, and was killed at Second Manassas. [33]

This officer's death separated him from his company more decisively than resignation would have done. As the war went on, casualties rent the cohesion of some veteran regiments almost to the vanishing point. Cohesion is a renewable resource, with new men bonding to old and veterans bonding more closely. In time, however, attrition became a deadly foe to cohesion—and therefore to the qualitative as well as quantitative combat effectiveness of a unit. By August 1862 the South Carolina infantryman who had refused to leave his company to join the cavalry the preceding May left it to join the artillery because his company had "been stripped of some of my best friends" by casualties in the Peninsula campaign. A sergeant in the 55th Illinois found it "very lonely here" after Shiloh. "Most of the boys from the village are either in their long home or have been sent down

the river on account of wounds." After the Shenandoah Valley campaign of 1864 had decimated Jubal Early's army, a Confederate officer
lamented that "my best friends have fallen so fast, that in the army I
feel as if I were left alone."[34]

One of the most influential studies of primary group cohesion attributed the persistent fighting power of the Wehrmacht even as the
Third Reich collapsed around them to the bonds of camaraderie
among squads and platoons in the German army.[35] The principal cri-
tique of this interpretation, however, points out that the enormous
casualties and consequent turnover of personnel in the Wehrmacht by
1942 left no core primary group around which to cohere. "*Real* 'primary groups' do not fully explain combat motivation due to their un-
fortunate tendency to disintegrate when they are most needed," wrote
Omar Bartov in his study of *Hitler's Army,* but "the *idea* of attachment
to an *ideal* 'primary group' . . . clearly does have a powerful integra-
ting potential." By ideal primary group Bartov meant the Nazi ideology
of Aryan racial brotherhood. "The Wehrmacht began to manifest its
most remarkable 'fighting power' precisely at a time when the network
of 'primary groups' which had ensured its cohesion during previous
Blitzkrieg campaigns began to disintegrate." Nazi ideology portrayed
the Soviet Union as a mortal threat to German civilization. These
"ideological arguments . . . [and the] ideological cohesion of the
troops" enabled the Wehrmacht to continue fighting after 1942 "with
far greater determination and against far greater odds than at any other
time."[36]

Bartov's thesis, while perhaps overstated, offers a suggestive way to
analyze the ideological attachments of Civil War soldiers to something
beyond their comrades in squad or company: to nationalism, liberty,
democracy, self-government, and so on. When primary groups disinte-
grated from disease, casualties, transfers, and promotions, these larger
ideals remained as the glue that held the armies together. Whether or
not these commitments constituted "combat motivation," they certainly provided "sustaining motivation" for armies composed mainly of
volunteers. Sustaining motivation is not unrelated to combat motivation, for armies cannot fight if they do not exist. And with respect to
Civil War armies, a strong case can be made that the most patriotic
and ideologically committed volunteers were the best combat soldiers,
because they believed in what they were fighting for. It is time to
examine what Civil War soldiers called "the Cause."

CHAPTER 7

ON THE ALTAR OF MY COUNTRY

THE EMPHASIS ON primary group cohesion that emerged in studies of combat motivation after World War II had a significant corollary: the unimportance of patriotic or ideological convictions. The detailed analysis of *The American Soldier* quoted one G.I.: "Ask any dogface on the line. You're fighting for your skin on the line. When I enlisted I was as patriotic as all hell. There's no patriotism on the line. A boy up there 60 days on the line is in danger every minute. He ain't fighting for patriotism." A British officer said that "it would be foolish to imagine that the average British or American soldier went into battle thinking he was helping to save democracy. . . . He never gave democracy a thought."[1] Another study of World War II soldiers found that "considerations of ideology, patriotism, and politics seem remarkably remote from the concerns of the front-line soldier." Questionnaires administered by social scientists to American soldiers found that their "convictions about the war and its aims" ranked low among various reasons for fighting. Indeed, among enlisted men there was "a taboo against any talk of a flag-waving variety."[2]

Likewise, American soldiers in Vietnam dismissed ideological and patriotic rhetoric as a "crock," "crap," "a joke." Some of these same American soldiers, however, explained the extraordinarily high combat motivation of enemy soldiers by reference to *their* ideological convictions. The North Vietnamese, said one American, were "the toughest fighters in the world" because "they knew what they were fighting for." A black American machine gunner described a North Vietnamese soldier as the bravest man he had ever seen "because he really believed in something."[3] One student of the American army in Vietnam insisted that primary group cohesion alone cannot motivate men to fight; on the contrary, it might cause them to refuse combat in order to ensure group survival. "Primary groups maintain the soldier in his combat role only when he has an underlying commitment to the worth of the larger social system for which he is fighting." Nevertheless, the primacy of group cohesion and the relative unimportance of ideology remain the orthodox interpretation. In the heat of combat, writes a British military analyst, "the soldier will be thinking more of his comrades in his section or platoon than of 'The Cause,' Democracy, Queen and Country."[4]

Most American soldiers in World War II and Vietnam were draftees or professional regulars; most soldiers in the Civil War were volunteers. Did that make a difference? Some historians think not. "American soldiers of the 1860s appear to have been about as little concerned with ideological issues as were those of the 1940s," according to Bell Irvin Wiley, the foremost student of Johnny Reb and Billy Yank.[5] Another scholar who examined the letters, diaries, and memoirs of fifty enlisted men concluded that "the Civil War soldiers studied here were notoriously deficient in ideological orientation." An analysis of Tennessee soldiers based on questionnaires completed in the early 1920s by surviving veterans concluded that "few Tennesseans were conscious of the major issues of the Civil War, and fewer still had any concept of the South's goals." In 1992 the commander of the New York chapter of the Sons of Union Veterans said that "it wasn't because our fathers knew what they were fighting for that they were heroes. They didn't know what they were fighting for, exactly, and they fought on anyway. That's what made them heroes."[6]

Research in the letters and diaries of Civil War soldiers will soon lead the attentive historian to a contrary conclusion. Ideological motifs almost leap from many pages of these documents. A large number of those men in blue and gray were intensely aware of the issues at stake and passionately concerned about them. How could it be otherwise? This was, after all, a *civil war*. Its outcome would determine the fate of the nation—of two nations, if the Confederacy won. It would shape the future of American society and of every person in that society. Civil War soldiers lived in the world's most politicized and democratic country in the mid-nineteenth century. They had come of age in the 1850s when highly charged partisan and ideological debates consumed the American polity. A majority of them had voted in the election of 1860, the most heated and momentous election in American history. When they enlisted, many of them did so for patriotic and ideological reasons—to shoot as they had voted, so to speak. (See Chapter 2.) These convictions did not disappear after they signed up. Recruits did not stop being citizens and voters when they became soldiers. They needed no indoctrination lectures to explain what they were fighting for, no films like Frank Capra's "Why We Fight" series in World War II. The spread-eagle speeches they heard at recruiting rallies merely reinforced the ideas they had absorbed from the political culture in which they had grown up. And their army experiences reinforced these ideas even more powerfully.

Newspapers were the most sought-after reading material in camp— after letters from home. Major metropolitan newspapers were often available only a day or two after publication, while hometown papers came weekly when the mail service functioned normally. "I receive the 'Chronicle' regularly," wrote a lieutenant in the 50th Ohio to his brother back home in 1863. "The boys all want to read it. . . . The officers subscribed $4.75 each for papers for the benefit of the boys. [We] get *four daily* papers, all loyal and right on politics"—that is, Republican. In January 1862 a private in the 17th Mississippi sta- tioned near Leesburg, Virginia, wrote in his diary: "Spend much time in reading the daily papers & discussing the war question in general. We allways close by coming to the conclusion that we will after much hard fighting succeed in establishing our independence."[7] Two years later a lieutenant in the 4th Virginia reported that the "boys" spent much of their time in winter quarters reading the papers. We "make comments on the news and express our opinions quite freely about the blood and thunder editorials in the Richmond papers, smoke again and go to bed." Even in the Petersburg trenches later that summer, soldiers in the 43rd Alabama "have daily access to the Richmond pa- pers. . . . We spend much of our time in reading these journals and discussing the situation."[8]

Some European officers who attached themselves to Civil War ar- mies expressed astonishment at this phenomenon. One of them was Gustave Paul Cluseret, a graduate of St. Cyr and a French army officer for two decades before he wangled a brigade command under General John C. Frémont in 1862. Looking back on his American adventure a few years later, Cluseret wrote that "if the American volunteers accomplished prodigies of patience, energy, and devotion it is because they fought with knowledge of the cause. In the midst of the messiest business one could hear the squeaking voice of the 'news boy' over the sound of the fusillade, crying 'New York Tribune, New York Herald.' The soldier paid up to 10 cents for the newspaper. . . . After reading it . . . there would be a redoubling of his zeal and drive." The discipline of European regulars, concluded Cluseret (a radical who would support the Paris Commune in 1871), could never have produced "the sentiment of abnegation and the force of resistance" that his brigade of Union volunteers "obtained through their love of liberty and country."[9]

Several regiments or brigades established debating societies while in winter quarters. A thrice-wounded sergeant in the 20th Illinois stationed near Vicksburg described some of the debates in his brigade during the winter of 1863–1864.

> *November 30:* "Took part on the affirmative of Resolved that the Constitutional relations of the rebel states should be fixed by Congress only. . . . Witnessed some rare outbursts of untutored eloquence."
>
> *December 14:* "Had an interesting debate at the Lyceum on the subject of executing the leaders of the rebellion. Made my speech on the negative. The affirmative carried by just one vote in a full house."
>
> *December 24:* "Discussed the question of reducing rebel states to territories."
>
> *Dec. 31:* "Sergeants Rollins & Need discussed ably the rights of the South. Sergt. Miller expanded on the revolution of ideas."[10]

In the Army of the Potomac, the debate topic in one brigade during November 1863 was "Do the signs of the times indicate the downfall of our Republic?" This topic must have been popular, for a soldier in the 103rd Illinois of Sherman's army reported a debate on the same proposition in February 1864. Not surprisingly, the negative carried the day in both debates, as did the affirmative in a debate the following winter at the convalescent ward of a Union army hospital in Virginia: "Resolved that the present struggle will do more to establish and maintain a republican form of government than the Revolutionary war." [11]

Some officers were not pleased with these disputatious activities. "A soldier [should have] naught to do with politics," wrote an Ohio colonel. "The nearer he approaches a machine . . . the more valuable he becomes to the service. . . . Our soldiers are too intelligent, for they will talk and they will write, and read the papers." But this was distinctly a minority opinion, even among high-ranking officers. "Our soldiers are closer thinkers and reasoners than the people at home," wrote a New York captain in 1864, a few weeks before he was killed at the battle of Plymouth. "It is the soldiers who have educated the people at home to a true knowledge . . . and to a just perception of our great duties in this contest." [12] None other than Ulysses S. Grant noted with pride after the war that "our armies were composed of men who were able to read, men who knew what they were fighting for." The same could be said for Confederate soldiers. If the assertion of John Keegan that "the Blue and the Gray [were] the first truly ideological armies of history" is an exaggeration, it is closer to the truth than Bell Wiley's remark that they were "as little concerned with ideological issues" as G.I.s in the 1940s were alleged to have been. [13]

Ideology is defined here both in the dictionary sense of "the doctrines, opinions, or way of thinking of an individual, class, etc.; specif., the body of ideas on which a particular political, economic, or social system is based" and in historian Eric Foner's usage as "the system of beliefs, values, fears, prejudices, reflexes, and commitments . . . of a social group." [14] These broad definitions embrace simple patriotism as well as more complex and systematic ideas about the meaning and purpose of the war. The most frequent affirmations of "The Cause" on both sides were uncomplicated avowals of patriotism that sometimes shaded into more sophisticated notions of nationalism.

When the war began, the Confederacy was a distinct polity with a fully operational government in control of a territory larger than any European nation save Russia. Although in the minds and hearts of some Southern whites, American nationalism still competed with Confederate nationalism, the latter had roots several decades deep in the antebellum ideology of Southern distinctiveness. [15] Thus it seemed natural for many Confederate soldiers to express a patriotic allegiance to "my country." "Sink or swim, survive or perish," wrote a young Kentuckian who had cast his lot with the Confederacy, "I will fight in defense of my country." Another Confederate Kentuckian insisted in

August 1862 that "we should yield all to our country now. It is not an abstract idea. . . . We have no alternative: we must triumph or perish." A sergeant in the 8th Georgia told his family in 1863 that "if my heart ever sincerely desiered any thing on earth . . . it certainly is, to be useful to my Country. . . . I will sacrifice my life upon the alter of my country." He did, at Gettysburg.[16]

Sacrifice on the "alter" (a frequent misspelling) of one's country was a typical phrase in soldier letters. So were the words written by a Missouri Confederate soldier to his wife in 1862 that she should take comfort in "knowing that if I am killed that I die fighting for my Country and my rights." Two months later she learned that this grim foreboding had come true. A lieutenant in the 47th Alabama wrote his wife in 1862: "I confess that I gave you up with reluctance. Yet I love my country [and] . . . intend to discharge my duty to my country and to my God." He too never returned to his wife and two children he missed so much.[17]

The conflict between love of family and love of country troubled some married Confederate soldiers. A homesick Arkansas sergeant wondered "why can I not be better satisfied here for surely my duty is to serve my country but I am restless. . . . [Not] money nor anything else could keep me from home and my little family except love of country and freedom for which I think every man ought to bear almost anything."[18] Many soldiers reconciled their dual responsibilities to country and family by the conviction that in fighting for the one they were protecting the other. A yeoman farmer from Alabama who had seven children wrote home from his cavalry battalion after one of the children had died in 1862: "If it were not for the love of my country and family and the patriotism that burn in my bosom for them I would bee glad to come home and stay there but I no I have as much to fite for as any body else." Another Alabama cavalryman wrote to his fiancée in 1863 that "if we fail I expect that my own home will be wrested from me, and would not be surprised if my own Cellie did not soon have the vandals at her door to rob and insult her." And a private in the 30th Georgia assured his wife that "if I fall it will be in a good Cause in the defence of my Country defending my home and fire side."[19]

The urge to defend home and hearth that had impelled so many Southerners to enlist in 1861 took on greater urgency when large-scale invasions became a reality in 1862. A Shenandoah Valley farmer serving with the 10th Virginia Cavalry learned that the Yankees had entered his county in April 1862. "I intend to fight them to the last," he assured his wife. "I will kill them as long as I live even if peace is made I never will get done with them." Another Virginian declared to his wife two weeks before he was killed at Malvern Hill that to drive "the insolent invader . . . from the soil polluted by their footsteps . . . has something of the glorious in it, that appeals to other feelings than those of patriotism and duty." Men who had opposed secession were nevertheless roused to fighting pitch by Northern invasion. "If I am killed tomorrow," said a major in the 2nd Virginia Cavalry on the eve of the battle of Fredericksburg, "it will be for Virginia, the land of my fathers, and not for the damned secession movement."[20]

Tennesseeans and Louisianians who saw large parts of their states including the principal cities fall to the "insolent invader" in the spring of 1862 felt a redoubled commitment to the Cause. A captain in the 16th Tennessee wrote after the surrender of Fort Donelson that his men were "now more fully determined than ever before to sacrifice their lives, if need be, for the invaded soil of their bleeding Country. . . . The chivalrous Volunteer State will not be allowed to pass under Lincoln rule without . . . the fall of a far greater number of his hireling horde than have yet been slain at the hands of those who are striking for their liberties, homes, firesides, wives and children." Rather grandiloquent prose, but it was echoed in plainer terms by a private in the 9th Tennessee who was incensed to think of his mother "being left there and Exposed to there insults and perhaps take what little you have got I feel a stronger Determination never to quite the field untill they are driven from that beautiful land." More succinctly, a Louisiana planter from Bayou La Fourche serving with his artillery unit in northern Mississippi wrote to his wife after the fall of New Orleans that "now I must fight to return to you."[21]

By 1863 much of Mississippi had also come under Union occupation, causing a thirty-three-year-old private in the 37th Mississippi, a former schoolteacher, to vent his spleen in diary entries: "Let me liberate my home from the varlet's tread, and then . . . my country shall be freed from the fiendish vandals who thirst for the extermination of a people who are actuated by motives as far above those that influence and characterize the enemy as is the soaring Eagle above the most insignificant reptile."[22]

Some Northern soldiers acknowledged the extra incentive that animated Confederates fighting in defense of hearth and home. "There is much more dash in the Southern troops and more real war spirit," wrote a lieutenant in the 12th New York, "for they feel they are fighting for their homes." An Illinois sergeant declared in 1862 that they "fight like Devils in tophet" because they were "fighting to keep an enemy out of [their] own neighborhood & protect [their] property. . . . Not that I consider their cause just but, right or wrong, if we thot or believed we was right it would be the same to us."[23]

The morale advantage of fighting for one's neighborhood could be a two-edged sword, however. This point first became evident among pro-Southern troops from border states that had fallen under Union control. Their principal desire was to regain their states for the Confederacy, a goal that did not necessarily fit with the overall purposes of Confederate strategy. An officer in the 8th Missouri Battalion stationed in Arkansas became convinced by the summer of 1862 that Missouri "is to be abandoned in this struggle. . . . Dont you think it too great a tax on ones patriotism to be asked to abandon all he has for the sake of [a] government that wilfully throws away the country that holds remains of his friends—the graves of his fathers?"[24]

Similar bitterness boiled up in regiments from Confederate states partly controlled by Union forces. Soldiers in the 2nd Arkansas resented their assignment to Georgia when much of their own state was under enemy occupation. They vowed to fight to the last "provided they are transferred to Arkansas," declared a captain in the regiment, "but not under any other circumstances." When the Army of Tennessee retreated (for the second time) from its namesake state in the Tullahoma campaign of 1863, hundreds of Tennessee soldiers deserted. "It is very mortifying that so many should have left," lamented an officer in the 1st Tennessee. "It is caused by the fact that the Army has no confidence in [Braxton] Bragg and thought he was giving up their homes without proper attempt to defend them."[25] One of the reasons for General John Bell Hood's quixotic invasion of Tennessee in November 1864 was a hope to revitalize the morale of troops from that state. Instead, after the devastating defeats at Franklin and Nashville forced Hood to retreat to Mississippi, few Tennesseeans remained with the now almost nonexistent Army of Tennessee.

Many Confederate soldiers understood, however, that the best way to defend their state was to win the war, even if that meant fighting on a front a thousand miles from home. The war experience molded an incipient Southern nationalism into the genuine article. "No amount of description can convey the most remote idea of the hardships" of soldiering, wrote a private in the 21st Mississippi serving in

Virginia, but "I am perfectly content to remain five years or until there is not a Yankee south of the Mason & Dixon's line." A sergeant in the 16th Mississippi, also part of the Army of Northern Virginia, likewise expressed his intention "never to lay down my rifle as long as a Yankee remains on *Southern* soil."[26] A private in the 9th Tennessee insisted that he was fighting "for our *national* rights. . . . We will fight them until Dooms Day or have our independence. I believe that we will be one of the greatest nations on the Globe." A University of Georgia student who left school to enlist wrote his sweetheart from Virginia in 1862 assuring her that the Confederacy would "become a nation among the nations of the earth, designed to fulfill a glorious destiny."[27]

This glorious destiny was much on the mind of twenty-one-year-old "Sandie" Pendleton, Stonewall Jackson's right-hand staff officer, when he wrote to his father (who was chief of artillery for the Army of Northern Virginia) in 1862 that "our men are thinking too much of a whole skin, and too little of their country and the future. What difference does a few hours more or less here of life make in comparison with the future destiny of the people?" Pendleton lived and died by this creed of Confederate nationalism; he was killed at Fishers Hill in 1864.[28]

PATRIOTISM AND NATIONALISM were also powerful sustaining motivations for Union soldiers. This truth has sometimes been difficult to grasp. Southern motives seem easier to understand. Confederates fought for independence, for a way of life, for their homes, for their very survival as a nation. But what did Northerners fight for? Why did they persist through four years of the bloodiest conflict in American history, which cost 360,000 Northern lives?

Puzzling over this question in 1863, Confederate War Department clerk John Jones wrote in his diary: "Our men *must* prevail in combat, or lose their property, country, freedom, everything. . . . On the other hand the enemy, in yielding the contest, may retire into their own country, and possess everything they enjoyed before the war began." A Texas private likewise insisted that "we are fighting for matters real and tangible . . . our property and our homes," while Yankees fought only for "matters abstract and intangible." Even an Illinois colonel seemed to agree with this assessment. "We are fighting for the Union," he wrote in 1864, "a high and noble sentiment, but after all a sentiment. They are fighting for independence and are animated by passion and hatred against invaders. . . . It makes no difference whether the cause is just or not. You can get up an amount of enthusiasm that nothing else will excite." [29]

It is perhaps true that Northern nationalism was more "abstract and intangible" than its Southern counterpart. But it was nonetheless just as real and as deeply felt. Union soldiers did not think that they could "retire into their own country" if they lost the war "and possess everything they enjoyed before the war began." Most of them believed that they would no longer have a country worthy of the name. "If we lose in this war, the country is lost and if we win it is saved," wrote a New York captain in 1863. "There is no middle ground." Another captain, in the 12th New Jersey, spelled out this idea in more detail in a letter to his brother and sister in January 1863, a time of profound Northern discouragement. "Though my nightly prayer is for peace," wrote this veteran, " 'tis for an honorable peace. I would rather live a soldier for life [than] see this country made a mighty sepulcher in which should be buried our institutions, our nationality, our flag, and every American that today lives, than that our Republic should be divided into little *nothings* by an inglorious and shameful peace." [30]

Again and again one finds similar phrases in the letters of Northern soldiers: "Home is sweet and friends are dear, but what would they all be to let the country go to ruin." "I do not want to live if our free Nation is to die or be broken [by] . . . the foul hand of treason." "Far better would it be if the war should continue until every home should be made desolate [than] . . . to surrender to those miserable despots who are trying to destroy our country." [31]

Sometimes the Victorian idioms in which soldiers expressed their patriotism became almost cloying. One wonders what the mother of a Pennsylvania cavalry corporal thought of a letter from her son in 1863 that listed his duties in the following order: "first my God, second my country, third my mother. Oh my country, how my heart bleeds for your welfare. If this poor life of mine could save you, how willingly would I make the sacrifice." Enlisted men in two renowned regiments, the 1st Minnesota and the 5th Iowa, used phrases that by 1862 had become clichés: "Thousands of precious lives will have to be sacrificed" to "support the best Government on God's footstool . . . the best Government ever made." A fifty-four-year-old captain in the 85th New York, a farmer from the dairy belt, wrote his wife in 1863 that "if I never get home you will not say my life has been thrown away for naught. My country, glorious country, if we have only made it truly the land of the free . . . I count not my life dear unto me if only I can help that glorious cause along."[32]

Glorious cause. Lives sacrificed on the country's altar. Hearts bleeding for the country's welfare. Some modern readers of these letters may feel they are drowning in bathos. In this post-Freudian age these phrases strike many as mawkish posturing, romantic sentimentalism, hollow platitudes. We do not speak or write like that any more. Most people have not done so since World War I which, as Ernest Hemingway and Paul Fussell have noted, made such words as *glory, honor, courage, sacrifice, valor,* and *sacred* vaguely embarrassing if not mock-heroic.[33] We would justly mock them if we heard them today. But these words were written in the 1860s, not today. They were written not for public consumption but in private letters to families and friends. These soldiers, at some level at least, *meant* what they said about sacrificing their lives for their country.

Our cynicism about the genuineness of such sentiments is more our problem than theirs, a temporal/cultural barrier we must transcend if we are to understand why they fought. Theirs was an age of romanticism in literature, music, art, and philosophy. It was a sentimental age when strong men were not afraid to cry (or weep, as they would say), a time when Harriet Beecher Stowe's great novel and Stephen Foster's songs could stir genuine emotions. What seems like bathos or platitudes to us were real pathos and convictions to them. Perhaps readers will take another look at the expressions by soldiers quoted two paragraphs above when they learn that all four of them were subsequently killed in action. They were not posturing for public show. They were not looking back from years later through a haze of memory and myth about the Civil War. They were writing during the immediacy of their experiences to explain and justify their beliefs to family members and friends who shared—or in some cases questioned—those beliefs. And how smugly can we sneer at their expressions of a willingness to die for those beliefs when we know that they did precisely that?

An important question remains. How representative were these assertions of patriotic motivations for fighting? Of the 429 Confederate soldiers and sailors whose letters or diaries form the basis for this book, 283, or 66 percent, affirmed such motivations at one time or another after enlisting. For the 647 Union fighting men, the proportion was virtually the same: 441, or 68 percent. These percentages need some interpretation and qualification, however. On the one hand, the absence of references to patriotic convictions in a soldier's letters or diary does not necessarily mean that he was unmoved by such convictions. By their nature, most personal letters and diaries were descriptive rather than reflective, concerned with day-to-day events in the army and at home—weather, food, sickness, gossip, and other mundane matters. Many soldiers who were motivated by patriotism probably found it unnecessary to mention the fact in such writings. On the other hand, the samples of both Confederate and Union soldiers are biased toward the groups most likely to be moved by patriotic and ideological motives: officers, slaveholders, professional men, the middle class, and 1861–62 volunteers rather than post-1862 conscripts, substitutes, and bounty men. Officers comprised 47 percent of the Confederate sample but only about 10 percent of all soldiers. And the proportion of officers who expressed patriotic motives was 82 percent, compared with 52 percent of Confederate enlisted men. Some 35 percent of the Union sample were officers, and 79 percent of them, compared with 62 percent of the enlisted men, expressed patriotic convictions.

Using army rank as a surrogate for class, patriotic motivations appear to have been shared more evenly across class lines in the Union army than among Confederate troops. This finding is borne out by other data from the samples. In the Confederate army the highest-status groups—members of planter families and of slaveholding professional families—voiced patriotic sentiments at almost twice the rate of nonslaveholding soldiers. A similar though less marked pattern occurred between the deep South, with its higher percentage of slaves and slaveholders, and the upper South. The contrast between South Carolina and North Carolina soldiers was particularly notable: 84 percent from South Carolina avowed patriotic convictions, compared with 46 percent from North Carolina. In the Union army there was no such regional variation, and the disparity between higher-status and lower-status groups was much less marked than between Confederates of slaveholding and nonslaveholding status. Thus there was a greater democratization of patriotic motivations across class and regional lines in the Union sample. It is impossible to know whether the same contrast held true for all three million Civil War soldiers. If so, it might help to explain the dogged determination that sustained

Union volunteers through four long years of fighting in enemy territory against a foe sustained by the more concrete motive of defending that territory.

In both the Confederate and Union samples the draftees, substitutes, and men who enlisted after conscription went into effect are underrepresented. To the extent that they *are* represented, the percentages expressing patriotic convictions were much smaller than among the volunteers of 1861–62. Among yeomen farmers in the Confederate army, for example, 57 percent of those who enlisted in the first year of the war asserted such sentiments, compared with only 14 percent who enlisted or were drafted after conscription went into effect. Among farmers and blue-collar workers in the Union army the disparity was less: 61 percent of those who enlisted before the conscription act of March 1863 avowed patriotic convictions, compared with 43 percent of those who went into the army after this date.[34]

The prototypical unwilling soldier who expressed no patriotic sentiments and would have preferred to be at home was a nonslaveholding Southern married farmer with small children who was drafted in 1862 or enlisted only to avoid being drafted. This is not meant to suggest that only those men who fell into this category were unwilling soldiers—there were many such, from all walks of life and every state, North and South, and they included a substantial number of 1861 volunteers who later regretted their impulsive act. But Southern nonslaveholding married farmers seemed particularly bitter on this matter. They gave substance to the theme of a "rich man's war and a poor man's fight" that is prevalent in modern scholarship on class tensions in both North and South during the Civil War.[35]

There is less emphasis on these tensions in soldiers' letters than in recent scholarship. But there is some. A dirt farmer in the 60th North Carolina complained to his wife in 1863 that "this is a Rich mans Woar But the poor man has to do the fiting." Another farmer drafted into the 57th North Carolina lamented that "I could be at home if it warent for a fiew big rulers who I cannot help but blame for it. . . . These big fighting men cant be got out to fight as easy as to make speaches. . . . They lay at home feesting on the good things of the land . . . while we poor soldiers are foursed away from home." Similar sentiments came from a German-born bricklayer in the 8th New Jersey, who exclaimed in 1862: "By God, I don't know for what I should fight. For the rich man so he can make more money the poor man should risk his life and I should get slaughtered."[36]

The soldiers who felt this way furnished a disproportionate number of deserters and skulkers—according to the letters of highly motivated volunteers. They may have been right. If the sample is biased toward those who expressed patriotic convictions, it is also biased toward those who did most of the fighting. The startling fact noted in the preface is relevant here. While 7 percent of all Civil War soldiers were killed or mortally wounded in action, 21 percent of the soldiers in the samples lost their lives in this way. In the Civil War patriotism was not the last refuge of the scoundrel; it was the credo of the fighting soldier.

CHAPTER 8

THE CAUSE OF LIBERTY

THE PATRIOTISM OF Civil War soldiers existed in a specific historical context. Americans of the Civil War generation revered their Revolutionary forebears. Every schoolboy and schoolgirl knew how they had fought against the odds to forge a new republic conceived in liberty. Northerners and Southerners alike believed themselves custodians of the legacy of 1776. The crisis of 1861 was the great test of their worthiness of that heritage. On *their* shoulders rode the fate of the great experiment of republican government launched in 1776. Both Abraham Lincoln and Jefferson Davis appealed to this intense consciousness of parallels between 1776 and 1861. That is why Lincoln began his great evocation of Union war aims with the words: "Four score and seven years ago our fathers brought forth . . . a new government, conceived in Liberty and dedicated to the proposition that all men are created equal." Likewise, Davis urged his people to "renew such sacrifices as our fathers made to the holy cause of constitutional liberty." [1]

The profound irony of the Civil War was that, like Davis and Lincoln, Confederate and Union soldiers interpreted the heritage of 1776 in opposite ways. Confederates professed to fight for liberty and independence from a tyrannical government; Unionists said they fought to preserve the nation conceived in liberty from dismemberment and destruction. These conflicting impulses, which had propelled many volunteers into the armies at the war's beginning, became more intense as the fighting escalated.

Patriotic holidays had a special tendency to call forth meditations by Confederate soldiers on the legacy for which they fought. "How trifling were the wrongs complained of by our Revolutionary forefathers, compared with ours!" wrote a captain in the 5th Alabama on Washington's Birthday in 1862. "If the mere imposition of a tax could raise such a tumult what should be the result of the terrible system of oppression instituted by the Yankees?" On the Fourth of July that same year a Kentuckian who had cast his lot with the Confederacy reflected upon George Washington, "who set us an example in bursting the bonds of tyranny." On the same date a year later an Alabama corporal who had just been captured at Gettysburg was not disheartened. Soldiers of the Revolution had endured many setbacks, he noted in his diary, and in fighting for "the same principles which fired the hearts of our ancestors in the revolutionary struggle" the Confederacy too would ultimately prevail.[2]

This folk memory of snatching victory from the jaws of defeat four score years earlier sustained the morale of Confederate soldiers during times of discouragement. A wealthy South Carolina planter and a North Carolina farmer's son who both served in elite regiments on the Virginia front wrote similar letters to boost spirits at home after a string of Confederate reverses in early 1862. "Times may grow a great deal worse than they now are," wrote the South Carolinian, "and still we can stand it—And even then not go through what our Grandparents went through, when they were struggling for the same thing that we are now fighting for." The North Carolinian told his father that "instead of indulging in feelings of despondency let us compare our situation and cause to those of our illustrious ancestors who achieved the liberties we have ever enjoyed and for which we are now contending." During the retreat from Gettysburg, a captain in the 50th Georgia learned of the surrender of Vicksburg. "What a calamity!" he wrote to his wife. "But let us not despair. . . . Our forefathers were whipped in nearly every battle & yet after seven years of trials & hardships achieved their independence."[3]

The rhetoric of liberty that had permeated the letters of Confederate volunteers in 1861 grew even stronger as the war progressed. A corporal in the 9th Alabama celebrated his twentieth birthday in 1862 by writing proudly in his diary that "I am engaged in the glorious cause of liberty and justice, fighting for all that we of the South hold dear." The lieutenant colonel of the 10th Tennessee declared in May 1862 that "my whole heart is in the cause of the Confederacy, because I believe that the perpetuity of Republican principles on this Continent depends upon our success." A year later he was killed in the battle of Raymond.[4] In a letter to his Unionist father early in 1863, the son of a Baltimore merchant tried to explain why he was fighting for the Confederacy as a private in the 44th Virginia. The war, he wrote, was "a struggle between Liberty on one side, and Tyranny on the other," and he had decided to "espouse the holy cause of Southern free-dom"—for which he gave his life three months later at Chancellorsville. A lieutenant in the Confederate 3rd Missouri wrote in his diary while recovering from a wound he suffered at Pea Ridge that if he was killed, it would be while "fighting gloriously for the undying principles of Constitutional liberty and self government." Two years later he was killed in action near Atlanta.[5]

The opposites of independence and liberty were "subjugation" and "slavery." These two words continued to express the fate worse than death that awaited Confederate soldiers if they lost the war. "If we was to lose," a Mississippi private wrote his wife in 1862, "we would be slaves to the Yanks and our children would have a yoke of bondage thrown around there neck." An enlisted man in the 8th Georgia was "ready to fight them 50 years rather than have them subjugate so noble a people as we are." And a Texas cavalryman who rode with Forrest agreed that the issue was "either subjugation, slavery, confiscation" or "victorious, glorious, and free."[6]

These soldiers were using the word *slavery* in the same way that Americans in 1776 had used it to describe their subordination to Britain. Unlike many slaveholders in the age of Thomas Jefferson, Confederate soldiers from slaveholding families expressed no feelings of embarrassment or inconsistency in fighting for their own liberty while holding other people in slavery. Indeed, white supremacy and the right of property in slaves were at the core of the ideology for which Confederate soldiers fought. "We are fighting for our liberty," wrote a young Kentucky Confederate, "against tyrants of the North . . . who are determined to destroy slavery." A South Carolina planter in the Army of Northern Virginia declared a willingness to give his life "battling for liberty and independence" but was exasperated when his supposedly faithful body servant ran away to the Yankees. "It is very singular and I cant account for it."[7] A captain in the 15th Georgia who owned forty slaves wrote to his wife in 1863 of "the arch of liberty we are trying to build." When she voiced apprehension about the future of slavery, he assured her that if the Confederacy won the war "it is established for centuries." In 1864 a South Carolina lieutenant who professed to fight for "the land of liberty and freemen" told his mother that he intended to sell his no-account body servant, who then ran off before he could do so. Good riddance, said this soldier, "but [I] would rather had converted him into money."[8]

Before the war many Southern whites had avoided using the words *slaves* and *slavery*, preferring instead *servants* and *Southern institutions*. Some Confederate soldiers kept up this custom even in private letters, referring to "our own social institutions," "the integrity of all our institutions," "the institutions of the whole South" as the cause for which they fought.[9] In June 1863 a lieutenant in the 2nd North Carolina stopped for a meal at the home of a Pennsylvania farmer during the Gettysburg campaign. "They live in real Yankee style wife & daughters . . . doing all the work," he wrote to his mother. "It makes me more than ever devoted to our own Southern institutions."[10]

A lieutenant in the 53rd Georgia, however, indulged in no euphemisms or circumlocutions. "Pennsylvania is the greates country I ever saw," he wrote to his wife on the eve of the battle of Gettysburg. "If this state was a slave state and I was able to buy land here after the war you might count on living in Pennsylvania." In January 1865 this same officer whipped his body servant for stealing some of the company's meat allotment. "I give him about four hundred lashes. . . . Mollie you better belive I tore his back and legs all to pices."[11]

Other soldiers were equally plain-spoken. "This country without slave labor would be completely worthless," wrote a lieutenant in the 28th Mississippi in 1863. "We can only live & exist by that species of labor: and hence I am willing to fight to the last." A captain in the 8th Alabama also vowed "to fight forever, rather than submit to freeing negroes among us. . . . [We are fighting for] rights and property bequeathed to us by our ancestors."[12]

Some Confederate soldiers welcomed Lincoln's Emancipation Proclamation for bringing the real issue into the open. "The Proclamation is worth three hundred thousand soldiers to our Government at least," wrote a Kentucky cavalry sergeant who rode with John Hunt Morgan. "It shows exactly what this war was brought about for and the intention of its damnable authors." A captain in the 27th Virginia, a small slaveholder in the Shenandoah Valley, believed that "after Lincoln's proclamation any man that would not fight to the last should be hung as high as Haman." Several Union soldiers regretted the Proclamation on just these grounds that it would make the enemy fight harder. "My hopes (if I had any) of a speedy termination of the war is thereby nocked in [the] head," wrote a New York corporal, "for I know enough of the southern spirit that I think they will fight for the institution of slavery even to extermination."[13]

Confederate prospects for victory appeared brightest during the months after the Emancipation Proclamation, partly because this measure divided the Northern people and intensified a morale crisis in Union armies. Slave prices rose even faster than the rate of inflation during that springtime of Southern hope. A number of soldiers wrote home advising relatives to invest in slaves. "Every species of property is selling now at a very high price—Negroe men for $1500 to 2000, fancy girls & women with one or two children at about the same," wrote a navy captain commanding the CSS *Morgan*. "I will buy five or six more if I can get them right." The famous "boy colonel" of the Confederacy, the planter's son Henry Burgwyn, who became colonel of the 26th North Carolina at the age of twenty-one, urged his father to put every dollar he had into slaves. "I would buy boys & girls from 15 to 20 years old & take care to have a majority of girls," he wrote. "The increase in the number of negroes by this means would repay the difference in the amount of available labor. . . . I would not be surprised to see negroes in 6 mos. after peace worth from 2 to 3000 dollars." Gettysburg cut short his life before he could witness the collapse of his dreams.[14]

But Gettysburg did not discourage Colonel E. Porter Alexander, Longstreet's chief of artillery who directed the barrage that preceded Pickett's charge. Three weeks after the battle, Porter told his wife to buy a wet nurse for their twins, for "Carline and her baby wd. be a fine *speculation* at $2000." Even as late as January 1865 an officer from low-country South Carolina wrote to his fiancée that "now is the time for Uncle to buy some negro women and children on the principle that if we don't succeed the money won't be worth anything and if we do slaves will be worth a 1000 times more than now."[15]

These soldiers, of course, belonged to slaveholding families. They tended to emphasize the right of property in slaves as the basis of the liberty for which they fought. This motive, not surprisingly, was much less in evidence among nonslaveholding soldiers. But some of them emphasized a form of property they did own, one that was central to the liberty for which they fought. That property was their white skins, which put them on a plane of civil equality with slaveholders and far above those who did not possess that property. Herrenvolk democracy—the equality of all who belonged to the master race—was a powerful motivator for many Confederate soldiers.

Even though he was tired of the war, wrote a Louisiana artilleryman in 1862, "I never want to see the day when a negro is put on an equality with a white person. There is too many free niggers . . . now to suit me, let alone having four millions." A private in the 38th North Carolina, a yeoman farmer, vowed to show the Yankees "that a white man is better than a nigger."[16] Similarly, a farmer from the Shenandoah Valley informed his fiancée that he fought to assure "a free white man's government instead of living under a black republican government," while the son of another North Carolina dirt farmer said he would never stop fighting Yankees, who were "trying to force us to live as the colored race." Many Northern soldiers shared the bewilderment of a private in the 25th Wisconsin who wrote home describing a conversation with Confederate prisoners captured in the Atlanta campaign: "Some of the boys asked them what they were fighting for, and they answered, 'You Yanks want us to marry our daughters to the niggers.' "[17]

Such sentiments were not confined to nonslaveholders. Many slaveholding soldiers also fought for white supremacy as well as for the right of property in slaves. An Arkansas captain was enraged by the idea that if the Yankees won, his "sister, wife, and mother are to be given up to the embraces of their present 'dusky male servitors.' " After reading Lincoln's Proclamation of Amnesty and Reconstruction in December 1863, which required Southern acceptance of emancipation as a condition of peace, another Arkansas soldier, a planter, wrote his wife that Lincoln not only wanted to free the slaves but also "declares them entitled to all the rights and privileges as American citizens. So imagine your sweet little girls in the school room with a black wooly headed negro and have to treat them as their equal." Likewise, a Georgia infantry captain wrote to his wife from the trenches on the Chattahoochee in 1864 that if Atlanta and Richmond fell, "we are irrevocably lost and not only will the negroes be free but . . . we will all be on a common level. . . . The negro who now waits on you will then be as free as you are & as insolent as she is ignorant."[18]

It would be wrong, however, to assume that Confederate soldiers were constantly preoccupied with this matter. In fact, only 20 percent of the sample of 429 Southern soldiers explicitly voiced proslavery convictions in their letters or diaries. As one might expect, a much higher percentage of soldiers from slaveholding families than from nonslaveholding families expressed such a purpose: 33 percent, compared with 12 percent. Ironically, the proportion of Union soldiers who wrote about the slavery question was greater, as the next chapter will show. There is a ready explanation for this apparent paradox. Emancipation was a salient issue for Union soldiers because it was controversial. Slavery was less salient for most Confederate soldiers because it was not controversial. They took slavery for granted as one of the Southern "rights" and institutions for which they fought, and did not feel compelled to discuss it. Although only 20 percent of the soldiers avowed explicit proslavery purposes in their letters and diaries, *none at all* dissented from that view.[19] But even those who owned slaves and fought consciously to defend the institution preferred to discourse upon liberty, rights, and the horrors of subjugation.

CONFEDERATES WHO PROFESSED to fight for the same goals as their forebears of 1776 would have been surprised by the intense conviction of Northern soldiers that *they* were upholding the legacy of the Revolution. A sergeant in the 1st Minnesota proudly told his parents that he fought for "the same glorious ensign that floated over Ticonderoga, [and] was carried triumphantly through the Revolution." A schoolteacher with several children of his own, who had enlisted in the 20th Connecticut on his thirty-sixth birthday, celebrated his thirty-seventh by writing that he had never regretted his decision to fight for "those institutions which were achieved for us by our glorious revolution . . . in order that they may be perpetuated to those who may come after." An Illinois farm boy whose parents had opposed his enlistment in 1862 asked them tartly a year later: "Should We the youngest and brightest nation of all the earth bow to traters and forsake the graves of our Fathers?" He answered his own question: "No no never never."[20]

As with Confederate soldiers, patriotic holidays had a special power to prompt such reflections. An officer in the 22nd Kentucky (Union) rejoiced at the surrender of Vicksburg on the Fourth of July, for that day "will now be sanctified to the lovers of freedom as the day of a second deliverance of the land from a danger greater, more potent and more to be dreaded than any our British progenitors threatened us with."[21]

The theme of parallel sacrifice with the patriots of 1776 appeared in the letters of many Union soldiers. An officer in the 101st Ohio wrote in December 1862 that "our fathers in coldest winter, half clad marked the road they trod with crimson streams from their bleeding feet that we might enjoy the blessings of a free government," and therefore "our business in being here [is] to lay down our lives if need be for our country's cause." Two weeks later he was killed at Stones River. A young private in the 2nd Michigan was killed in action less than a year after he had written a letter to his uncle describing the hardships of a soldier's life. But "did the revolutionary patriots in valley forge," he asked rhetorically, "complain [when] they had to march in the snow with there bare feet and to stand the cold twenty degrees below zero without blankets? We will show our fathers and mothers wifes sisters brothers and sweethearts that we are" worthy of that heritage.[22]

Some of those wives, however, told their soldier husbands that they had a greater responsibility to their present families than to the Founding Fathers. A lieutenant in the 41st Ohio received several such letters from his wife complaining about the burdens of raising three children while worrying about his fate. In response, he asked her to "bear your trouble with good cheer. . . . It only gives another trouble on my mind to know that you are so discontented. . . . If you esteem me with a true woman's love you will not ask me to disgrace myself by deserting the flag of our Union. . . . Remember that thousands went forth and poured out their lifs blood in the Revolution to establish this government; and twould be a disgrace to the whole American people if she had not noble sons enough who had the spirit of seventy six in their hearts." Justifying to *his* wife a decision to stay in the army instead of seeking a medical discharge after he was wounded, a thirty-three-year-old Minnesota sergeant, also a father of three children, wrote that "my grandfather fought and risked his life to bequeath to his posterity . . . the glorious Institutions" now threatened by "this infernal rebellion. . . . It is not for you and I, or us & our dear little ones, alone, that I was and am willing to risk the fortunes of the battle-field, but also for the sake of the country's millions who are to come after us."[23]

What were those "glorious Institutions"? An officer in the 54th

Ohio defined them as "the guaranty of the rights of property, liberty of action, freedom of thought, religion [and] . . . that kind of government that shall assure life liberty & the pursuit of happiness." But a Confederate soldier would have said that he fought for the same things. His Union adversary might have replied, like Lincoln, that secession was "the essence of anarchy," a challenge to constitutional law and order without which liberty becomes license and leads in turn to despotism. The Founding Fathers fought a revolution and adopted a Constitution to achieve *ordered* liberty under the rule of law. Southern states had seceded in response to Lincoln's election by a constitutional majority in a fair vote held under rules accepted by all parties. To permit them to get away with it, said Lincoln, would be to "fly to anarchy or to despotism."[24]

Many Union soldiers echoed Lincoln's words. We are "fighting for the maintenance of law and order," they wrote, "to assert the strength and dignity of the government" against the threat of "dissolution, anarchy, and ruin."[25] "This is not a war for dollars and cents," wrote a captain in the 12th Indiana, "nor is it a war for territory—but it is to decide whether we are to be a free people—and if the Union is dissolved I very much fear that we will not have a Republican form of government very long." To an Ohio blacksmith, the cause for which he fought as a private in the 70th Ohio was "the cause of the constitution and law. . . . Admit the right of the seceding states to break up the Union at pleasure . . . and how long will it be before the new confederacies created by the first disruption shall be resolved into still smaller fragments and the continent become a vast theater of civil war, military license, anarchy, and despotism? Better settle it at whatever cost and settle it forever."[26]

Northern soldiers also picked up Lincoln's theme that the United States represented the last best hope for the survival of republican government in a world bestrode by kings, emperors, and despots of many stripes. If secession fragmented America into the dis-United States, European aristocrats and reactionaries would smile in smug satisfaction at the confirmation of their belief that this harebrained experiment in government of, by, and for the people would indeed perish from the earth. "I do feel that the liberty of the world is placed in our hands to defend," wrote a private in the 33rd Massachusetts in 1862, "and if we are overcome then farewell to freedom." A private in the 27th Connecticut agreed that if "traitors" destroyed the government that cost "our forefathers long years of blood" to establish, "all the hope and confidence in the capacity of men for self government will be lost."[27] But "if we succeed in establishing our Gov[ernment]," added a private in the 122nd Illinois, *"then you may look for European struggles for liberty."* In 1863 on the second anniversary of his enlistment, a thirty-three-year-old private in the 2nd Ohio Cavalry wrote that he had not expected the war to last so long, but no matter how much longer it took it must be prosecuted "for the great principles of liberty and self government at stake, for should we fail, the onward march of Liberty in the Old World will be retarded at least a century, and Monarchs, Kings and Aristocrats will be more powerful against their subjects than ever."[28]

All of the Union soldiers quoted in the preceding paragraphs were born in the United States. Many of their forebears *had* fought in the Revolution. Foreign-born soldiers are underrepresented in the Union sample, and some who are represented expressed few if any ideological convictions. Of those who did, however, the theme of the Union as a beacon light for the oppressed in their homelands shone brightly. In 1864 a forty-year-old corporal in the 39th Ohio who had been born in England wrote to his wife after he had reenlisted for a second three-year hitch: "If I do get hurt I want you to remember that it will be not only for my Country and my Children but for Liberty all over the World that I risked my life, for if Liberty should be crushed here, what hope would there be for the cause of Human Progress anywhere else?" Four months later he was killed near Atlanta.[29]

Irish-American soldiers drew some of the clearest parallels between their fight for the Union and the struggle for liberty in the old country. An Irish-born carpenter, a private in the 28th Massachusetts of the famous Irish Brigade, angrily rebuked both his wife in Boston and his father-in-law back in Ireland for questioning his judgment in fighting for the Black Republican Lincoln administration. "This is my country as much as the man who was born on the soil," he wrote in 1863. "I have as much interest in the maintenance of . . . the integrity of the nation as any other man. . . . This is the first test of a modern free government in the act of sustaining itself against internal enemys . . . if it fail all tyrants will succeed the old cry will be sent forth from the aristocrats of europe that such is the common lot of all republics. . . . Irishmen and their descendents have . . . a stake in [this] nation. . . . America is Irlands refuge Irlands last hope destroy this republic and her hopes are blasted." A year later he too was killed in action. Another Irish-born soldier, a sergeant in the 2nd New Jersey, gave this argument a different twist. After he and his brother had been in the army for about a year, their mother rued the day they had enlisted. He told her curtly that "you are not a fit subject to live in a free and prosperous country. Ireland is the place for those who possess such sentiments—there is where the iron heel of despotism grinds the Patriot heart."[30]

As noted in the preceding chapter, two-thirds of both Confederate and Union soldiers in the samples expressed generalized patriotic motives for fighting. Likewise an almost identical proportion—42 percent Confederate and 40 percent Union—discoursed in more depth on ideological issues such as liberty, constitutional rights, constitutional law, self-government, resistance to tyranny, republicanism, democracy. Among Confederate soldiers, 47 percent of those from slaveholding families but only 28 percent from nonslaveholding families emphasized one or more of these themes. The greater disparity between officers and men in the Confederate than in the Union army that characterized simple expressions of patriotism also prevailed with respect to more sophisticated ideological comments. Some 53 percent of Confederate officers and 30 percent of Southern enlisted men discussed ideological themes; the comparable figures for Union soldiers were 49 and 36 percent.

PATRIOTIC AND IDEOLOGICAL convictions were an essential part of the sustaining motivation of Civil War soldiers. But how important were they for combat motivation? Were soldiers who avowed such convictions better fighters than those who did not? Or were the factors of primary group cohesion, religion, adrenalin, and the fear of showing cowardice that were discussed in earlier chapters the only things that counted when the bullets started flying?

No unequivocal answer is possible. American soldiers in World War II and those social scientists who studied them relegated patriotism and ideology to a marginal role in *combat* motivation. On the other hand a questionnaire administered to their slightly older contemporaries, American volunteers in the Abraham Lincoln Brigade in the Spanish Civil War, found that "belief in war aims" helped 77 percent of them to overcome fear in battle—a far higher percentage than any other factor.[31] But these volunteers were exceptional both in the degree of their ideological convictions and in their motivation. What about soldiers in the *American* Civil War? Nobody gave them a questionnaire. But several of them tried to answer the question anyway.

Some answered it in the same way as the G.I. who said that "a boy up there 60 days on the line is in danger every minute. He ain't fighting for patriotism. You're fighting for your skin on the line." A lieutenant in the 1st Virginia of Pickett's division wrote after he survived the famous charge at Gettysburg that "when you rise to your feet as we did today, I tell you the enthusiasm of ardent breasts in many cases *ain't there*, and instead of burning to avenge the insults of our country, families, altars and firesides, the thought is most frequently, *Oh*, if I could just come out of this charge safely how thankful *would I be!*" Similarly, a private in the New Hampshire company of the 2nd U.S. Sharpshooters wrote in his diary after the battle of the Wilderness that "when I first started on the charge this morning I felt that I could fight & do any thing for my bleeding country. But after I had got out the first time my patriotism had died & I thought of nothing but to keep clear of the enemy's bullets—zip, zip, zipping around me."[32]

But in the opinion of a good many others, it was the men whose patriotism did *not* die when the bullets zipped around them who made the best combat soldiers. "The Only thing that bears me up . . . in the hour of Battles is the Consciousness . . . that I am in discharge of a duty that all good sitizens owe there country," wrote a captain in the 37th North Carolina. "It is the caus that makes a man fight," agreed a sergeant in the 59th Illinois after the battle of Pea Ridge. Another Illinois sergeant expressed pride in his company after the battle of Stones River because "they are too patriotic to be cowards . . . and are willing to do or suffer anything for their country."[33]

During the siege of Port Hudson a strongly ideological sergeant in the 90th New York wrote his parents that "this place has been attacked again and again for the past two months and without success as in every regiment there are cowardly fellows who on a charge will fall out, drop behind logs, etc and that cripples the efforts of those who would go forward." On two occasions, therefore, Union commander Nathaniel Banks called for volunteers to form a special unit of shock troops to lead assaults. "You may wonder why I volunteered to undertake a work of such danger," this soldier said. "I thought of the mighty interests at stake . . . and I concluded that the great results which it promised were worth the sacrifice." A lieutenant in the 30th Massachusetts who also volunteered to lead one of these charges wrote in his diary before the attack: "Although we are going into a terrible conflict, the boys feel gay and happy. We came to fight for our country, and why should we falter?"[34]

These two men survived the assaults. But as an ideologically committed sergeant in the 8th Illinois Cavalry pointed out to his fiancée in 1863, it was "the *best, truest,* and *bravest* of the nation" who went forward and often got killed while the beats lagged to the rear and saved their skins. A few months later he was killed in action. The same fate befell a corporal in the 57th Massachusetts shortly after he wrote home in August 1864: "Mother if all our army felt as I feel when I go into battle, the war would soon be over but I am sorry to say that we have got too many in the army that are not fighting for there country but for money and all they think of when they go into battle is how to . . . skulk behind the first stump . . . [and] keep out of danger."[35]

This observation became almost a litany among the volunteers of 1861–62 as they tried to absorb the substitutes, draftees, and bounty men of 1863 and after. These new men "are far inferior to the old patriotic vols. who came 'without money and without price,' " wrote a division commander in the Union 12th Corps. "One of the old is worth ten of the new." A private in the 85th New York agreed that "thoes *money* soldiers are not worth as much as they *cost* for when you heer firing ahead you may see them hid in the woods." The same was true of substitutes and draftees in the Confederate army, according to a Texas captain, who in 1864 contrasted "the old soldiers, the original volunteers" who were "patriotic and sacrifice everything to Country" with the "whining, cowardly Georgians and Alabmians" who had been drafted into his division and "resort to every means to avoid" combat.[36]

The ideological commitment of so many of those volunteers of 1861 and 1862 was one reason for the high casualty rates of Civil War armies. Fighting for liberty was a dangerous business. The kind of liberty that most Americans today associate with the Civil War was the liberation of four million slaves. But that was not the liberty for which most Civil War soldiers initially fought. "I have been talking all my life for the cause of liberty," a recruit to the 5th Wisconsin had written in August 1861, and "now the time is nigh at hand when I shall have a chance to aid by deed this cause and I shrink not from doing my duty."[37] He did not mean freedom for the slaves. He meant the republican liberty and constitutional government of 1776 and 1789—which had left slavery intact. But by 1864 most Northern soldiers had broadened their conception of liberty to include black people.

CHAPTER 9

SLAVERY MUST BE
CLEANED OUT

A YEAR BEFORE LEE surrendered at Appomattox, a Texas private predicted that Confederate victory was certain because "we are fighting for our property and homes; they, for the flimsy and abstract idea that a negro is equal to an Anglo American."[1] He was wrong in more ways than one. Few Union soldiers professed to fight for racial equality. For that matter, not many claimed even to fight *primarily* for the abolition of slavery. In his study of Billy Yank, Bell Wiley wrote that scarcely one in ten Union soldiers "had any real interest in emancipation per se." If by "per se" Wiley meant "in and of itself alone," one in ten may be an exaggeration. Rare indeed were two soldiers, one from Wisconsin and the other from Maine, whose letters home contained such sentiments as: "I have no heart in this war if the slaves cannot go free." Our cause is "nobler even than the Revolution for they fought for their own freedom, while we fight for that of another race. . . . If the doom of slavery is not sealed by the war I shall curse the day I entered the Army or lifted a finger in the preservation of the Union."[2]

But if "emancipation per se" meant a perception that the abolition of slavery was inseparably linked to the goal of preserving the Union, then three in ten Union soldiers whose letters and diaries form the basis of this book took that position during the first eighteen months of the war, and many more were eventually converted to it. While restoration of the Union was the main goal for which they fought, they became convinced that this goal was unattainable without striking against slavery. "I believe that Slavery (the worst of all curses) was the sole cause of this Rebellion," wrote a private in the 5th Iowa in January 1862, "and untill this cause is removed and slavery abolished, the rebellion will continue to exist." A corporal in the 64th Ohio likened secession to a cancer. "We are now fighting to destroy the cause of these dangerous diseases, which is slavery and the slave power." A private in the 1st Minnesota put the point succinctly: "The war will never end until we end slavery."[3]

Experience in the South reinforced the antislavery sentiments of many soldiers. After talking with a slave woman in Virginia who described the brutal whipping of her husband, a private in the 83rd Pennsylvania wrote to a cousin in January 1862: "I thought I hated slavery as much as possible before I came here, but here, where I can see some of its workings, I am more than ever convinced of the cruelty and inhumanity of the system." A sergeant in the 90th New York stationed on the South Atlantic coast in 1862 likewise vented his wrath at "this cursed slavery that gives one man power over another to whip or to do as he pleases with him."[4]

Several soldiers wrote home after a few months in the South that slavery was a "blight" that "withered all it touched." This was not necessarily an abolitionist position grounded in a humanitarian concern for the plight of slaves. It stemmed from personal observation as well as from the antebellum free-labor ideology that portrayed the South as mired in backwardness and ignorance. "I am no abolitionist," wrote the colonel of the 53rd Indiana to his wife from Tennessee in 1862. "But the more I see of slavery in all its enormity the more I am satisfied that it is a curse to our country. . . . Outside the towns in the South the people are a century behind the free states." An Ohio farmer's son who marched through Tennessee as an artilleryman remarked on "how far they are behind the North in improvements. . . . The institution of slavery is as much a curse to the whites as the blacks and kills industry and improvements of every kind. Slavery has deadened all enterprise and prosperity." Tennessee did not stand alone as a target of such comments. A prewar Democrat, now a brigade commander in the Army of the Potomac, was converted to emancipation by what he saw in Virginia. "There is scarcely a man in this county

(Prince William) who can read and write," he told his wife in 1863, "another of the results of the peculiar and beautiful system."[5]

As Northern armies invaded the South they became agents of emancipation by their very presence. "It is all humbug about Slaves liking to stay with their masters," wrote an Ohio colonel in 1862. "Men women & children run off whenever they can get a chance." Attempts by their masters to reclaim these runaways turned many soldiers into practical abolitionists. They hid fugitives in camp and laughed at the rage of owners who went home empty-handed. Officers sometimes winked at this activity despite orders to the contrary. A lieutenant in the 10th Massachusetts stationed in Maryland vowed in March 1862 that "I never will be instrumental in returning a slave to his master in any way shape or manner, I'll die first."[6]

A lieutenant in the 8th Michigan recounted what happened when a "secesh" came into camp near Annapolis to reclaim his slave. The soldiers "pounced on him," and if he had not quickly decided that discretion was the better part of valor, "he would have lost his life in this Negro Hunt. As it was he got well frightened, & I presume will think twice before he goes into a Camp of northern Soldiers to reclaim biped property." From Tennessee a private in the 10th Wisconsin wrote home in March 1862 that "whe have got lots of contraband negroes in our regt now and there is no less than two negro hunters in camp every day hunting for negroes   Our colonel tells them if they can get them out of the lines they can have them but that is the trouble a negro hunter finds himself in a hot bed when he gets into the Regt they stone them out in a hurry."[7]

The attitudes of a good many soldiers on this matter were more pragmatic than altruistic. They understood that every slave laborer who emancipated himself by coming into Union lines weakened the Confederate war effort. It also strengthened the Union army. "I don't care a damn for the darkies," wrote an Illinois lieutenant, but "I couldn't help to send a runaway nigger back. I'm blamed if I could. I honestly believe that this army [in Tennessee] has taken 500 niggers away with them." In fact, "I have 11 negroes in my company now. They do every particle of the dirty work. Two women among them do the washing for the company." Another Illinois soldier, an infantry sergeant, wrote from Corinth, Mississippi, in 1862 that "every regt has nigger teamsters and cooks which puts that many more men back in the ranks. . . . It will make a difference in the regt of not less than 75 men that will carry guns that did not before we got niggers."[8]

By the summer of 1862, antislavery pragmatism and principle fused into a growing commitment to emancipation as both a means and goal of Union victory. This development represented a significant hardening of Northern attitudes toward "traitors," whose rights of property—especially property in slaves—were entitled to little respect. "We have been . . . playing with *Traitors* long enough," wrote an Iowa private. "We have guarded their property long enough, now is the time for action." A Wisconsin major insisted that "the only way to put down this rebellion is to hurt the instigators and abettors of it. Slavery must be cleaned out." By July 1862 the colonel of the 54th Ohio had decided that "we [must] teach these ingrates that we can punish with a rod of iron, that we can not only meet and vanquish them on the field but that we have the nerve and the will to sweep them & all they hold dear clear off from the face of the earth. . . . Slavery is doomed."[9]

Officials in Washington had come to the same conclusion. In July 1862 Congress passed the second confiscation act, and Lincoln made his momentous decision to issue an emancipation proclamation. It would not become public for two months, but meanwhile the work of practical emancipation went on. "That bill to confiscate the rebel property is just what we want," wrote a Rhode Island sergeant. "If a rebels property gits eney favers from eney of our Soldiers you can call me a poor judge." The colonel of the 5th Minnesota wrote from northern Alabama in September 1862: "I am doing quite a business in the confiscation of slave property. . . . It certainly makes the rebels wince to see their 'niggers' taken off which is a source of private satisfaction to me. . . . Crippling the institution of slavery is . . . striking a blow at the heart of the rebellion."[10]

But a good many Union soldiers strongly opposed the idea of freeing the slaves. A backlash of anti-emancipation sentiment began to surface in their letters. This sentiment brewed up from a mixture of racism, conservatism, and partisan politics. "No one who has ever seen the nigger in all his glory on the southern plantations . . . will ever vote for emancipation," wrote a private in the 19th Indiana, part of the famous Iron Brigade. "If emancipation is to be the policy of this war . . . I do not care how quick the country goes to pot." A sergeant in the 56th Illinois, which was recruited from the heavily Democratic southern part of the state, wrote in his diary when news of the second confiscation act reached the regiment: "It is rumored, that the negroes are freed, quite a dissatisfaction in our camp. . . . Some of our boys contend, that the war has now become an abolition war, and used insulting langige in regard to the same."[11] From the 29th Massachusetts of the Irish Brigade a sergeant wrote in July 1862 that "if *anyone* thinks that this army is fighting to free the Negro . . . they are terribly mistaken." And an artillery major from New York, a Democrat like so many officers in the Army of the Potomac under McClellan, wrote that if Lincoln caved in to "these 'black Republicans' " and made it "an abolition war . . . I for one shall be sorry that I ever lent a hand to it."[12]

A large minority of Union soldiers felt this way in 1862. After all, some two-fifths of them came from Democratic backgrounds and another tenth from the border states. Their resistance to any notion of turning a war for Union into a war against slavery had been one reason for Lincoln's hesitancy to embrace emancipation. The cause of Union united Northern soldiers; the cause of emancipation divided them. Letters and diaries mention vigorous campfire arguments about slavery. A Massachusetts sergeant made the following entry in his diary for February 4, 1863: "Had a jaw on slavery in the evening, & Jim did n't agree with the rest of us, & so he got mad." At about the same time an Indiana corporal wrote in his diary: "At night got into an argument, with a man that believed Slavery is right.—Had a warm time." A New York lieutenant wrote to his sister in January 1863 that in his officers' mess "we have had several pretty spirited, I may call them *hot,* controversies about slavery, the Emancipation Edict and kindred subjects."[13]

It was no accident that these heated discussions took place during the winter of 1862–63. The Emancipation Proclamation had given a sharper edge to the controversy. Soldiers who had advocated an antislavery war from the beginning naturally welcomed the Proclamation. As a captain in the 46th Pennsylvania put it, Lincoln's action made the war no longer merely a contest "between North & South; but a contest between human rights and human liberty on one side and eternal bondage on the other." A Minnesota corporal wrote to his wife: "Abraham 'has gone and done it' at last. Yesterday will be a day hallowed in the hearts of millions of the people of these United States, & also by the friends of liberty and humanity the *world* over."[14] "Thank God," wrote a private from the burned-over district of upstate New York, "the contest is now between Slavery & freedom, & every honest man knows what he is fighting for." A sergeant in the 5th Iowa not only thanked God; he was also confident that "the God of battle will be with us . . . now that we are fighting for *Liberty* and Union and not Union and Slavery."[15]

These were the idealists. The pragmatists weighed in with equally forceful if less elegant expressions. "I am no abolitionist," wrote a non-com in the 55th Ohio, "in fact i despise the word," but "as long as slavery exists . . . there will be no permanent peace for America. . . . Hence I am in favor of killing slavery." Likewise a Pennsylvania artilleryman assured his father that "I am no Nigger worshiper," but Lincoln's Proclamation "is striking at the root of the Evil   nothing will end this war sooner."[16] A private in the 72nd Pennsylvania pointed out to his father, a life-long Democrat who opposed emancipation, that after Lincoln's Proclamation "foreign nations will now have to come out flat-footed and take sides; they dare not go with the South, for slavery, and consequently they will all be ranged on our side." As for those who howled that Northern soldiers were now "fighting for the nigger" rather than for the Union, wrote an Ohio private to his wife, "if they are such fools as not to be able to see the difference between the means employed, and the end in view, let them remain blind."[17]

But plenty of soldiers believed that the Proclamation *had* changed the purpose of the war. They professed to feel betrayed. They were willing to risk their lives for Union, they said, but not for black free-dom. "I don't want to fire another shot for the negroes and I wish that all the abolitionists were in hell," wrote a German-born bricklayer in a New York artillery battery. An Illinois private told his family that "I am the Boy that Can fight for my Country, But not for the Negros."[18] Another Illinois soldier, married with children, assured his wife that "I consider the life & Happiness of my family of more value than any Nigger." The lieutenant colonel of the 3rd New York, an outspoken Democrat, wrote angrily that "I did not come out to fight for the nigger or abolition of Slavery." Lincoln "ought to be lashed up to 4 big fat niggers & left to wander about with them the bal[ance] of his life."[19]

Many Union soldiers from the border states expressed bitter disaf-fection. "I dont want the negro freed," wrote a private in the 33rd Missouri. "I dont think I will do much fighting to free the nasty thing. . . . I say the Democrats ougt to go in with the south and kill all the Abolitionists of the north and that will end this war." A farmer's son in the 7th Kentucky said that he and his comrades "volunteered to fight to restore the Old Constitution and not to free the Negroes and we are not a-going to do it." A previously patriotic private in the 5th Maryland said that he was now "sick and tired" of the war because "it really seems to me, that we are not fighting for our *country*, but for the freedom of the negroes."[20]

The Emancipation Proclamation intensified a morale crisis in Union armies during the winter of 1862–63, especially in the Army of the Potomac. The removal of McClellan from command, the disaster at Fredericksburg, and the fiasco of the Mud March had caused esprit in that army to plunge to an all-time low. Things were little better in Grant's army on the Mississippi, where the first attempts against Vicksburg had come to grief. Desertion rates rose sharply. Many soldiers blamed the Proclamation. In the Army of the Potomac, according to a New York captain, men "say it has turned into a 'nigger war' and all are anxious to return to their homes for it was to preserve the Union that they volunteered." A private in the 66th Indiana of the Army of the Tennessee wrote to his father in February 1863 that he and his messmates "will not fight to free the niger. . . . There is a Regement her that say they will never fite untill the proclamation is with drawn . . . nine in Comp. G tride to desert." A captain in the 91st New York of the Army of the Gulf reported from Baton Rouge that "there is an astonishing amount of dissatisfaction among officers & men in this army. . . . The emancipation act is alarmingly unpopular. . . . There has been a great many Resignations. . . . Twelve officers from one Regiment tendered their resignations."[21]

How widespread were such attitudes? How dangerous were they to the morale and cohesion of Union armies? The answers are difficult to quantify. For several months during the winter of 1862–63, those who expressed hostility to emancipation seemed to outnumber those who supported it. And morale certainly declined, though defeatism and lack of faith in Union leaders probably had more to do with this than the Emancipation Proclamation. In any case the decline of morale proved short-lived, for Union armies did not fall apart and soon won some of their most notable victories of the war. Of the Union soldiers in the sample who expressed a clear opinion about emancipation as a war aim at any time through the spring of 1863, more than twice as many favored it than opposed it: 36 percent to 16 percent. If we apportion those who did not comment on the subject evenly between the two sides, the picture would conform with the results of a poll in March 1863 in the 15th Iowa, a fairly typical regiment. Half of the men endorsed the Emancipation Proclamation, a quarter opposed it, and the other quarter did not register an opinion.[22]

These figures undoubtedly understated anti-emancipation sentiment, for the regiment's colonel supported the Proclamation and the poll was an open one. In the sample, pro-emancipation sentiment was strongest among those groups that are overrepresented: officers and men from professional and white-collar occupations. Forty-two percent of the officers, compared with 33 percent of the enlisted man in the sample, explicitly supported emancipation. Among soldiers with prewar professional and white-collar occupations, those who favored emancipation outnumbered opponents by four to one, while among blue-collar soldiers and farmers the margin was less than two to one.

In any event, the evidence seems to indicate that pro-emancipation convictions did predominate among the leaders and the fighting soldiers of the Union army. And that prevalance increased after the low point of early 1863 as a good many anti-emancipation soldiers changed their minds. Two factors played a part in their conversion. The first was an ominous rise of Copperheadism on the home front during the first half of 1863. Peace Democrats zeroed in on the Emancipation Proclamation in their denunciations of Lincoln's unconstitutional war and their demands for a negotiated peace. This attack on the Union war effort produced an anti-copperhead backlash among Northern soldiers, including many Democrats, that converted some of them to emancipation. This transformation can be traced in the letters of two Ohio soldiers, one a private and the other a colonel.

From January to March 1863 Private Chauncey Welton of the 103rd Ohio damned the Emancipation Proclamation up and down and backward and forward in a dozen letters to his family, staunch Democrats all. "I enlisted to fight for and vindicate the supremacy of the constitution," he wrote, but "we did not enlist to fight for the negro and I can tell you that *we never shall* . . . sacrafise [our] lives for the liberty of a miserable black race of beings. . . . Abolitionism is traitorism in its darkest collar."[23]

But then Welton began to change his tune, especially after Clement L. Vallandigham won the nomination for governor of Ohio on an antiwar platform, which "fell like a thunderbolt on this regiment," he reported in June 1863. "There is no one on the face of the earth that is dispised as mutch as the copperhead is." Welton now believed that the abolition of slavery would be "a means of haistening the speedy

Restoration of the Union and the termination of the war." This letter fell like a thunderbolt on his father, who regarded it as rank heresy. The elder Welton nearly suffered apoplexy a year later when his son proclaimed himself a Republican and praised Lincoln as well as the Emancipation Proclamation, which had been issued at "exactly the right time. . . . It was intended to weaken the rebellion and I can asshure you it was a great blow to them." By 1865 young Welton sounded just like an abolitionist when he wrote in joyful anticipation of a restored nation "*free free free* yes free from that blighting curs *Slavery* the cause of four years of Bloody Warfare."[24]

As commander of the 120th Ohio, Colonel Marcus Speigel was one of the highest-ranking Jewish officers in the Civil War. As a Democrat he denounced the Emancipation Proclamation, writing to his wife in January 1863: "I am sick of the war. . . . I do not fight or want to fight for Lincoln's Negro proclamation one day longer." But when his men began to say the same thing, repeating what they had heard from home or read in Democratic newspapers, Speigel grew alarmed. "Stand by the government right or wrong," he told his regiment. By April 1863 he had repudiated the Democratic party; in January 1864, a few months before he was killed in the Red River campaign, he wrote his wife from Plaquemines Parish, Louisiana, that "since I [came] here I have learned and seen more of what the horrors of Slavery was than I ever knew before. . . . I am [in] favor of doing away with the . . . accursed institution. . . . I am [now] a strong abolitionist."[25]

The second factor that converted many soldiers to emancipation was a growing conviction that it really did hurt the enemy and help their own side. "I have always untill lately been opposed to abraham linkins proclamation," wrote a private in the 18th Pennsylvania Cavalry, a distiller by trade, in May 1863, "but i have lately been convinced that it was just the thing that was neded to weaken the strength of the rebls   this has been proven by the raids that our cavalry have made into their country." A soldier in the 86th Indiana reported in March 1863 that comrades who had two months earlier damned the "abolition war" now favored emancipation on pragmatic grounds. "We use all other kinds of rebel property," he pointed out, "and they see no reason why we should not use negroes. Every negro we get strengthens us and weakens the rebels."[26]

Like Chauncey Welton and Marcus Spiegel, some soldiers progressed from this pragmatic position to one closely resembling abolitionism. Writing of the government's emancipation policy in July 1863, an artillery sergeant from Illinois acknowledged that "I would never have enlisted for that purpose, but now, since that has become the issue and things have progressed so far, I wish to see the system go. I believe . . . we would be a far happier and more prosperous people if the 'bone of contention' was once removed." A lieutenant in the 2nd Minnesota who had once bitterly denounced emancipation had come so far by February 1863 that he agreed with Thaddeus Stevens. "Slavery and Aristocracy go hand in hand," he told his fiancée, who did not agree with his new opinions. "An Aristocracy brought on this war— that Aristocracy must be broken up . . . it is rotten and corrupt. . . . God intends that it and slavery its reliance & support must go down together. . . . We did not think so one year ago & you will think differently too a year hence."[27]

Even some border-state soldiers traveled this road to Damascus. A Kentucky lieutenant who had once threatened to resign his commission if Lincoln moved against slavery had executed an about-face by the summer of 1863. "The 'inexorable logic of events' is rapidly making practical abolitionists of every soldier," he informed his sister. "I am afraid that [even] I am getting to be an Abolitionist. All right! better that than a Secessionist."[28]

One of those events whose inexorable logic converted Union soldiers was the recruitment of black regiments. At first many white soldiers opposed this policy—generally the same soldiers who opposed emancipation, and for similar reasons. Black men wearing the same uniform they wore carried disturbing implications. "Woud you love to se the Negro placed on equality with me?" a private in the 17th Indiana asked his father, who had suggested the idea of enlisting black soldiers. "If you make a soldier of the negro you can not dispute but he is as good as me or any other Indiana soldier   I hope you will se your wrong and reform." Then, too, complained a sergeant in the 9th New Jersey, arming the slaves would be "a confession of weakness, a folly, an insult to the brave Solder."[29]

But this soon became a minority position as it dawned on white soldiers that blacks in uniform might stop bullets otherwise meant for them. And the organization of enough black regiments might bring the war to a quick and victorious end. A sergeant in another Indiana regiment reported that the men in his company "say if there can be negroes enough raised to conquer the rebels let them do it." A private in the 9th Illinois declared that "i wouldant lift my finger to free them if i had my say, but if we cant whip the rebils without taking the nigers I say take them and make them fite for us any way to bring this war to a close."[30] A sergeant in the 34th Illinois considered it "no disgrace to me to have black men for soldiers. If they can kill rebels I say arm them and set them to shooting. I would use mules for the same purpose if possible." By the summer of 1863, wrote a quarter-master in the Army of the Cumberland, "you would be surprised at the change of sentiment this Army has undergone latterly, not a man have I heard but what is in favor of putting the colored pusson right into the front of the fight."[31]

At Port Hudson, Milliken's Bend, and Fort Wagner black soldiers in 1863 proved their willingness and ability to fight. That began a process of converting many skeptics into true believers. A naval officer whose ship came into the Union base at Beaufort, North Carolina, for repairs was impressed by the black regiment there under the command of James Beecher, brother of Henry Ward Beecher and Harriet Beecher Stowe. "There is a firmness & determination in their looks & in the way in which they handle a musket that I like," he wrote his wife. "It looks like fight & Port Hudson has proved that they will do so. I never [would] have believed that a common plantation negro could be brought to face a white man. I supposed that everything in the shape of spirit & self respect had been crushed out of them generations back, but am glad to find myself mistaken." By October 1863 a lieutenant in the 50th Ohio could declare that "there is not a Negro in the army that is not a better man than a rebel, and for whom I have not a thousand times more respect that I have for a traitor."[32]

Such change of mind was not confined to officers. After black troops had assaulted and captured a portion of the Confederate line at Petersburg on June 15, 1864, a sergeant in the 20th Indiana ex-pressed surprise at "how civilly our boys treated them. They used to make fun of, and ill treat every negro, soldier or slave, that we passed." After the battle of Nashville on December 15–16, 1864, a private in the 89th Illinois, a railroad section hand before the war, wrote to his mother: "I have often herd men say that they would not fight beside a negro soldier but on the 16th the whites and blacks charged together and they fell just as well as we did. . . . When you hear eney one say that negro soldiers wont fight just tell them that they ly for me. . . . I have seen a great meny fighting for our country. Then why should they not be free."[33]

Black soldiers themselves perceived a great personal stake in the war. They fought for their own freedom, and beyond that for the freedom of all four million slaves. Many, especially those who had been free before the war, also fought for equal citizenship in a restored Union. Free and slave alike, they fought to prove their manhood in a society that prized courage as the hallmark of manhood.

Regrettably, most wartime evidence for the thinking of African-American soldiers comes from letters of Northern blacks written for publication, mainly in black newspapers. Very few personal letters or diaries have survived, and even fewer written by freed slaves—most of whom, of course, could not read and write. There is no reason to believe, however, that the genuine feelings of black soldiers were different from the published letters of their most articulate spokesmen. A sergeant in the 107th U.S. Colored Infantry wrote from Louisville in September 1864 that he was fighting "to break the chain and exclaim 'Freedom for all!'" This affirmation was echoed by a Connecticut private in the famous 54th Massachusetts in a personal letter to his fiancée at the end of the war, in which he explained why he had not written for several months: "We have been almost constantly on the move, marching and fighting for the good old cause—LIBERTY."[34]

By 1864 freedom alone was not enough for many black soldiers. In August of that year a thirty-eight-year-old barber from Philadelphia who fought through all the battles of the 54th Massachusetts proclaimed that "if we fight to maintain a Republican Government, we want Republican privileges. . . . All we ask is the proper enjoyment of the rights of citizenship," which a corporal in the 55th Massachusetts defined as "the same rights that the white man has." Perhaps the best summary of what blacks fought for was provided by a literate slave who escaped from his master in North Carolina and joined the Union navy in September 1862. In a diary he kept during his service on a blockading warship he wrote that he fought "for the holiest of all causes, Liberty and Union." In April 1865 he added "the cause of Right and Equality."[35]

BY THE WAR'S last year, the example of black soldiers fighting for Union as well as liberty had helped convince most white soldiers that they should fight for black liberty as well as Union. There were some holdouts, to be sure. A private in the 20th Indiana explained his refusal to reenlist for a second three-year term on the grounds that "this war has turned out very Different from what I thought it would. . . . It is a War . . . to Free the Nigars . . . and I do not propose to fight any more in such A cause." A private in the 21st Kentucky also complained in the spring of 1864 that "this is nothing but an abolition war. . . . I am a strait out Union and Constitution man I am not for freeing the negroes." His brother in the same regiment added a wish that "old abe lincoln . . . had to sleep with a negro evry night as long as he lives and kiss ones ass twice a day." A New York artilleryman expressed disgust with what he (unjustly) considered the cowardly performance of a black regiment in the fighting at the Petersburg Crater. "All that I am Sorry for is that the Rebs did not Capture every niger there was there and Shoot them for I think that we have got white men enough in the north to fight our battles."[36]

But these were distinctly minority views among Union soldiers by 1864. When Lincoln ran for reelection on a platform pledging a constitutional amendment to abolish slavery, he received almost 80 percent of the soldier vote—a pretty fair indication of army sentiment on slavery by that time. A private in the 6th Wisconsin battery in Sherman's army wrote just before the election: "In the evening a general discussion took place on the 'nigger question,' politics, etc. All agree on 'Old Abe' for president." The battery voted 75-0 for Lincoln. After the election this artilleryman thanked God that "the sin of slavery" would soon be no more. "I can cheerfully bear all the discomforts of a soldier's life for the overthrow of the monster evil."[37]

Emancipation actually brought into the army some white men for whom freedom provided a greater incentive to fight than nationalism. Two Quaker brothers from Bucks County, Pennsylvania, enlisted in the 20th Pennsylvania Cavalry in July 1863 because they no longer felt right "allowing others to make all the sacrifices to liberty. . . . Thee knows how I have always felt about war. . . . Still I never regret that I am a participant in the struggle . . . [to] advance the cause of universal freedom. . . . Remember, Mother, that while we strike strong telling blows for liberty . . . we need not hesitate as to the means employed." This philosophy that the end justified the means did not appeal to all Quaker abolitionists, including their mother. But even when one of the brothers was killed in the battle of Sayler's Creek, the other remained "glad that I was a soldier and have done my part for the cause of universal liberty." Another Quaker, an officer on Admiral David G. Farragut's flagship USS *Hartford,* believed that "slavery is such a horrible blot on civilization, that I am convinced that the war will exterminate it and its supporters, and that it was brought about for that purpose by God."[38]

A good many Union soldiers in addition to Quakers came to see God's hand in this war to free the slaves. They embraced this purpose with an ideological fervor they had not felt for the cause of restoring the Union with slavery still in it. A lieutenant in the 59th Illinois, a farmer by trade, wrote as early as May 1863 that "it is astonishing how things has changed in reference to freeing the Negros. . . . It allwais has been plane to me that this rase must be freed befor god would recognise us. . . . We bost of liberty and we Should try to impart it to others. . . . Thank god the chanes will Soon be bursted . . . now I belive we are on gods side . . . now I can fight with a good heart." Another lieutenant, in the 5th Iowa, also declared in 1863 that "the hand of God is in this, and that in spite of victories and advantages he will deny us Peace until we grant to others the liberties we ask for ourselves . . . and sweep every vestige of the cursed institution from our land."[39]

In the spring of 1864 a forty-three-year-old farmer, a sergeant in the 19th Michigan who had lost one stepson in the war, wrote to his wife from Georgia that "the more I learn of the cursed institution of Slavery, the more I feel willing to endure, for its final destruction. . . . After this war is over, this whole country will undergo a change for the better. . . . Abolishing slavery will dignify labor; that fact of itself will revolutionize everything. . . . Let Christians use all their influence to have justice done to the black man."[40] He never experienced disappointment with this vision of the future; an enemy sharpshooter ended his life near Atlanta in August 1864.

CHAPTER 10

WE KNOW THAT WE ARE
SUPPORTED AT HOME

CONVICTIONS OF DUTY, honor, patriotism, and ideology functioned as the principal sustaining motivations of Civil War
soldiers, while the impulses of courage, self-respect, and
group cohesion were the main sources of combat motivation. But
without a firm base of support in the homes and communities from
which these citizen soldiers came, their morale would have crumbled.
Even the solidarity with comrades in arms was insufficient to sustain
their commitment if it lacked sustenance on the home front. In the
Vietnam War the erosion of that sustenance was one reason for a
decline in the motivation and fighting power of the American army. A
century earlier the potential for a similar erosion threatened at times
to undermine the fighting power of Civil War armies. But the Northern people rallied from their moments of despair, as did the Southern
people until the last months of the war.

Homesickness was a dominant theme in the letters of many soldiers. At the same time, however, their consciousness of fighting for
those at home buoyed them up. As a private in the 39th Indiana
expressed it in a letter to his sister: "I can only think of home. And
but for those at home I might feel less like serving my country." A
private in the 12th Georgia wrote that the hardships and homesick-

ness of campaigning in Virginia made it only "natural that the spirits of a man at times should be gloomy and cast down, but to receive a letter from home . . . stirs our sleeping patriotism, it makes us firm in our purpose to conquer or perish." Across the lines a private in the 5th Wisconsin was gratified that "we have the sympathy of nearly all in the North . . . [which makes it] almost impossible for the greatest coward to be anything but a brave man here."[1]

An efficient mail service played a large part in maintaining morale. Both armies understood this and made strong efforts to provide one. The Union army succeeded; letters from the North reached Yankee soldiers in Virginia or Tennessee almost as quickly in 1861–65 as they take to travel between the same points today. At first the Confederate postal service also worked well, but it broke down as the war went on because of the deterioration of Southern railroads and Union occupation of ever-larger portions of the South. The degree to which Confederate morale consequently suffered is difficult to measure, but it was undoubtedly significant.

Mail call was the brightest part of a soldier's day—*if* he received a letter from home. If he did not, his spirits sank. "The mail is *the event* of the camp," wrote an officer in the 11th Georgia to his fiancée on the eve of Lee's invasion of Pennsylvania. "Could our friends witness the crowding round the post-man—the beaming look of expectation on the swarthy, weather-beaten faces—the cloud of disappointment upon the brows of those who receive nothing . . . they would never again imagine that it matters little with soldiers whether or not they receive frequent letters." Charles Francis Adams, Jr., a captain in the 1st Massachusetts Cavalry, made a similar point, also during the Gettysburg campaign. "After long marches and great exposure . . . when you have gone through all that a man can go through," he wrote to his brother Henry, who was serving at the American legation in London, "to get into camp at last and hear that a mail has come! You should see the news fly round the camp and the men's faces light up." Failure to receive a letter had the same dispiriting effect on Northern as on Southern servicemen: the "glow of hope the moment before," wrote a sailor on the USS *Powhatan*, "fades away and the very life seems crushed out of them. . . . It is really surprising to see what effect it has upon some."[2]

Soldiers chided loved ones for laziness and selfishness when they did not write often enough. "It is the bitterest of all my privations not to get letters from home," went a typical complaint, from a lieutenant

in the 10th Massachusetts during the Peninsula campaign in the summer of 1862. "Letters are the only thing that makes existence tolerable
in this God forsaken country. . . . You all seem to think that because
you have no great events to write about . . . you have nothing.
Whereas, it is the little common place incidences of everyday life at
home which we like to read. . . . You do not realize how everything
that savors of home, relishes with us." Married soldiers were particularly susceptible to the extremes of despair and elation at mail call.
When a captain in the 67th Ohio, father of three children, received
no letter from his wife for several days, "it makes me sad; it makes
me feel uneasy." But when the next mail brought a letter from home,
"My God what a weight that takes from my mind. I feel young, well,
cheerful . . . and could have licked a thousand Rebels myself."[3]

Letters from home have been of crucial importance in sustaining
morale in all literate armies. "Letters represent the soldier's major contact with the social unit that reinforces his desire to serve faithfully
and under great hardship," wrote an expert on modern armies. For the
volunteer regiments of the Civil War composed of community-based
companies, the point is doubly relevant. As a lieutenant in the 9th
Alabama put it, "letters from home . . . have much more to do with
keeping up the spirits and morale of the army than is generally supposed. When each individual member of a company or regiment feels
that his labors are appreciated by his friends and neighbors at home,
he asks no other recognition of his services."[4]

But the wrong kind of letter could have the opposite effect. From
almost the first month of their service, many married soldiers received
letters from their wives complaining of loneliness and hardship and
expressing fears that the war would leave them widows and their children fatherless. "I experience such constant dread and anxiety that I
feel all the time weary and depressed," wrote one Southern woman to
her husband in the army. "What do I care for patriotism?" wrote another. "My husband is my country. What is country to me if he be
killed?"[5] Almost every letter to a Texas cavalryman from his wife described a new crisis at home: the children were sick, the farm was
going to rack and ruin. "If you could only be at home I would not feel
so bad," she wrote. "I do not know what will become of you or us."
Far to the north a Pennsylvania woman wrote to her husband: "I
awaken up at night and lay for hours wondering if I ever shall see my
dear Pet again. . . . *You are my all* in this world and without *you* now
my Pet I *feel* as though I could not live." Some wives pleaded with

their husbands to get out of the army by fair means or foul. The wife of a German-born private in the 8th New Jersey thought that his sore foot should be enough to get him a medical discharge. "Dear husband, come home," she wrote. "Get your discharge. . . . If you will give one of the doctors a couple of dollars you can be home here with us."[6]

Such letters had a baneful impact on morale. An unmarried officer in the 103rd Illinois described two married captains in the regiment who "each gets five letters a week [from his wife] and looks a little sicker after each letter." The colonel of the 15th Wisconsin, a renowned Norwegian-American regiment, lamented that several of his married soldiers received letters filled with "complaints, and whinings, asking him to 'come home' etc., [which] has more to do with creating discouragement and finally sickness and disease than the hardships he has to endure." In an effort to arrest this demoralizing process, the lieutenant colonel of the crack 6th Wisconsin of the Iron Brigade gave a speech at home during a furlough in March 1863: "If you wish success, write encouraging letters to your soldiers. . . . Do not fill the ears of your soldiers with tales of troubles and privations at home, caused by their absence."[7]

Married soldiers confronted a dilemma caused by competing ideals of manhood and honor. In one direction lay their responsibilities as husbands, fathers, and breadwinners for dependents to whom they had made a sacred pledge to cherish and support. In the other direction lay their duty as able-bodied citizens to defend their country. To evade either obligation would dishonor their manhood. But in time of extreme national peril, the manly call of duty to country seemed more urgent. A twenty-five-year-old soldier in the 2nd Vermont who married his fiancée during a furlough was able to live with her for only one month of their first year of marriage. "It seems like crushing the feelings out of one's soul," he wrote on their anniversary which he spent in dreary winter camp in Virginia, "but a soldier must not be faint-hearted or babyish nor tied to a woman's apron strings for it is unmanly and unworthy." When a private in the 7th Minnesota said good-bye to his wife after a brief furlough, "it seemed as though it would break my heart but the thought that I was a *man* nurved me up to the task."[8]

Some 700,000 or 800,000 married men made a voluntary choice to enlist. Most of them reconciled the the dilemma of competing obligations by denying that it existed. In fighting for their country, they insisted, they were defending the security and liberty of their families.

"The man who loves his family the best now," wrote a lieutenant in the 3rd Virginia Cavalry to his wife in 1862, "is he who is the most anxious and will risk the most and suffer the most to repel the invader."[9]

This argument was easier for Confederates than for Union soldiers to make. But many of the latter also worked out an elaborate rationale that in fighting for country they were also fighting for their families. "It is for the future welfare of your selfe and children, that causes me to be seperated from you," wrote a lieutenant in the 41st Ohio to his wife. "If you esteem me with a true womans love you will not ask me to disgrace myself by deserting the flag of our Union. . . . Remember that however much I would like to be at home, to enjoy the sweet comforts of life, the society of a dear wife, and children, yet what is life worth, without a government under which it can be enjoyed. . . . I will again return to you as soon as honor alone will permit." To his nine-year-old son this soldier wrote in 1863 that he wished he could come home but he must stay in the army to fight the bad men who "would soon bring anarchy and ruin to the whole American people, and would soon deprive you and every other honest little boy and girl of many blessings and privileges you now enjoy."[10] Another Ohio officer lectured his wife that "without Union & peace our freedom is worthless . . . our children would have no warrant of liberty. . . . You are interested in the future of our government—the welfare of our children depends on it, therefore why denounce the war when the interest at stake is so vital." A forty-year-old captain in the 18th Massachusetts whose sons would soon enter their teenage years wrote his wife in August 1862 that "I am fighting for my children. . . . I know if this war is not fought through and settled as it should be that our boys will have to be soldiers and pass through what I have. I had rather stay here for years than they should ever go on the battle field." Four months later he was killed at Fredericksburg.[11]

Three additional and related themes emerged in soldiers' letters to wives trying to justify their absence in the army. The first was an appeal to women's own patriotic duty, their heritage of "republican motherhood" from the Founding Mothers who had labored to give birth to the nation by sustaining the Founding Fathers. "Be a woman," wrote a lieutenant in the 28th Mississippi to his wife who had expressed her loneliness and anxiety. "Think of the noble women of ancient and modern times—Think of our Revolutionary mothers daily." An Ohio officer rebuked his wife for her complaining letters in 1862:

"It only gives another trouble on my mind to know that you are so discontented. . . . You could not claim to be a daughter of this proud and beautiful mother America, were you to be guilty for one moment of sutch selfish weakness. No it will never do, cheer up and show to the world that there flowes in your veins the noble blood of your mother country." A forty-one-year-old captain in the 1st North Carolina, father of several children, felt certain—or at least hopeful—that his wife shared his commitment "to a country & a cause which we love. . . . We both (I think) have more than the ordinary degree of 'sense of duty' to sustain us." She would need that sense of duty to sustain her, for the battle of Mechanicsville left her a widow.[12]

Soldiers appealed not only to their wives' obligation of womanly *duty* but also to their sense of family *honor*. Failure to fight for one's country would dishonor wife, children, and posterity as well as the husband himself. "I know you would rather see my body dead, with honor, than alive with disgrace attached," wrote an officer in the 26th Illinois to his wife, who clearly wished nothing of the kind. A Virginia cavalry lieutenant likewise assumed that his wife would "rather that I should die honorably in the discharge of my duty than live a coward and thereby bring lasting disgrace on myself and my family." If he was killed in the next battle, wrote a captain in the 7th Louisiana after his company was almost wiped out at Stones River, "God would take care of you although I could bequeath you nothing but my sword and the knowledge that I have done my duty to my country . . . and my children would be prouder of their father than if he had staid at home while his countrymen were struggling for liberty."[13]

If appeals to womanly duty and family honor did not work, some married soldiers fell back on the necessity of upholding their own manhood. A lieutenant in the 47th Virginia could probably have resigned for reasons of health after a severe bout of typhoid fever. But he refused, to his wife's dismay, and upon returning to his regiment he wrote her: "Nothing but stern necessity and the salvation of my reputation and honor (without which a man is not a man) could have by any possible means induced me to leave you again." The major of the 24th South Carolina whose wife had just given birth to a sickly child told her that he could not leave the army during active operations to come home: "If I were to give way to the *moral pain* . . . I would be held up before my fellow countrymen in disgrace,—would be below the noble spirit of my heroic brother," who had been killed in Virginia. An officer on Stonewall Jackson's staff insisted to his wife that "my duty and my self-respect" made it necessary for him to be away from home. "Would you have me return there the subject of such conversation as has been freely lavished upon those who remained behind? . . . My manhood is involved in a faithful and fearless sticking to the job until it is finished, or it finishes me." It finished him; he was killed at Chancellorsville.[14]

Because officers had the privilege of resigning their commissions— or trying to—many wives could not understand why they did not do so after a year or two, which they considered sufficient to satisfy honor. After he fought at Shiloh, where his company suffered 45 percent casualties but he came out unharmed, a lieutenant in the 9th Arkansas heard from his wife, who urged him to resign: "If you could come home now, I think you ought to be satisfied; you have been in a hard fought battle; and won glory enough, certainly for me."[15]

Most husbands who received such letters replied that to resign while an enemy was still in the field would disgrace their reputation; to have the resignation accepted, implying incompetence, would add injury to insult. "I could not come back to you with honor," wrote the colonel of the 54th Ohio after almost two years and several battles, which had prompted both his wife and mother to suggest that he could resign. "The filing of a resignation would cover me with disgrace, no officer can resign in the face of the enemy." After more than two years of hard service, an officer in the 28th Mississippi Cavalry could not resign "without being everlastingly dishonored and disgraced," he told his wife, "thus involving you & my innocent little babe in my own personal ruin." And the Norwegian-born colonel of the 15th Wisconsin urged his wife not "to fret about me now. I cant come home honorably by resigning. . . . All who have resigned without any good reason will never hear the last of it. It will stick to them as long as they live." A year later he was killed at Chickamauga.[16]

This credo of honor and manhood transcended section and nationality. It did not transcend rank and class quite so universally. All of the evidence cited so far came from officers. They seemed to be more concerned about the question than enlisted men. Certainly they wrote more about it. One reason they did so, of course, is that because they were generally a few years older than enlisted men, a much higher percentage of officers than men were married (51 percent of officers and 26 percent of enlisted men in the sample). Wives of enlisted men undoubtedly felt the same as officers' wives, but they realized that their husbands' only way out of the army was by desertion. While it may have been dishonorable for an officer to resign, it was at least legitimate; desertion was both dishonorable and illegitimate.

Nevertheless, several married enlisted men, after a few months or a year in the army, found themselves wishing to be home. This was especially true among those who had enlisted for bounties or had been drafted. In 1862 a private in the 1st Ohio wrote his wife that "I am sick and tird of the war and I want to see you and the children the worst in the world. . . . I wood give my monthly wages and my hundred dollars bounty to be at home." About the same time a yeoman farmer from Georgia wrote in a similar vein to his wife: "I would give all I possess if I could be back with you and the childreng. . . . I have the blews the worst that I ever had them in my lief." A Virginia farmer wrote to his wife seven months after he had enlisted in the spring of 1862, probably to avoid being drafted, that "if I cant get home no other way I will run away and come home as soon as I can get a good chance. I hate mity to runaway but I want to see you all so bad that I think I shall try that trick."[17]

Desertion rates were probably higher among married than unmarried soldiers, especially in the Confederacy where Union invasions and food shortages threatened soldiers' families with danger and hunger. A good many Confederate soldiers deserted in response to such letters from their wives as this one from Alabama in 1864: "We haven't got nothing in the house to eat but a little bit o meal. . . . If you put off a-coming, 'twont be no use to come, for we'll all hands of us be out there in the grave yard with your ma and mine."[18]

But there were married privates with a sense of duty and honor as highly developed as any officer's. "I came to the war because I felt it to be my duty," wrote a private in the 18th Georgia in 1863 to his wife, who had told him that his two daughters were pleading for him to come home. "I am not going to run away if I never come home I had rather di without seeing them than for peple to tell them after I am dead that their father was a deserter. . . . It [is] every Southern mans duty to fight against abolition misrule and preserve his Liberty untarnished which was won by our fore Fathers. . . . I never yet regeted the step I have taken." A Tennessee cavalryman who also had two daughters said he "would rather die an honorable Death than to Bring Reproach or Dishonor upon my family or friends."[19]

Many Northern enlisted men felt the same way. "I would give anything in my possession to be with you," a sergeant in the 14th Indiana wrote his wife in 1863, "but I am in the service of my country and I will serve it faithfully and do my duty and if I never see you more I will do nothing that will disgrace you or my Children." A forty-one-year-old farmer with several children who enlisted in the famed 24th Michigan of the Iron Brigade rebuked his wife, who kept pressing him to get a discharge on grounds of family responsibilities. Any such course, he lectured her, "would be attended with dishonor. . . . People at home would call me a coward." His wife and children never saw him again; he was captured at Fredericksburg and died of erysipelas in prison.[20]

The impression that most women opposed their men's decision to volunteer or complained frequently while they were in the army may be a false impression—an artifact created by the nature of the documentary evidence. That is, those women who did not complain but instead wrote encouraging letters to their husbands or sweethearts did not evoke the kinds of responses that have been quoted in the preceding pages. Most evidence of women who encouraged their husbands' or lovers' commitment to duty, honor, and country is lost to history, for most collections of soldiers' letters home do not include letters coming the other way.

One that does, however, suggests the kind of determined moral support from home that helped sustain morale in the army and navy. The fiancée of one of the best young officers in the Union navy, who repeatedly volunteered for hazardous duty, expressed her loneliness and her fears for him in letters of tenderness and love. "I would not be worth your true love if I could wish to keep you home in such a time as this," she wrote. "I am proud of having you where you are. I am proud of your courage and patriotism and I will never knowingly keep you back from any duty. . . . For any thing else I *could* not let you go, but . . . I am glad dear that I *can* give something for my country, and will try and be as brave as many others who too have sent their dearest ones."[21]

Of course a fiancée did not have the same claim on a man's allegiance as did wife and children. A good many wives, however, wrote similar letters. A sergeant in the 21st Ohio was grateful to his wife, who had written him that "the country needs your services. . . . Your country's cause is *my* cause." "Oh Minie," he replied, "I am doubly proud of you for this sacrifice. May God bless you sweet one for this encouragement." Late in the war an Ohio officer with a distinguished record who had been promoted up the ranks from lieutenant colonel to brigadier general praised his wife for her encouraging letters over the years despite the hardships of "providing for a large family, and the birth and death of a loved infant. . . . Had you written me such letters as a majority of officers get from their wives, I am sure that I would have been the most errant coward in the world. When exposing myself to the fire of the enemy . . . my first thought has always been my family, but the certainty that I had the approval . . . of my dear wife that I should be just where I was, gave my heart courage."[22]

Some soldiers, however, wondered whether married men might always hold something back when going into combat. "I begin to think no Soldier ought to be married," mused a Wisconsin infantry colonel in 1863. "It helps to make him a coward." An unmarried South Carolina artillery lieutenant remarked that "all the married men down here seem to take wonderful care of their lives." A widower who commanded the high-casualty 4th North Carolina remarried in the middle of the war, even though he worried that "marriage will have a tendency to make a skulker of me."[23]

But in his first battle after marrying, reported this same colonel, "much to my surprise I felt no more hesitation or reluctance to venture my life in the chances of battle than heretofore." And a captain in the 123rd Illinois wrote to his new wife, whom he had married during a furlough in 1863, that when he got back to the regiment his colonel had chewed him out. "He tells me my getting married was the worst thing I could do as a soldier; he says it will make me a coward, that I will never go into a fight without thinking of my wife and endeavoring to shelter myself as much as possible on her account. He says it is the case with himself, and that he wishes he had no wife. I don't believe him for he has been in the battles of Belmont, Fort Henry, Fort Donelson, Shiloh and Perryville, and was promoted for gallantry on the field at Fort Donelson, so I think he forgets all about wife, self and everything else but doing his best when he gets in a fight." This colonel was subsequently killed in action. So was a Massachusetts captain who had promised his wife that he would be "cautious," but was shot down leading his company in an assault at Fredericksburg. It is worth noting that in the sample of soldiers whose letters and diaries form the basis for this book, 23 percent of the married men, compared with 20 percent of the single men, were killed in action.[24]

SEVERAL STUDIES OF soldiers in wartime have discerned a growing estrangement between men at the front and their own civilian populations. The impossibility of describing what war is really like to the folks back home creates a vast gulf between those who have been in combat and those who have not. A strange sense of fraternity toward enemy soldiers develops, for they too have seen the elephant and are therefore more worthy of respect—even comradeship—than the shirkers, slackers, war profiteers, and soft-living civilians back home. Soldiers hardened by the suffering and killing they have experienced grow weary and cynical toward the values and goals for which they are supposedly fighting and the superpatriots back home who continue to shout the same old slogans of "the Cause." An influential study of soldiers on the Western Front in World War I found "estrangement from those values and beliefs upheld and affirmed" at home. " 'Courage,' 'honor,' 'self-sacrifice,' 'heroism' now belonged to those distant, 'unreal' worlds outside the trench system."[25]

In an important interpretation of Civil War soldiers, Gerald Linderman maintains that they experienced the same estrangement from their civilian populations and a growing affinity for the brotherhood of soldiers on the enemy side. "The men grew to resent unchanging civilian allegiance to the precepts with which the war began," he states. Their "intense anger was directed at civilians who continued to voice the old values and to invoke the 1861 rituals that summoned them. . . . Those who continued to kill one another in battle often felt less estrangement from their victims than those in whose behalf they had gone to fight."[26]

There is an element of truth in this thesis. Soldiers often expressed hostility toward those who had remained at home. "It is outrageous and abominable that the Army must be slandered and abused by the cowards that stay at home," wrote a lieutenant in the high-casualty 10th Massachusetts in 1864. "I wish that the cowards at home who sneer at the noble Army of the Potomac, might be forced out here to take their share." An artillery sergeant from Pennsylvania wanted "some of those who can live in affluence at home [to] come out. . . . But I tell you the greater part of these men are cowards at heart and despise the common soldier and would see their country fall to ruins before they would volunteer their services." Far to the south in the defenses of Mobile an officer in the 21st Alabama likewise denounced "the miserable gilded coward who remains in the rear to fatten like a hyena over the grave of his country."[27]

These maledictions were specifically aimed at "cowards" and those "who would see their country fall to ruins." To generalize these sentiments into estrangement from "those in whose behalf they had gone to fight" is misleading. And even more so is the argument that soldiers repudiated the "old values" of courage, honor, and patriotism that civilians continued to voice. In fact, almost the opposite was true. Soldiers' anger was selectively targeted at civilians who *failed* to adhere to the values of 1861: those who "shirked their duty," "croakers," "Copperheads" in the North, and "Tories" in the South. In contrast to World War I, soldiers at the front remained more vocal in their patriotism and more faithful to the values of duty and honor than many civilians back home, and it was precisely *those* civilians toward whom soldiers expressed hostility.

By 1863, especially after Gettysburg and Vicksburg, some civilians in the South who had been reluctant secessionists in 1861 cautiously started talking about the possibility of a compromise peace that might include reconstruction of the Union. A nineteen-year-old private who rode with Forrest in the 7th Alabama Cavalry denounced this "miserable class of men that now infest the country,—shirking every duty they owe to their country." Another Alabamian, a captain in the 44th, deplored the lack of "patriotism of a great many of the people at home. The army cannot be sustained without the cooperation of the people. . . . Is Bibb County for the Union, with the Yankees? God forbid. If so, I am ashamed for the county that gave me birth." Even in South Carolina a few Tories seemed to surface after Gettysburg and Vicksburg, causing a nineteen-year-old veteran from that state to cry: "Shame for South Carolina! Go back into the *union,* degraded despised dishonorable. . . . This is the way we are rewarded—our own people forsake us in the trying hour—and after our all—honour—and everything else is at stake. . . . Degrading, wretched, unpatriotic, infamous thought!" [28]

These soldiers exaggerated the decline of patriotism on the Confederate home front in 1863. By 1865, however, demoralization was indeed widespread in the South. Civilians had become "craven hearted and weak kneed," lamented an officer in the 61st Alabama. "Our people are not the same as they were four years ago. Their courage, spirit and pride are gone. . . . I don't know what can be done to save us." [29]

If one can judge from the volume of soldier complaints, however, dry rot on the Northern home front was far more pervasive than in the South. "I hate and despise" the "puny cravens at home, whose fears make them tremble at shadows," wrote a Quaker captain in the

5th New Jersey as early as July 1862, after the Seven Days battles had discouraged many Northern people. "These poltroons deserve the scorn of all true patriots." A similar decline of home-front morale in the summer of 1864 caused a Pennsylvania captain in Sherman's army to deplore "the dastardly apathy of the people who sent these noble men here to fight for their liberties. . . . We with the few who still stand firm at home are the *people* and will wield the destinies of the country for the future."[30]

One of the things that most embittered Union soldiers in the last two years of the war was the opportunity for drafted men to hire a substitute or pay a commutation fee of $300. "The columns of the daily papers [from the North] I see filled with advertisements of Northern cowards, offering large sums for substitutes to take their places in the ranks," wrote an Illinois captain with Sherman's army before Atlanta in August 1864. "Oh! how such men are despised here! . . . We who are already in the field must do our whole duty now, for it is daily becoming painfully evident those at home do not intend to do theirs."[31]

More even than those who evaded the draft, however, Union soldiers despised those who were part of an organized group that opposed it along with other measures for a relentless prosecution of the war— the Copperheads. The political strength of Copperheads, or Peace Democrats, as they preferred to call themselves, rose and fell inversely with Union fortunes on the battlefield. When Northern military prospects appeared bleak from the late summer of 1862 until July 1863 and again in July and August of 1864, Copperhead political prospects appeared bright. The greatest estrangement between soldiers and civilians on either side occurred between Union soldiers and Peace Democrats. "Copperheadism has brought the soldiers here together more than anything else," wrote a corporal in the 101st Ohio in April 1863. "Some of the men that yoused to be almost willing to have the war settled any way are now among the strongest Union soldiers we have got."[32]

Many soldiers lamented the destructive impact on morale of newspaper editorials or letters from home branding the war a failure and calling for an armistice and peace negotiations. Democratic gains in the congressional and state elections of 1862 fell like a wet blanket on the army. The troops were "not in as good spirits and as cheerful as they were before the elections," wrote the surgeon of the 13th Iowa in November 1862. "The election of men whose antecedents prove them to be at least sympathizers with the South . . . all prove the strength of the opposition at home, and it is a common saying here that if we are whipped, it will be by Northern votes, not by Southern bullets." An enlisted man from Iowa added the observation that the Peace Democrats not only discouraged the boys in blue but also encouraged the enemy. "The Rebels in the South well know how we are divided in the North," he wrote in March 1863. "It encourages them to hold out, with the hopes that we will get to fighting in the North, well knowing that 'a house divided against itself cannot stand.' "[33]

During the winter and spring of 1863 the Peace Democrats pressed their antiwar campaign full tilt in Congress and the press. Their efforts culminated in the nomination of arch-Copperhead Clement L. Vallandigham for governor of Ohio after a military court had convicted him of treason and Lincoln had exiled him to the Confederacy. Vallandigham escaped to Canada, where he ran his campaign for governor. During this Copperhead blitz a captain in the 8th Connecticut wrote that "the papers (many of them) published at the North & the letters recd by the soldiers are doing the Army an immense amount of evil." From the western theater came similar testimony from a captain in the 103rd Illinois: "You can't imagine how much harm these traitors are doing, not only with their papers, but they are writing letters to the boys which would discourage the most loyal of men. . . . I put in a great deal more of my time than I would wish to, in talking patriotism at the boys . . . to counteract the effect of these letters . . . and doing good solid cursing at the home cowardly vipers."[34]

Many soldiers were immune to the propaganda of Peace Democrats. This same Illinois captain noted proudly that "the copperhead letters in our company have been answered as patriots and soldiers should answer them." Some of the answers were pungent and to the point. A farmer's son in the 94th Ohio whose parents had immigrated from Germany learned in 1864 that his sister was dating one of the "infernal traitors." "You think more of traitors than you do of yor brothers" in the army, he wrote to her. As for her new beau, "he can just kiss my royal bengall I shall never go to see him if ever I life to get back." This soldier's mother had also expressed Copperhead sentiments, to which he responded angrily: "You think more of the butternuts [another term for Copperheads] than you do of your country and of your son yes and of your god. . . . Shame on you all abuse your dear son for fighting for your liberties why did you leave germina and come to this country . . . you would do better to go back to germina and live there . . . it appears you are dissatisfied with a free government. . . . I shall never want to see any of my relations that worked against me while I was in the surves."[35]

A few soldiers swore a deadlier vengeance than harsh words and ostracism. "I could shoot one of them copperheads with as good heart as I could shoot a wolf," wrote a private in the 25th Wisconsin. "I would shoot my own father if he was one." His father was not, so the threat in this case was an empty one. But a private in the 114th Ohio wrote to a lifelong friend in 1863 denouncing his Copperhead sentiments. "I would rather be at home killing Such men as you and Some of your comrades . . . if I live to get home [you'll see] if I dont Shoot there hearts out So help me god. . . . I tell you that you could Stay about my house no longer than I could raise my foot and kick you out."[36]

Threats to shoot Copperhead relatives were rare. But soldiers' letters were full of fire and brimstone against Peace Democrats in general, especially prominent ones like Vallandigham. "My *first* object is to crush this infernal Rebellion the *next* to come North and bayonet such fool miscreants as Vallandigham Reed &c.," wrote a captain in the 46th Pennsylvania. In a typical comment, a private in the 49th Ohio told his sister in June 1863 that "it would give me the greatest pleasure in the world to be one of a regiment that would march through Ohio and Indiana and hang every Copperhead in the two States." There seemed to be few Union soldiers who did not agree that "every copperhead, peaceman, anti-draft man, every cursed mother's son of them that does not support the war by word and deed ought to be hung or sent to the south where they belong. There is no middle ground. Every man who is not for us is against us."[37]

Many soldiers expressed greater regard for their open and honest enemies in front than for the sneaking Copperhead enemies in the rear. On this particular point the thesis of estrangement from one's own civilian population and identity with enemy soldiers is valid. "We have more respect for those that actually took up arms against us and showed themselves men and not cowards," declared a Wisconsin soldier, "than we can [have] of sneaking, low-lived, miserable cowards . . . that have cried our cause down at our backs." A Maine private spoke for many of his comrades: "If I could shoot a copperhead I should feel more elated than to have the privilege of bayoneting a Rebel captain."[38]

After the twin Union victories at Gettysburg and Vicksburg, both

the shrillness of Copperhead rhetoric and the bloodthirstiness of soldiers' responses faded for a time. Vallandigham was buried under a
100,000-vote majority in the 1863 Ohio gubernatorial election, in
which 94 percent of the soldier vote went to his Republican opponent.
The Republicans also swept other off-year elections that fall, helped
by the soldier vote. The huge anti-Vallandigham rallies in Ohio
cheered a soldier in that state's 55th Infantry. "We are glad to hear
that we have so many lovers of our Cause at home yet," he wrote his
father. "You don't know what good it does a soldier to hear such news."
A sergeant in the 16th Iowa reported after that state gave a solid
Republican majority in the gubernatorial election: "Before the election
the boys were considerably disheartened. They heard so many reports
about the copper heads and their doings. But the election dispelled all
doubt. We know that we are supported at home by a loyal majority."[39]

In the summer of 1864, however, Northern home-front morale
plummeted and Copperhead activity rose again as Grant's campaign
came to a halt at Petersburg after horrendous casualties and Sherman
seemed similarly stymied before Atlanta. Peace Democrats wrote the
crucial plank in the Democratic platform for the presidential election,
which shaped up as a referendum on the war. Republican prospects
brightened in September after Sherman's capture of Atlanta and Sheridan's victories in the Shenandoah Valley. These military triumphs propelled Lincoln to a decisive reelection, helped by almost 80 percent
of the soldier vote.

Union soldiers, whose morale had remained higher than civilian
morale during the dark days of July and August 1864, were gratified
by the way in which a majority of the folks at home came through for
them in November. Lincoln's reelection was "a grand moral victory
gained over the combined forces of slavery, disunion, treason, tyranny,"
rejoiced a forty-year-old antislavery sergeant in the 120th New York
whose son and brother-in-law had both been killed in action. The
"true hearted lovers of country & liberty & Freedom have not bowed
the knee to the Baal of slavery." A thrice-wounded sergeant in the
14th Indiana wrote to his wife after the election that "this does me
good to know that there is So many union men in the north and that
the traitors are So few . . . the Soldiers are in good Spirits they all
think we are Sure to win."[40]

He was right. Lincoln's reelection marked a final, decisive turning
point in the mutually reinforcing morale of soldiers and civilians, in
both North and South. It ended the Confederacy's last hope for inde-

pendence by a negotiated peace; it signaled a Northern determination to achieve peace and reunion by military victory.

But the will to fight was not only a function of war aims and positive cultural values shared by soldiers and the society for which they fought. The darker passions of hatred and revenge also motivated men to kill. These passions became more powerful as the war went on.

CHAPTER 11

VENGEANCE WILL BE OUR MOTTO

A N ESSENTIAL COMPONENT of the masculine code of honor was revenge for insult and injury. Hatred of the object of vengeance often accompanied this code. Both revenge and hatred were incompatible with Christian ethics. But many American men in the Civil War era were quite capable of reconciling Christianity and vengeance, just as they were able to suspend the Commandment "Thou shalt not kill" for the duration of the war. Otherwise the concept of a Christian soldier would have been an oxymoron. As the Civil War escalated in scope and intensity, the fury of hatred and revenge against the perpetrators of death and destruction crowded out Christian charity.

These sentiments played a stronger role in the motivation of Confederate than of Union soldiers—partly because the code duello had persisted longer in the South, but mainly for the obvious reason that the South suffered so much more death and devastation than the North. Even before any significant Union invasions occurred, however, Southern soldiers vowed vengeance against "the Vandal hordes, who would desecrate and pollute our Southern Soil." [1] The antebellum propaganda war between North and South had created in Southern minds an image of the hated Yankees as an amalgam of money-

grubbing mudsill Black Republican abolitionist thieves. From the outset, Confederate soldiers' letters bristled with stereotypes of "a low,
degraded set of Northern people," the "thieving hordes of Lincoln,"
the "lowest and most contemptible race upon the face of the earth."[2]

Once large-scale invasions and fighting began in earnest, vengeance
against "these fiends in human shape" became almost an obsession
with some Confederates. For reasons not entirely clear (the state was
scarcely touched by Union invasion), Texans seemed particularly ferocious on this score. When the popular colonel of the 12th Texas Cavalry was killed in a skirmish, a sergeant in the troop reported that "the
men were too much exasperated after the death of our colonel to take
prisoners—they were shot down." The same sergeant, now promoted
to captain, later expressed the hope that many thousands of the
"narrow-minded, bigoted, parsimonious, hypocritical, nasal-twanged
Yankee[s]" would "rot and lie unburied on the soil they came to lay
waste." Another Texas captain told his wife to teach their children "a
bitter and unrelenting hatred to the Yankee race" that had "invaded
our country and devastated it . . . [and] murdered our best citizens.
. . . If any luckless Yank should unfortunately come into my way he
need not petition for mercy. If he does I'le give him lead. . . . [I
intend] to *Massacre* the last one of them that ever has or may hereafter
place his unhallowed feet upon the soil of our sunny South."[3]

Soldiers from other states were not far behind Texans in the rhetoric of revenge. "Teach my children to hate them with that bitter hatred, that will never permit them to meet under any circumstances
without seeking to destroy each other," a Georgia lieutenant instructed
his wife. A Louisiana cavalry sergeant, the headmaster of a boys'
school before the war, had a pen as sharp as his saber. He had enlisted
for patriotic reasons, he reflected in 1863, but by the time Vicksburg
and Port Hudson had fallen the "only thing" that kept him going was
"absolute hatred of . . . the hyperborean vandals with whom we are
waging a war for existence. . . . I expect to murder every Yankee I
ever meet when I can do so with impunity if I live a hundred years.
. . . I don't intend ever to take prisoners. I think anybody who should
see the destruction they have caused in this country would applaud
the resolution." Confederates from border states professed a special
desire for revenge against their Unionist neighbors. Once they had
regained their state, promised a Missouri Confederate, "*vengeance* will
be our motto."[4]

A good many Confederate soldiers demanded an eye-for-an-eye re-

taliation for the destruction of Southern property. A sergeant in the
8th Georgia on his way into Pennsylvania in June 1863 voiced the
conviction that "we [should] take horses; burn houses; and commit
every depredation possible upon the men of the North. . . . I certainly love to live to kill the base usurping vandals." As matters turned
out, he had little opportunity to burn or kill; he was himself killed at
Devil's Den on July 2. But a soldier in the 3rd South Carolina who
survived the Gettysburg campaign reported that "most of the soldiers
seem to harbor a terrific spirit of revenge and steal and pillage" in
Pennsylvania. Lee had issued orders against plundering, "but the soldiers paid no more attention to them than they would to the cries of
a screech owl . . . and did every thing in their power to gratify their
revenge. . . . The brigadiers and colonels made no attempt to enforce
Lee's general orders. And Lee himself seemed to disregard entirely the
soldiers' open acts of disobedience."[5]

By 1864 the retributive cycle of revenge had intensified. A captain
in the 5th Alabama described with pleasure the burning of Chambersburg, Pennsylvania, by Confederate cavalry in retaliation for Union
destruction in the Shenandoah Valley. "Our men soon became
drunk & mad for plunder," he wrote to his cousin. "Some would come
to a man's house with a torch & demand $500 or so, or else they wd.
fire his house. This he wd. give, and fancy himself safe, when another
would come, and make a similar demand. This was continued untill
all his money was gone, when the last party would set fire to it. . . .
It was one of the best strokes we have ever inaugurated, its effects
have been most beneficial."[6]

In some Confederates this passion became almost pathological. A
Maryland-born officer in Longstreet's corps, a grandson of the archi-
tect Benjamin Latrobe (who helped design the United States Capitol
and the White House), directed the artillery fire of Confederate guns
from Marye's Heights during the battle of Fredericksburg. Afterward
he rode over the battlefield and, as he described the experience in his
diary, "enjoyed the sight of hundreds of dead Yankees. Saw much of
the work I had done in the way of severed limbs, decapitated bodies,
and mutilated remains of all kinds. Doing my soul good. Would that
the whole Northern Army were as such & I had my hand in it." Similarly, a Texas officer rode over the Chickamauga battlefield viewing
"the black and swollen [Yankee] corpses that will never be buried and
whose bones will be bleached by the pelting rains of the coming winter. . . . It actually done me good to see them laying dead, and every

one else that I heard expressed [the same] opinion." A corporal in the 4th Virginia was not satisfied with the death only of enemy soldiers: "I really think that it would be for the good of mankind, if the whole Yankee race could be swept from the face of the earth."[7]

Several Confederate soldiers picked up grisly battlefield trophies. After the battle of Manassas in 1861 a private in the 3rd South Carolina, son of a wealthy planter, offered to his sister to "send you some yankee bones." A soldier in the 21st Mississippi, also a planter's son, wrote to his parents after Antietam that there were hundreds of dead Union soldiers lying in the sector of the battlefield controlled by the Confederates before they retreated. "Tell Miss Anna [his sister] that I thought of collecting her a peck of Yankee finger nails to make her a sewing basket of as she is ingenious at such things but I feared I could not get them to her." A Virginia cavalryman had better luck when he camped on the battlefield of Brandy Station ten weeks after the cavalry battle there and found himself "laying on Yankee bones" at the very spot where his regiment had fought. He wrote to his wife that his brother, in the same regiment, "is now making a ring of some portion of the leg bone of the dead yankee."[8]

Perhaps the ultimate in vindictiveness was expressed by an officer in an artillery battery defending Charleston, who was cheered by news of the burning of Chambersburg. "I long to hear," he wrote his fiancée, like him a member of a prominent low-country family, "that we are paying the Yankees off in the same coin we have been enduring for the last 4 years—burn! and slay! until Ft. Pillow with all its fancied horrors shall appear as insignificant as a schoolboy's tale." A month later, after Sherman's capture of Atlanta, many of the Union prisoners at Andersonville were moved to Charleston. The South Carolinian wrote again to his fiancée that "I never saw a worse looking set than the Yankee prisoners. They have all wasted away from starvation and are fortunately dying rapidly. . . . That is much better than exchanging them." Yellow fever had broken out in Charleston, and "if it only gets among those 15,000 [prisoners] encamped on the race course it will make them beautifully less."[9]

Civil War lore is full of stories about fraternization between the men in blue and gray. Such contacts occurred quite often, to be sure. And so did incidents like the one in which Sergeant Richard Kirkland of the 2nd South Carolina risked his life to carry water to wounded Yankees in front of the stone wall at Fredericksburg, memorialized by a larger-than-life sculpture on the battlefield. But exaggeration and

romanticization have magnified the examples of fraternization. If soldiers' letters and diaries are an accurate indication, bitterness and hatred were more prevalent than kindness and sociability.

Toward black Union soldiers and their white officers, Confederate
enmity was unremitting. No fraternization or tacit truces took place
along the lines where they confronted each other. As a captain in the
8th Texas Cavalry expressed it, when the chance arose of attacking a
post defended by black troops, "all of our command determined if we
were put in a fight there to kill all we captured." After his capture at
Gettysburg, a lieutenant in the 9th Alabama imprisoned at Johnson's
Island learned that the Union government had suspended prisoner
exchanges because the Confederates refused to exchange black captives. The lieutenant approved: "I hope there may never be another
exchange. . . . One thing I think is very certain and that is that the
army in Virginia will not take negro prisoners. Much as we would
deplore such a state of affairs I say let it come rather than take the
alternative. If we lose everything else, let us preserve our honor."[10]

Many Confederates did preserve their honor by killing black soldiers who were trying to surrender. As a North Carolina private explained to his mother after a skirmish with a black regiment: "several
[were] taken prisoner & afterwards either bayoneted or burnt." A number of well-documented massacres of black captives occurred: at Fort
Pillow, Tennessee; Poison Springs, Arkansas; Plymouth, North Carolina; and the Crater at Petersburg, Virginia. After the battle of the
Crater the famous young Virginia artillerist Willie Pegram wrote to his
family that four hundred of the dead Union soldiers "were negroes.
As soon as we got upon them, they threw down their arms to surrender, but were not allowed to do so. . . . You could see them lying
dead along the route to the rear. . . . It seems cruel to murder them
in cold blood, but I think the men who did it had very good cause for
doing so. . . . I have always . . . wished the enemy to bring some
negroes against this army . . . it has had a splendid effect on our
men."[11]

The most notorious massacre of black prisoners took place at Fort
Pillow after Nathan Bedford Forrest's cavalry had overrun Union defenses on April 12, 1864. A great deal of controversy has swirled
around the question of Forrest's responsibility for the massacre. A lieutenant in the 20th Tennessee Cavalry who fought under Forrest had
no doubts. In a letter to his sister he described the scene after they
had captured the fort: "The poor deluded negroes would run up to our

men fall upon their knese and with uplifted hands scream for mercy but they were ordered to their feet and then shot down. . . . I with several others tried to stop the butchery and at one time had partially succeeded, but Gen. Forrest ordered them shot down like dogs and the carnage continued." [12]

MOST UNION TROOPS did not come from areas that experienced enemy invasion or occupation. But those from the border states and from East Tennessee, where a majority of the population was Unionist, constituted an exception. Among East Tennesseans, whose homeland was occupied by Confederates until the fall of 1863, the motives of hatred and revenge burned with a white-hot intensity. "Them rebs that cos us to leave . . . have not sead any thing yet," wrote an exile from East Tennessee who fled to Kentucky and joined the 5th Tennessee Cavalry (Union). "[We] will have an eye for eye and toth for toth." Another East Tennessean who became a lieutenant in the 19th Kentucky (Union) vowed that "if I live, I will be revenged. Yes I will draw their blood and mutilate their dead bodies and help send their souls to hell." [13]

Passions ran equally high in areas of Union border states where Confederate guerrillas were active. An Ohio captain serving with West Virginia Unionists expressed awe at their animosity toward rebels. "Hate rankled in their breasts," he wrote his wife. "Oh, how strong is this passion, this desire for revenge." The bushwhacking war in Missouri fired Unionists there with a desperate conviction "that it is to be a war of extermination. . . . It is life or death. . . . Union men will have to Leave or Pitch in and Kill as Many secesh as they can before Thay Kill [us]." [14]

The desire to avenge comrades or relatives killed by enemy bullets burned as hotly in Northern as in Southern hearts. A sergeant in the 1st Michigan Cavalry, which became a crack regiment in George A. Custer's brigade, wrote to his mother in 1862 that two of his friends had been killed from ambush in the Shenandoah Valley. "Those that are left of us are determined to visit a terrible vengence upon their murders. We are to take no prisoners after this." After the battle of Cedar Mountain, in which several of his close friends were killed, Captain Robert Gould Shaw of the 2nd Massachusetts "long[ed] for the day when we shall attack the Rebels with an overwhelming force and annihilate them. May I live long enough to see them running before us hacked to little pieces." A New York lieutenant whose younger brother, a corporal in the same regiment, had been killed at Cold Harbor, itched for a chance "to cut one of the Rebs into pieces [to] pay them back." Three weeks later a Confederate counterattack on his sector of the Petersburg lines gave him his chance: "We let them get within 3 rods of us & then we jumped up & gave them a volley. O how we did mow them down. We thought of Cold Harbor & the Boys just went in as fast as they could."[15]

Some Union soldiers avowed a more abstract motive of revenge for Confederate atrocities elsewhere, even the Fort Pillow massacre. Whether or not Billy Yank liked black soldiers personally, he identified with the uniform they wore. A Wisconsin soldier with Sherman's army in Georgia wrote to his fiancée that when his regiment charged Confederate works at Resaca in May 1864, "twenty-three of the rebs surrendered but the boys asked them if they remembered Fort Pillow and killed all of them. Where there is no officer with us, we take no prisoners. . . . We want revenge for our brother soldiers and will have it. . . . Some of the [rebels] say they will fight as long as there is one of them left. We tell them that is what we want. We want to kill them all off and cleanse the country."[16]

As this letter suggests, punishment for treason and a determination to "clean out" the rebels, whom they held responsible for starting the war, motivated many Northern soldiers. "I want to fight the rest of my life if necessary," wrote an Illinois sergeant to his sister, "before we recognize them as anything but Rebels and traitors who must be humbled." A captain in the 91st New York believed that "a rebel against the *best Government* the world ever saw is worthy only of one of two things to wit a *bullet* or a *halter*. . . . If I hated a rebel before I left home I hate him double now." A Minnesota captain who had fought for three years would hear of no peace terms except "utter submission" of "these traitors to the government. . . . When they have submitted I would propose to hang the leaders and let the poor *dupes* of Soldiers go."[17]

More than a few Union soldiers drew a similar distinction between Southern leaders and followers, between an arrogant "aristocracy" and the deluded common people. They were familiar with the famous Senate speech by James Hammond of South Carolina in 1858 labeling the Northern working class as mudsills. Several soldiers echoed the words of a farmer's son in the 93rd Illinois, whose two brothers also fought in the war. All three of them itched for the "chance to try our *Enfields* on some of their villainous hides and let a little of that *high*

Blood out of them, which I think will increase their respect for the *northern mud sills.*" Another soldier from Lincoln's state wanted Southerners to "eat of the bitter fruits of secession I want them poor so that they can appreciate the feelings of those they have so often made feel that they were poor."[18]

This feeling underlay the well-advertised resolve of Sherman's soldiers to take South Carolina apart. "No man ever looked forward to any event with more joy," wrote an Ohio soldier, "than did our boys to have a chance to meet the sons of the mother of traitors, 'South Carolina.'" After leaving a fiery trail through the state, another Ohio infantryman wrote to his brother that "her black ruins will stand as a warning of more terrible things to come" if the inhabitants persisted in treason. This soldier was particularly contemptuous of the self-styled Carolina aristocracy that "can talk of nothing but the purity of blood of themselves & their ancestors. . . . Their cant about aristocracy is perfectly sickening. . . . If you hear any condemning us for what we have done, tell them for me and for Sherman's Army, that *'we found here the authors of all the calamities that have befallen this nation . . . and that their punishment is light when compared with what justice demanded.'*"[19]

THIS RHETORIC OF revenge reflected a broad spectrum of opinion on the Southern and Northern home fronts. It revealed the dark underside of the patriotic symbiosis of community and army necessary to sustain the morale of volunteer soldiers. Another crucial component of morale, however, was internal to the armies themselves. They were instruments of the societies that called them into being, but they also became entities that took on a life of their own. Victory in battle pumped up their internal morale and gave them a more positive attitude toward the next battle; defeat lowered morale and caused many soldiers to wonder whether it was worthwhile to continue risking their lives. "In defining morale," wrote the historian of a crack British unit in World War I, "there is no better tonic for soldiers than to win a battle." Even in the highly motivated Abraham Lincoln Brigade in the Spanish Civil War, defeats and retreats were the foremost causes of demoralization.[20]

In the early months of 1862 the momentum of victory rode with Union soldiers. "We whip them every where," exulted a sergeant in the 66th Illinois who fought at Fort Donelson. On the eve of Shiloh he speculated about the possibility of a big battle: "Well let it come the sooner the better." After that bloody Union victory he remained confident. "You need not fret yourself about our staying in 3 years," he assured his wife, "for we are whipping them too fast for that." Confederate discouragement mirrored this confidence. Even in Virginia, Joseph Johnston's retreat up the Peninsula in the face of McClellan's Army of the Potomac in May 1862 caused an Alabama captain "for the first time . . . to despond. . . . I wont attempt to describe to you the horrible sensation I experienced, when I for the first time conceived it possible that we might be overrun."[21]

But then came the successful counteroffensives of Jackson and Lee in Virginia and of Kirby Smith and Bragg in Kentucky, which plunged many Union soldiers into gloom. "If you ever saw a discouraged regt it is this," wrote a lieutenant in the 10th Massachusetts. "No courage, no ambition, no hope." Units that fought well at South Mountain and Antietam were temporarily buoyed up by their success. In these two battles the famous 23rd Ohio (which contained future Presidents Rutherford B. Hayes and William McKinley) suffered 200 casualties but performed superbly. "We were victorious all the time," boasted the wounded Lieutenant Colonel Hayes from his hospital bed. "How happy the men are—even the badly wounded ones."[22]

After the removal of McClellan from command and the defeat at Fredericksburg, however, morale in the Army of the Potomac plummeted. At the same time the rise of the Copperheads, political bickering in Washington, and divisive controversy over emancipation interacted with discouragement in the ranks to plunge the army's willingness to fight to the lowest point of the war. Desertion reached alarming proportions. Soldiers' letters made clear the depth of demoralization. Over and over again occurred similar phrases: These "are the darkest days I have ever known in the army." "Never saw so many discouraged and discontented men in the regiment before." "What disgrace is greater than to belong to the Army of the Potomac?"[23] The war has cost more in "*blood* and *misery* . . . than I would give for the *whole south*." "I have made up my mind that we are not going to whip them at all." "The boys seem to be all discouraged they say they wont get them in another battle if they can get out of it any way   they say the union may go to the Devil."[24]

The Army of the Potomac seemed on the verge of disintegration when Joseph Hooker took command on January 26, 1863. Hooker's greatest contribution to ultimate Union victory was his success in reorganizing the army and reviving its morale. But he threw part of that success away by his indecision and wrong decisions that lost the battle of Chancellorsville. "Every breath of air has seemed a moan over our great misfortune," wrote a sergeant in the 22nd Massachusetts after the battle. "We feel as if we had wasted our strength on long, weary marches . . . wet, cold, and hungry, and fought all in vain. . . . Call it what you please, demoralization or discouragement, we dare not ford rivers, sleep standing and fight running, when sure defeat always awaits such a *doomed army.*" A private in the 124th New York, which had suffered 40 percent casualties at Chancellorsville, told his wife that "the lord is for the South he is not for us at all events."[25]

Yet the Army of the Potomac somehow picked itself up from the canvas and fought courageously with its back on the ropes at Gettysburg. Perhaps a private in the 6th New York Cavalry best explained the remarkable resilience of this army despite repeated defeats: "Yet I tell you I will fight for it, because it is on the right side, because Freedom will come out of it." A captain in the 18th Massachusetts offered an important observation as the armies began to move northward in the fateful campaign that climaxed at Gettysburg. "This Army of the Potomac is truly a wonderful army," he wrote to his mother on June 10, 1863. "They have something of the English bull-dog in them. You can whip them time and again, but the next fight they go into, they are in good spirits, and as full of pluck as ever. . . . Some day or other we shall have our turn."[26]

Their turn came three weeks later. As a Massachusetts private wrote ten days after Lee's retreat from Gettysburg: "We went into the bloody battle of Gettysburg feeling that we had suffered too much from the wretches, not to give them a *licking,* and we fought like *devils.* . . . Father, I am proud to say that I have . . . fought one of the most terrible battles on record, and *whipped*—GLORY!!! and chased them by thunder!!!!" The tonic of this victory did wonders for morale in the Army of the Potomac. "Those who a few weeks ago were almost willing to give up everything are now the most hopeful for the future," commented a corporal in the 57th New York.[27] Despite the ghastly losses of the Iron Brigade at Gettysburg (1,153 men killed, wounded, and missing), the commander of the 6th Wisconsin would "cheerfully abide the terrible risk of another battle . . . if we can end this war right here." As the fighting shifted back to Virginia, a corporal in the 10th Vermont spoke for many of his comrades when he wrote home that "I'm ready and willing to march to Richmond if we can whip the rebels up nice and clean. . . . Our army never was in such good spirits. . . . I want to help end this war *now*."[28]

More gyrations of morale were in store for the Army of the Potomac. In the meantime Grant's Army of the Tennessee experienced a similar cycle of despair during the winter of 1862–63 followed by elation with success at Vicksburg. In December 1862 Sherman's failed assault at Chickasaw Bluffs and Grant's retreat to Memphis after the destruction of his Holly Springs supply base had the same dispiriting effect on this army as the battle of Fredericksburg and the Mud March had on the Army of the Potomac. "I never in my life saw such a change in an Army in two weeks," wrote an officer in the 120th Ohio after the bloody repulse at Chickasaw Bluffs. "Men, Officers, who 60 days ago were in favor of fighting till the last man . . . are now in favor of Compromise." A captain in the 4th Iowa was "very much discouraged. . . . I have lost all my enthusiasm, a large portion of my patriotism and all my confidence."[29]

Things had not improved much three months later, after the failure of several efforts to flounder through the swamps and bayous that barred the approaches to Vicksburg except from the east. "I have never been so low spirited since I have been in the army," wrote a private in the 93rd Illinois who had participated in the failed Yazoo Pass expedition. But within a week Grant launched his movement past the Vicksburg batteries to close in on the bastion from the south and east. After winning several battles and placing Vicksburg under a siege that would force its surrender on the Fourth of July, Union soldiers who had written despondent letters in April reported that "the army is at present in excellent spirits. . . . They used to talk of going home, but hear none of that now. They say, 'As soon as we get this place we want to be sent east, we can whip them there.' "[30]

After Gettysburg and Vicksburg it was the turn of Confederate soldiers to sink into the slough of despond. "Everything has changed so in the last month that I have no heart for anything," wrote an enlisted man in the 21st Virginia on July 18, 1863. "This army is in no condition for active service. The men seem more depressed than I ever saw them & are in a bad way. . . . All things together have brought me to such a state that I feel more like cutting out my brains than I ever did before." A North Carolina private who survived Gettysburg concluded "that we are whiped. . . . The soldiers are all discouraged and they dread the thoughts of meeting the yankees again & loosing thier lives in a cause they consider to be nearly hopeless."[31]

Disaffection and desertion were particularly rife in North Carolina regiments. A soldier in the 5th North Carolina wrote that "there ain't fifty privates that wouldent leave if they had half a chance there is no secret talk about it they tell there offerciers so to there face they had an election last saturday two weeks wether we would fight any more or not and they souldiers all said no." A private in the 57th North Carolina was "the worst out of heart I Ever was yet the way Things is a going we lost nearley half of our men in Pensilvania. . . . I wouldent mind it if we Ever had gained any thing or Ever could Expect to gain any thing but . . . I believe in my heart that we are whiped git all our poor men kiled up and that is a bout all the good we Ever done yet. . . . Thare is more talk a bout Running a way than I Ever heard befor. . . . I wouldent care if they would all Runaway and then I am shure I would go to[o]."[32]

Not all soldiers in the Army of Northern Virginia felt this way, of course. Indeed, a majority probably would have agreed with the sentiments of a Georgia private who did "not think we should become discouraged when we meet with a few reverses" but rather should "fight the harder to make up for lost time. We know not but that it is for our own good as I fear we had become too self confident in our own strenth Instead of giving the praise unto Him who ruleth the destinies of men."[33] This sentiment underlay the remarkable wave of religious revivals in the Army of Northern Virginia after Gettysburg that did much to revive morale among the troops.

It was not only the "trip to Pennsylvania" that rendered "a most awful shock upon this army," wrote a Georgia lieutenant in Longstreet's corps, but also "the reverses in the West"—the fall of Vicksburg and Port Hudson and Bragg's loss of middle Tennessee.[34] Because of soldiers' access to a free press, news of battles in other theaters than their own soon reached them. Distant victories or defeats had an impact on morale second only to an army's own victories and defeats.

After a dispirited Confederate Army of Mississippi evacuated Corinth in 1862, news of Lee's victories in the Seven Days battles a thousand miles away "cheered our army a great deal," wrote a Mississippi artilleryman. But in the Union army that captured Corinth, "there is a universal *depression* in camp at the bad news from Virginia," ac-

cording to an Iowa sergeant. By September the Confederate victory at
Second Manassas and Lee's invasion of Maryland, plus Bragg's initially
successful invasion of Kentucky, caused a lieutenant of the 4th Iowa
in Arkansas to write his wife: "Our late defeats and disasters all over
the country has put a kind of damper on our feelings and spirits etc.
that we in the army cannot shake off." [35]

Even armies that had known nothing but success could be demoralized by failures of allied armies elsewhere. Burnside's expeditionary
force swept all before it along the North Carolina coast in 1862, "and
yet what does it all amount to?" asked a Massachusetts soldier in that
victorious army. "Richmond is not taken and probably never will be.
. . . It is useless to hope that the 'banner of freedom is to wave over
all the southern soil.'" But good news from elsewhere could wipe
away discouragement overnight. When word of Gettysburg, Port Hudson, and Rosecrans' Tullahoma campaign in Tennessee reached the
Union 15th Corps besieging Jackson, Mississippi, in July 1863, "we
hardly know how to contain ourselves over the unequalled good news,"
wrote a major in the 47th Ohio. "Everybody is electrified with it—the
army is on fire—as irresistible as an avalanch. . . . I never saw such
enthusiasm." [36]

In the Atlanta campaign of 1864, Sherman commanded an army
that had known mostly victory, while his adversary Joseph Johnston
commanded an army that had known mostly defeat. The experiences
of both armies in this campaign reinforced the corresponding morale
equation. After advancing sixty miles into the heart of Georgia, a captain in the 103rd Illinois felt "that to be connected with such a campaign as this is well worth risking one's life for." On the other side,
retreating rebels expressed despair. "We have run until I am geting out
of heart," wrote a sergeant in the 29th Georgia. "Evry retreat we make
only has a tendeincy to demoralize a portion of the Army." A lieutenant in the 46th Alabama could "hardley help from just given up everything when I see how bad we are doing." [37]

After he took part in the successful Union assault at Jonesboro that
ensured the capture of Atlanta, an officer in the 123rd Illinois described the elation of victorious troops. "I could have lain down on
that blood stained grass, amid the dying and dead, and wept with joy,"
he wrote his wife. "I have no language to express the rapture one feels
in the moment of victory, but I do know that at such a moment one
feels as if the joy was worth risking a hundred lives to attain it." After
part of this same Union army under George Thomas demolished the

Confederate Army of Tennessee at Nashville in December 1864, an Ohio artilleryman who fought there furnished one of the best descriptions of the tonic of victory: "We have had so many victories that we do not think there is any such thing as getting whipped; and so when we go into a fight expect to come out the best and are shure to do so."[38]

Through the grueling spring and summer of 1864, Union forces in Virginia experienced little of this heady success. Quite the contrary, they suffered such heavy casualties in the stalemated battles from the Wilderness to Petersburg that the men lost the high morale they had carried over from Gettysburg. A private in the 23rd Massachusetts, which was cut up badly at Drewry's Bluff and Cold Harbor, confessed that "in view of the fate of my regiment I must admit that my patriotism is somewhat shaken. . . . We are all very low spirited. . . . *All looks dark.* . . . It is time we should acknowledge that the northern army can never subdue the South."[39]

Yet those soldiers from the Army of the Potomac who won an unbroken string of victories as part of Sheridan's Army of the Shenandoah in the fall of 1864 sang a different tune. "I never felt in better spirits in my life," wrote a private in the 138th New York after the battle of Cedar Creek. "We have just given the Johnnies one of the worst thrashings they have ever had." As they went into winter quarters in the snow-covered valley, wrote the major of the 29th Maine, "we can bear cold and starvation" because "we have whipped the rebels. . . . The effect of victory extends to every portion of the army. . . . I see no reason why we cannot begin the final campaign next spring."[40]

By December 1864 many Confederate soldiers also foresaw the beginning of the end in the spring. At the battle of Nashville, wrote a staff officer in the much-defeated Army of Tennessee, "the men seemed utterly lethargic and without interest in battle. I never witnessed such want of enthusiasm." A private in the 28th Mississippi who fought at Nashville had "seen retreats before today, but none to compare with this—Disorganization, straggling, dissatisfaction & disaffection: bad—worse than bad." The army would never fight again, he believed; "I confess myself to be discouraged, & sick at heart. . . . Death, destruction, & slavery only present themselves to view."[41]

Even in the Army of Northern Virginia the will to fight seemed gone. "Our army is worst demoralized than it has ever been," wrote a corporal in the 27th North Carolina. At the battle of Hatcher's Run

(February 5–7, 1865), "the reason why we didnt whip those yanks . . . was that the men would not fight. The order was given to charge, but there was no charge in them . . . they would not go forward, if they had have charged as they have done before, we would have whiped the yanks." Desertion reached epidemic levels because, as a private in the 58th Virginia told his sister, "many have come to the belief that we will never whip the Yankees and it is only a question of time to bring us under. . . . Many are anxious for the war to stop and they don't care how [just] so they get out of the Army."[42]

By the time it surrendered at Appomattox, the once-mighty Army of Northern Virginia was a shadow of its former self. Its high morale bred by repeated victories had vanished. Without a similar tradition of success, the Army of Tennessee had cracked earlier. War weariness and economic breakdown on the home front accelerated the decline of the soldiers' will to fight. In the North, by contrast, military victories in September and October 1864 had revived flagging morale on the home front, ensuring Lincoln's reelection which in turn reinforced the determination of Union soldiers to fight to the finish.

The suddenness of the Confederacy's collapse in the spring of 1865 came as something of a surprise. But perhaps the greater surprise is that neither side had collapsed sooner. The military campaigns and battles of 1864 were unprecedented in duration and intensity. Combat fatigue and stress exhaustion mounted alarmingly. Yet no army broke until the Army of Tennessee did so after the battle of Nashville in December 1864. What sustained those men through that fateful year of 1864, more terrible than anything that had gone before?

CHAPTER 12

THE SAME HOLY CAUSE

C IVIL WAR SOLDIERS never heard of the terms "shell shock" or "battle fatigue" or "combat stress reaction" or "psychiatric casualties." But many of them experienced the symptoms these terms attempt to describe. A word that *was* familiar to them, however, was "courage." And they would have understood that combat stress reaction was a loss of courage, a loss of the will to go on fighting. They would also have understood the analysis of this loss by a British military doctor who served in the trenches during World War I and became Winston Churchill's personal physician during World War II: "Courage is will power . . . the fixed resolve not to quit." It can be used up by being spent too freely; in combat "a man's will power was his capital and he was always spending. . . . When their capital was done, they were finished."[1]

It was not only prolonged combat that caused soldiers eventually to break down; it was also the marching, loss of sleep, poor food or no food, bad water, lack of shelter and exposure to extremes of heat and cold, dust and mud, and the torments of insects. That was why a major in the 11th Georgia defined courage in 1863 as not merely bravery in battle but also "the nerve to endure rain, and snow, and sleet, and the privations of Winter, and the scorching sun of Summer

163

. . . to undergo extreme fatigue, to subdue the pangs of hunger . . . to do battle with sickness and despondency and gloom as with the Country's enemies. And above all to hold one's self patiently and cheerfully ready to meet the shocks of battle."[2] After a prolonged period of such fatigue and stress, however, even the best of soldiers will crack.

Combat stress reaction became more common in the last year of the Civil War than in the preceding three years. During those three years the continuous contact with the enemy over a long period of time that provokes combat fatigue was the exception rather than the norm. From 1861 through 1863 the armies usually maneuvered to bring themselves to battle, fought, and then separated when the loser retreated. The exceptions to this process, however, foreshadowed what was to come in 1864. During Stonewall Jackson's famous Shenandoah Valley campaign of 1862, some of his men marched 350 miles and fought five battles plus several skirmishes in a single month. A captain in the 27th Virginia of the famous Stonewall Brigade confessed to his wife that this activity "has broken me down completely. . . . [I am] in a state of exhaustion. . . . I never saw the Brigade so completely broken down and unfitted for service." They had little time to recover before going into the terrible Seven Days battles, after which a soldier in the 12th Georgia of Jackson's corps wrote home that "I am worn out . . . and also worn out in mind there is so much loss of sleep & excitement in every way. I never craved rest more in my life. . . . I would give the whole confederate states if I owned them to be with you all again." A soldier in the 3rd South Carolina reported three weeks after the Seven Days battles that one of his messmates had been "strangely afflicted" since the fighting ended. "He has almost lost the entire use of his hands and legs and is almost as helpless as poor little Johnnie. No one knows what is the matter with him."[3] A modern psychiatrist would probably know.

Many Union soldiers also succumbed to combat exhaustion in the three-months' Peninsula campaign that culminated in the Seven Days battles. After "living on eight or nine hard crackers from Thusday dinner till Monday near dinner and fighting and marching day and night nearly all the time," reported a Pennsylvania private and a Massachusetts lieutenant, they were "all reduced to shadows and look as though they were on thier last legs. They have a dreamy, listless look as though they were without hope." A lieutenant in the 13th New York was "worn out—ten years older than I was when we left Yorktown" two months earlier. "I must rest or lie down and die."[4]

Coming soon after the Seven Days, the six-weeks' campaign in which the Army of Northern Virginia marched more than 150 miles and fought two major battles (Second Manassas and Antietam), plus several smaller ones, produced unprecedented exhaustion and straggling. As a private in the 58th Virginia described it, "through the months of August and Sept we were under the sound of canon or musket the larger portion of the time. . . . We waded the Potomac 4 times, besides a good many other large water Courses" and "fought 4 and 5 days in succession without drawing any thing to eat." The Army of the Potomac was in better shape after these campaigns, but some of its soldiers nevertheless experienced severe combat stress reaction. The colonel of the elite 20th Massachusetts went to pieces after Antietam. The next morning he rode away from camp without telling anyone and was later found "without a cent in his pocket, without anything to eat or drink, without having changed his clothes for 4 weeks, during all which time he had this horrible diarrhea. . . . He was just like a little child wandering away from home."[5]

Some of these soldiers were clearly suffering from what is today termed post-traumatic stress disorder, the most serious and prolonged form of combat stress reaction. The battles of 1863 produced additional cases. But it was the campaigns of 1864 that caused the greatest toll of psychiatric as well as physical casualties. The opposing armies in Virginia and Georgia were never out of daily contact for months on end. Some portion of these armies fought or skirmished every day and marched or dug elaborate trench networks every night. In the seven weeks from May 5 to June 22, the Army of the Potomac and the Army of Northern Virginia experienced physical casualties (killed, wounded, and missing) equal to 60 percent of their original strength.

Little wonder that Captain Oliver Wendell Holmes, Jr., wounded three times in the previous three years, could write at the end of the bloody road from the Wilderness to Petersburg: "I tell you many a man has gone crazy since this campaign began from the terrible pressure on mind & body." Another prominent Massachusetts captain, Charles Francis Adams, Jr., wrote on June 19 that he had "never seen the Army so haggard and worn, so worked out and fought out, so dispirited and hopeless. . . . Grant has pushed his Army to the extreme limit of human endurance. It cannot and will not bear much more."[6]

A private in the 100th Pennsylvania drew a word picture of the experiences that caused the stress and exhaustion noted by Holmes and Adams. "For 25 days I did not sleep but a single night and this was the average for the whole army. . . . We would not more than get to sleep until we would be roused by the pickets being driven in or an order to move. Scarcely a day passed without an exchange of shots with the enemy." In those twenty-five days his regiment lost two-thirds of its men killed and wounded. The 20th Indiana also "lost about two thirds and what are left are Lousy and Dirty beyond be-lieving, some not having washed or changed since leaving camp now about 50 days," wrote a corporal in that regiment. "The Gettysburg campaign was thought a hard one but did any one ever hear of such A one as this." A major in the 14th New Jersey summed up the cam-paign succintly: "Nothing but fighting, starving, marching and cussing for 50 days with no cessation especially in the cussing."[7]

Studies of modern armies have shown that a unit is wrecked psy-chologically if it twice suffers casualties equivalent to one-third of its strength.[8] Many regiments in the Army of the Potomac, having been constantly on the attack against an entrenched enemy, had gone be-yond this breaking point by the time they reached Petersburg June 15–18, 1864. Some of them refused to obey orders to attack yet again. "Never has the Army of the Potomac been so demoralized as at this time," wrote a New York artillery officer. "A sicker set of wretches you never saw," wrote another New Yorker, a sergeant. "Our immense army has been wasted in battles and marches until it is now too weak to work with." A captain in the 20th Massachusetts acknowledged that his men were "utterly unnerved and demoralized" by the events of the previous fifty-three days, "*every day* under fire, every night either dig-ging or marching. . . . We, our brigade, have made fourteen charges upon the enemy's breastworks, although at last no amount of urging, no heroic examples, no threats, or anything else, could get the line to *stir one peg.*"[9]

Although they fought on the defensive and held interior lines, the Army of Northern Virginia also suffered many psychiatric casualties in 1864. A private in the 34th Virginia was "nearly broken down" from "fighting, working, day and night." A lieutenant in the 12th Georgia "was never so near worn out in my life" while a lieutenant in the 27th North Carolina felt he had "grown at least 10 years older in appearance."[10] After eighteen hours of continuous combat at the Bloody Angle of Spotsylvania, a Union lieutenant the next morning found enemy soldiers piled three or four deep in the trenches, mostly dead, but "one Rebel sat up praying at the top of his voice and others were gibbering in insanity."[11]

In Sherman's Atlanta campaign the armies did less heavy fighting but more strenuous marching and maneuvering than in Virginia. Sleep deprivation as well as casualties decimated many units. "There hasn't been a minute of time, night or day, that guns are not heard or that our regiment has not been losing men," wrote a private in the 25th Wisconsin. "A good many of the boys are breaking down for lack of sleep. The doctors are sending them back by the hundreds to rest." A captain in the 8th Alabama Cavalry thought he "had seen much of war but the last two weeks experience has been the most trying of any . . . sleeping has been almost out of the question—fighting all day & marching during the night." A lieutenant in the 16th Kentucky (Union) finally broke down after three months of almost continuous marching and fighting. At the battle of Utoy Creek near Atlanta his company was almost wiped out. "As my men were being carried by me to the rear, groaning, and terribly mangled, about a dozen of the survivors collected around me as if I were their only remaining support, I sat down on a log and cried like a child."[12]

ON JULY 1, 1864, a captain in the 103rd Illinois, which had suffered grievous casualties in the assault at Kenesaw Mountain four days earlier, told his sister that "this campaign is coming down to a question of muscle and nerve. It is the 62d day for us, over 50 of which we have passed under fire. I don't know anything more exhausting. One consolation is that the Rebels are a good deal worse off than we are. . . . We'll wear them out yet."[13]

Perhaps he was right. At least one Rebel, a private in the 40th Alabama, was worse off if one can judge from a poem he wrote in his diary in April 1864, *before* the fighting that year began for him:

> *I am weary of war, of powder [and] ball*
> *I am weary & sick of the glory & all. . . .*
>
> *Too much blood has already flowed like a river*
> *Too many fond hearts have been parted forever*
> *Too many farewells with tears have been spoken*
> *Too many fond circles already been broken*
> *Footsore and weary over paths steep and rough*
> *We have fought, we have bled, we have suffered enough.*[14]

Yet this bard fought on through another and more terrible year of war. What kept him going? What made the Illinois captain so confident that his side would wear out the enemy in the end? For many of the volunteers of 1861 and 1862, who did most of the fighting and suffered most of the casualties, the answer was pride and conviction. These words summed up the values of duty, honor, courage, and belief in the Cause that had initially propelled them into the army. The interpretation advanced here that these values persisted to the end is not universally accepted. Gerald Linderman's study of Civil War soldiers argued precisely the opposite: their harrowing adventures turned them into hardened skeptics who experienced a "harsh disillusionment" that caused them "to abandon many of the war's initial tenets." Another student influenced by Linderman maintained that "whatever idealism the soldiers brought with them into the army faded" in the latter part of the war. By then they fought not for a cause or for honor, but to stay alive and get the job done so they could go home—or even to go home without getting the job done.[15]

This conclusion seems consistent with common sense. How could soldiers sustain a high level of ideological commitment or belief in noble ideals through the grim experiences of disease, exhaustion, frustration, and death as the war ground on through its fourth year? The weary cynicism of Bill Mauldin's Willie and Joe in World War II, the bitter alienation of the "grunt" in Vietnam, must have had their counterparts in the Civil War. They did. Desertion rates rose in the latter part of the war. Many of the conscripts, substitutes, and bounty men who made up an increasing proportion of both armies were motivated marginally if at all by duty, honor, or ideology. The tone of some soldiers' letters as well as their behavior did take on a more negative, cynical, callous, even brutal quality as time went on. Without question there was a decline in the romantic flag-waving rhetoric of the war's first two years.

But this is not the whole story. Indeed, it is not the most important part of the story. For the fighting soldiers who enlisted in 1861 and 1862 the values of duty and honor remained a crucial component of their sustaining motivation to the end. Their rhetoric about these values was the same in the war's last year as in its first. In a letter of January 12, 1865, summarizing his three and a half years in the army, a young Illinois cavalryman used the word "duty" five times in a single sentence. A Maine veteran who reenlisted for a second three-year term explained why: *"Do your duty* is my motto even though it may clash with my own personal life."[16] The mother of a soldier in the 89th Illinois urged him to get a medical discharge after he was wounded at Pickett's Mills in May 1864. She had already lost one son killed in action and did not want to lose another. But he insisted on returning to the ranks in August. "Because I have done my Duty for the last 23 months," he wrote, "that is no reason why I should not return to the regiment and do my Duty again." After more than two years of fighting, a captain in the 28th Mississippi Cavalry was convinced that war was "an unmixed evil [of] . . . blood, butchery, death, desolation, robbery, rapine, selfishness, violence, wrong . . . palliated only when waged in self defence." He was "heartily sick" of it—*and* "sustained alone by a strong sense of duty."[17]

The belief in honor also remained alive and well for many soldiers to the end. To give up the Cause because of reverses, wrote a Tennessee cavalry officer in 1864, would mean "disgrace, dishonor, and slavery forever." When both the mother and wife of an officer in the 40th Tennessee urged him in 1864 to resign because he had done enough for the Confederacy, he rebuked them: "You know me too well to ever mention that to me to desert my country at this time would be awful. I had better die, by that I would not disgrace myself nor the woman I have sworn to love, cherish, & honor. . . . I want to be among the list who can return free from disgrace."[18]

These sentiments were not confined to officers. A private in the 27th North Carolina scorned the "dishonor" of desertion in February 1865 even as the Army of Northern Virginia melted around him. Likewise a private in the 11th Georgia told his mother proudly that for the past four years he had done his "Deuty while in the Noble Army of Northern Va and if I were to desert and lie out of this Strugle as many are doing I could not go any where but that the Eys of man and Woman would look at me. . . . I would feel worse than a Sheep killing Dog."[19]

The language of honor also persisted in the letters of married Union officers whose wives insisted that they had given enough to their country. "Darling you should not have done that," responded a captain in the 2nd Minnesota to his wife in January 1865. "I have risked my life too often for my own & Country's honor to throw both recklessly away." The major of the 10th New York said that in the future his children would look back on the war "either with pride or shame" in their father. This knowledge "has nerved me on & I would rather my children would mourn a Fathers death than his disgrace." When one of the Army of the Potomac's most celebrated soldiers, Joshua Lawrence Chamberlain, proposed to return to the army after partial recovery from a wound once thought to be fatal, his mother pleaded with him to reconsider: "Surely you have done & suffered & won laurels enough in this war." He replied in February 1865 that "I am not scared or hurt enough yet to be willing to face the rear, when other men are marching to the front." To return was the only course "which honor and manliness prompt." Surviving another life-threatening wound at White Oak Road on March 31, he fought through the campaign to Appomattox where Grant designated him to receive the formal surrender of the Army of Northern Virginia.[20]

FOR MANY CONFEDERATE soldiers in 1864–65 the motive of up-holding honor blended with the persistence of their ideological com-mitment to liberty, independence, and self-government as the only al-ternatives to the "degradation" of "vassalage" to the Yankees. "The old Troops are not as near whiped as the citizens at home," wrote a vet-eran in the 32nd Mississippi in early 1864. "Let [the war] be long or short meat or no meat shoes or no shoes [we are] Resolved to fight it out . . . for the sake of liberty . . . if we give it up now we will certainly be the most degraded people on earth." A sergeant in the 27th North Carolina admitted in September 1864 that "the soldiers are all tired of the war & would be glad for it to end," but "they are for it ending on honorable terms or none. . . . The south has lost too many of its noble sons to ever submit to A black republican form of government & be striped of its property & rights." If we give up, wrote a planter serving as an officer in the 28th Mississippi, "we lose every-thing of property—sacrifice our pride of character—of family—every-thing:—and descend to a depth of degradation unmeasurably below that of the Helots of Greece."[21]

The theme of fighting for liberty remained seemingly as uncompli-cated by the existence of slavery in 1864–65 as it had been in 1861. "I went in for the ware," wrote a private in the 47th Alabama in March 1864, "and I do expect to fite till the last for fredom." The last for him came two months later; he was killed at the Wilderness. Another Alabamian, an artillery captain, continued through the final months of the war to fill his diary with references to "the dear rights of freemen" and "the gigantic struggle for liberty," while a private in the 23rd Ten-nessee remained confident that he would see the "flag of liberty and peace floating to [the] breeze of a united and happy Confederate peo-ple."[22] At the end of 1864 a Mississippi officer declared that he was still determined to "battle for freedom a little longer," including the freedom to keep his slaves, for "without slavery little of our territory is worth a cent."[23]

By the winter of 1864–65, however, some Confederate soldiers had come to a new view of the relationship between slavery and liberty. "I can never bear to see the stars and stripes float over this country again," wrote an officer in the 23rd Mississippi. "We would simply be in a deplorable condition of slavery. . . . Almost anything else I am willing to accept, [even to] let the negro go."[24]

This soldier alluded to a great debate then occurring in the Confederacy: whether to arm slaves to fight for the South. The origins of this drastic proposal went back to the previous winter when General Patrick Cleburne had suggested that the Confederate army should remedy its manpower shortage by freeing and arming slaves. This heretical suggestion was squelched because, as one of Cleburne's fellow officers said, "its propositions contravene the principles on which we fight." But it did not stay squelched. By the following winter, discussions of the matter became widespread. In February 1865 Jefferson Davis and Robert E. Lee threw their weight behind a measure to enroll a limited number of slaves in the army—with the assumption, though not the explicit provision, that those enrolled would be freed. This was a desperate move, but these were desperate times. As a Mississippi newspaper put it: "Although slavery is one of the principles that we started to fight for . . . if it proves an insurmountable obstacle to the achievement of our liberty and nationality, away with it!"[25]

After contentious debate, the Confederate Congress finally passed the Negro soldier bill on March 13, 1865. The margin was three votes in the House and one in the Senate. Confederate soldiers who commented on the issue in their letters and diaries mirrored this split: about half reluctantly supported the measure and half angrily opposed it.

The latter condemned the proposal to arm slaves as one of "dishonor and humiliation," in the words of a Louisiana lieutenant. A South Carolina planter's son wrote from the Petersburg trenches that it "throw[s] away what we have toiled so hard to maintain."[26] A Missouri Confederate captain likewise reported that his men believed it contrary to "what they have fought for the last four years." A sergeant in the 17th North Carolina who had served through the whole war said in February 1865 that many men in his company were deserting because of the Negro soldier bill. He was thinking of deserting also if it passed. "Mother," he wrote, "I did not volunteer my services to fight for a free negroes country but to fight for a free white mans country & I do not think I love my country well enough to fight with black soldiers."[27]

Soldiers who favored the arming of slaves saw it as the only alternative to defeat. "Fight negro with negro," wrote an officer on Longstreet's staff, for it would be better even to free them "to gain our independence than be subjugated and lose slaves, liberty, and all that makes life dear." "If we continue to lose ground as we have for the last 12 months, reflected a Louisiana sergeant in January 1865, "we will soon be defeated, and then slavery will be gone any way, and I think we should give up slavery to gain our independence." The son of a wealthy Georgia planter still believed that "the negro's happiest condition is in slavery" but between abolition by the Yankees and emancipation by Confederates he was willing to take "the lesser of two evils."[28] A Tennessee officer agreed in January 1865 that "slavery is lost or will be, & we had better as well emancipate if we can make anything by it now. . . . We can certainly live without negroes better than with yankees and without negroes both." Perhaps reflecting the views of his chief, Robert E. Lee's adjutant Walter Taylor was willing to try the "experiment" of black Confederate soldiers. "It makes me sad however," he told his fiancée, "that the time honored institution will be no more, that the whole social organization of the South will be revolutionized."[29]

THE LETTERS AND diaries of many Union veterans in the later years of the war also reveal little if any of the disillusionment with their "initial tenets" of patriotism and ideological commitment that some historians have posited. "The cause [is] the same," wrote a lieutenant in the 7th Indiana to his fiancée who had urged him to secure a medical discharge because of his wound so they could get married. "My country [is] as dear. . . . Why should I lay down my arms? I love peace but I love my country more. I am now wedded to war . . . until the issue comes." An eighteen-year-old Illinois private conceded in 1863 that "i dont like [the army] very Well, and they hant many Does," but "Mother, i feal like fighting for My Country as mutch as i ever did. i don't play off Sick like som do to git their Discharge." The next year he was killed at Jonesboro. After more than three years in the army, a lieutenant who commanded his company of the 57th New

York from the Wilderness to Petersburg, losing two-thirds of his men, felt "as determined as the first time I took one of the U. S.'s Enfield Rifle Muskets, Ca. .577 into my hands, for the purpose of helping put down the Slave-holder's Rebellion" because "I still love my country."[30]

A key test of this determination came during the winter of 1863–64. Because the three-year terms of 1861 volunteers would soon expire, the Union army faced the dire prospect that many of its best regiments would melt away before the war ended. To meet this exigency the War Department offered several incentives for three-year veterans to reenlist: a $400 bounty (plus state and local bounties in many cases), a thirty-five-day furlough, a "veteran volunteer" chevron to wear on their sleeves, and an appeal to unit pride by allowing a regiment to retain its identity if three-quarters of its veterans reenlisted. This last provision put great pressure on holdouts when a given regiment neared the three-quarters mark. The bounty also helped, though many veterans hesitated to put a price on their lives. For some the furlough was the greatest inducement; they told themselves in January 1864 that since their terms still had five or more months to run, they stood a good chance of being killed anyway so why not seize the opportunity to spend a month with family and friends?

But all of these incentives together do not explain why 136,000 veterans reenlisted—more than half of those whose terms expired in 1864. The persistence of ideological convictions and a determination to finish the job were crucial factors for many soldiers. A reenlisted veteran in the 64th Ohio mentioned in his diary the bounty and furlough and a desire "to remain with my old companions" as reasons for his decision, but "more weighty than any of these [is] love of country and its institutions, and a determination to put down the rebellion." At the end of his reenlistment furlough, this soldier said goodbye to family and friends "to go forth with my life in my hands to fight the battle of freedom for another term of years." The parents of a reenlisted veteran in the 90th New York had opposed his decision, but he explained that although "it is hard to be separated from you so long . . . while duty calls me here and my country demands my services I should be willing to make the sacrifice. . . . Our country needs every man [now] in the service and as many more as possible." A forty-four-year-old father of three tried to assuage his wife's anger when he reenlisted as a captain in the 91st New York, but his choice of words may have made things worse: "I feel as keenly as any other the sacrifice made of home and those I love" as well as the dangers of a soldier's life, but these were "but dust in the balance for my Country's in the scale. . . . My children will remember me [proudly] for having been found among those who challenge treason and battle for the right."[31]

On New Year's Day in 1864, a reenlisted lieutenant in the 57th New York lamented the 50 percent of his comrades who had succumbed to bullets or disease during the past two and a half years. "Amongst the survivors," he wrote, "the excitement and enthusiasm of the early days has long since passed away, but the resolve still remains." They would need every ounce of this grim resolve during the coming campaigns. Writing from the trenches before Petersburg and Atlanta and from active fronts elsewhere in 1864, enlisted men echoed the themes of weariness coupled with determination to see it through. "There is nothing pleasant" about soldiering, wrote a corporal in the 105th Ohio, but "I can endure its privations . . . for there is a *big idea* which is at stake . . . the principles of Liberty, Justice, and of the Righteousness which exalteth a Nation."[32] A few months before he was killed at Fort Fisher, a sergeant in the 9th New York reproved his brother that "this is no time to carp at things which, compared with the success and reestablishment of the Republic, are insignificant." And in letters to his mother, an Irish-born sergeant in the 2nd New Jersey declared that neither the "horrors of the battlefield [nor] the blind acts of unqualified generals" had "chilled my patriotism in the least." "We are still engaged in the same holy cause," he wrote on the third anniversary of his enlistment, "we have yet the same Country to fight for."[33]

Not all Union soldiers felt this way, of course. The beats, the skulkers, the bounty men, substitutes, and draftees, the short-timers who had not reenlisted, the psychiatric casualties who could not take any more—these soldiers wanted nothing so much as to go home or at least to stay as far away from combat as possible. But there were enough who believed in the Cause and were willing to keep risking their lives for it to turn the war decisively in favor of the North in the fall of 1864. Their iron resolve underlay the message conveyed by a dispatch from the American correspondent of the London *Daily News* to his paper in September. "I am astonished," he wrote, by "the extent and depth of the [Northern] determination to fight to the last. . . . They are in earnest in a way the like of which the world never saw before, silently, calmly, but desperately in earnest; they will fight on, in my opinion, as long as they have men, muskets, powder . . . and would fight on, though the grass were growing in Wall Street." [34]

This was chilling news to Southerners who had counted on a waning of the Northern will to fight. Those Southerners might have experienced an even colder chill could they have read the letters of Northern soldiers confirming the observations of the *Daily News* correspondent. *"We must succeed,"* wrote an intensely Unionist Missouri officer to his wife in August 1864. "If not this year, why then the next, or the next. And if it takes ten years, why then ten years it must be, for we never can give up, and have a Country and Government left." A lieutenant in the 147th New York wrote from the Petersburg trenches that "I would rather stay out here a lifetime (much as I dislike it) than consent to a division of our country." When the wife of a captain in 28th Wisconsin wrote that she would prefer having him home to winning the war, he replied angrily: "Carrie, don't *ever again* say you don't care *how* they settle this war with the southern traitors—at least *not to me.* . . . I would see the war last twenty years—yes, a lifetime, & while my poor life lasted I would serve my country rather than see her dishonored by yielding to the demands of the wicked crew." [35]

The conviction of Northern soldiers that they fought to preserve the Union as a beacon of republican liberty throughout the world burned as brightly in the last year of the war as in the first. After marching up and down the Shenandoah Valley a couple of hundred miles in Sheridan's 1864 campaign, the last twenty-five miles barefooted, a private in the 54th Pennsylvania wrote to his wife from the hospital that he was ready to do it again if necessary, for "I cannot believe Providence intends to destroy this Nation, this great asylum for the oppressed of all other nations and build a slave oligarchy on the ruins thereof." A Kansas lieutenant who had spent more than a year in prison after his capture at Chickamauga longed for release but, he wrote his fiancée, he did not want the war to end short of unconditional victory, for if it did "the hope of the freedom of Nations and Millions in Europe and elsewhere [will be] driven back and obscured for ages." An Iowa officer who had risen from the ranks during three years of service while his father and younger sister had died at home and his brother was missing in action after the battle of Atlanta wrote to his distraught mother in September 1864 that he could not resign his commission and come home while the war's outcome remained in doubt. "Thank God," he counseled her, "that you have children that will support the Government that *your* Father supported in the Revolution."[36]

The 1864 presidential election shaped up as a decisive test of these convictions. The Democrats nominated McClellan, who professed to stand for restoration of the Union by military victory. But the Peace Democrats wrote the platform, whose crucial plank, drafted by none other than Clement Vallandigham, branded the war a failure and called for an armistice and peace negotiations. The vice presidential nominee George Pendleton was also a Peace Democrat. Most Northern voters viewed the election as a referendum on the war. So did many Confederates. If Lincoln won, the North would fight on to unconditional victory; if McClellan won, most observers expected a peace short of Union victory.

The overwhelming majority of Northern soldiers saw it this way. Unless they came from Illinois, Indiana, or New Jersey (states with Democratic legislatures) they could vote in camp by absentee ballot. As the election approached, sometimes heated arguments dominated soldiers' campfire bull sessions. The diary entries of a sergeant in the 8th Ohio Cavalry offer a typical chronicle:

Sept. 12, 1864: "Politics the principal topic of the day."
Sept. 13: "Spend a good portion of my time reading the news and argueing politics."
Sept. 21: "Politics keep up quite an excitement in our company."

The regiment then went on a raid (after all, there was a war on), but when they returned to camp the arguments continued.

Oct. 15: "Some considerable excitement on politics in camp."
Nov. 8: The regiment voted 367 for Lincoln, 16 for McClellan.[37]

Peer pressure in this regiment no doubt coerced some of the minority to mark their tickets for Lincoln. But a striking majority of all Union soldiers—78 percent, compared with 53 percent of the civilian vote—went for Lincoln. This was all the more remarkable because some 40 to 45 percent of soldiers had been Democrats (or came from Democratic families) in 1860, and McClellan retained some residual popularity among old soldiers in the Army of the Potomac. More than one of these veterans said, however, that while they still admired McClellan, they did not like the company he kept. So half of the former Democrats voted for Lincoln. As one of them explained it: "I can not vote for one thing and fight for another."[38]

McClellan's letter accepting the nomination had pledged to proceed with peace negotiations *only* on the condition of reunion. But most soldiers refused to take this seriously. It was the platform that counted, and in the words of a New York lieutenant that platform proclaimed the war "a miserable failure and ask[ed] for peace at the sacrifice of every sense of honor and right. . . . I do not see how any soldier can vote for such a man, nominated on a platform which acknowledges that we are whipped." A corporal in the 19th Michigan explained to his mother that "to ellect McClellan would be to undo all that we have don in the past four years. . . . Old abe is slow but sure, he will accept nothing but an unconditional surrender."[39] The noted cavalry commander Charles Russell Lowell feared that "McClellan's election would [leave] this country . . . in the condition of the South American republics, or worse. . . . Either half a dozen little republics, or *one despotism,* must follow." Lowell did not live to vote for Lincoln; he was killed at Cedar Creek on October 19. But a private in the 122nd New York did live to "give the rebelion another thump this fall by voting for old Abe. I cannot afford to give three years of my life to maintaining this nation and then giving them Rebles all they want."[40]

While service in the army converted many Northern Democrats into Lincoln voters, some of their families back home remained in the McClellan camp. This led to epistolary quarrels. A Connecticut artillery private could scarcely believe that his brother intended to vote Democratic. How could he "countenance such disloyalty? such infamy and such open insult to the patriots and soldiers of our land and to the martyred dead who have fallen—*they* say for nothing—but we say to save our country's freedom and liberty and . . . the universal cause of liberty and right throughout the world." An Ohio artilleryman sent word to his brother that if he voted for McClellan, "I will never speak to him. . . . He had better go and join the rebel army and have done with it at once." Another Ohioan, an infantry private who was too young to vote, told his father point blank that "when you vote for Mc & Pendleton you put yourself down and go to the ballot box hand in hand *with the vilest trators that America ever knew.*"[41]

When he learned the news of Lincoln's reelection, a naval officer wryly expressed his gratification that "McClellan meets with no better success as a politician than as a general." A private in the 17th Connecticut rejoiced that "our nation has been given new life and vigor and our glorious institutions [are] to be perpetuated."[42] When Lincoln reaffirmed at the Hampton Roads conference in February 1865 that his conditions for peace were unconditional surrender and the end of slavery, a private in the 1st New York Artillery was convinced that the sacrifice of his friends who "died fighting against cruelty and oppression" had been worth it, for "we shall come forth from the fire of trial and have proven to the world that the American people can and will govern themselves and that our country is indeed the land of the free and the home of the brave." After Lee surrendered at Appomattox, a fifty-one-year-old New Jersey colonel wrote to his wife that he could now come home proud that "it has been our privilege to live and take part in the struggle that has decided for all time to come that Republics are not a failure."[43]

ON THE THIRD anniversary of his enlistment, which also happened to be his thirty-first birthday, a carpenter who had risen to a captaincy in the 47th Ohio wrote to his ten-year-old son congratulating him on a neatly written birthday letter to the daddy he had scarcely seen during the past three years: "It tells me that while I am absent from home, fighting the battels of our country, trying to restore law and order, to our once peaceful & prosperous nation, and endeavoring to secure for each and every American citizen of every race, the rights garenteed to us in the Declaration of Independence . . . I have children growing up that will be worthy of the rights that I trust will be left for them."[44]

Americans at the end of the twentieth century are also children of that heritage. Whether we are worthy of it will remain a matter of constant reexamination. Civil War soldiers willingly made extraordinary sacrifices, even of life itself, for the principles they perceived to be at stake in the war. Whether Americans today would be willing to make similar wartime sacrifices is unanswerable. One hopes that it will remain unanswered.

APPENDIX

Table 1. Geographical Distribution of Confederate Soldiers
(number in sample = 429)

State	Sample (%)	Estimated % of All Confederate Soldiers	Region	Sample (%)	Estimated % of All Confederate Soldiers
Virginia	13.1	14	Upper South	38.0	41
North Carolina	14.9	15			
Tennessee	10.0	12			
South Carolina	7.7	6			
Georgia	12.4	11	Lower South	37.5	35
Florida	1.9	2			
Alabama	8.9	9			
Mississippi	6.8	7			
Louisiana	5.3	6	Trans-Mississippi	13.8	15
Arkansas	1.9	3			
Texas	6.5	6			
Maryland	2.8	2	Border States	10.0	10
Kentucky	4.4	5			
Missouri	2.8	3			

NOTE: The precise number of Confederate soldiers from each state is unknown because of the destruction of many records when Richmond was evacuated.

Percentages do not total exactly 100 because of rounding.

Table 2. Geographical Distribution of White Union Soldiers
(number in sample = 642)

State	Sample (%)	Estimated % of All Union Soldiers	Region	Sample (%)	Estimated % of All Union Soldiers
Maine	2.2	2.7			
New Hampshire	1.1	1.3			
Vermont	1.5	1.3	New England	15.9	13.7
Massachusetts	8.5	5.5			
Connecticut	1.9	2.1			
Rhode Island	.8	.8			
New York	12.7	17.1			
New Jersey	3.5	2.9	Middle Atlantic	29.2	32.7
Pennsylvania	13.0	12.7			
Ohio	11.4	11.8			
Indiana	6.5	7.5			
Illinois	10.0	9.8			
Michigan	5.6	3.3			
Wisconsin	4.5	3.5	Midwest	45.8	40.3
Minnesota	2.3	.9			
Iowa	5.1	2.9			
Kansas	.5	.6			
Delaware	.3	.4			
Maryland	.9	1.5			
Kentucky	2.0	2.0	Border states	7.3	9.2
Missouri	3.1	3.9			
West Virginia	.9	1.3			
Tennessee	.3	1.1	Confederate states	.6	2.0
Other Confederate states	.3	.9			
California, Oregon, and Territories	.3	.9	West	.3	.9

NOTE: The precise number of soldiers from each state is not known because the records were for *enlistments,* which must be adjusted to avoid double counting for reenlistments, which varied by state.

Percentages do not total exactly 100 because of rounding.

Table 3. Occupations of Confederate Soldiers

	Sample (%)			
	Officers (N=181)	Enlisted Men (N=209)	Combined (N=390)	Wiley Sample (%)
Professional	35.9	3.8	18.7	5.2
White-collar	21.0	13.9	17.2	7.0
Skilled labor	1.1	3.3	2.3	14.1
Unskilled	0	0	0	8.5
Planters	31.5	23.0	26.9	61.5
Farmers	10.5	56.0	34.9	

NOTE: The first three columns of percentages are from the sample of soldiers whose letters and diaries form the basis of this book. The line between planters and farmers is a thin and fuzzy one. Farmers include nonslaveholders and men who owned or rented a few slaves; planters ranged from large farmers who worked their land with, say, a dozen slaves up to those who owned scores. Soldiers who were too young to have an occupation (including numerous students in school or college) are designated by their fathers' occupations when known. For example, many soldiers listed here as "planters" were in fact the sons of planters ranging in age from the late teens to the mid-twenties who did not yet own land of their own.

Many soldiers listed in the "professional" and "white-collar" categories, such as lawyers, physicians, bankers, and merchants, owned farms or plantations as well; some listed as "planters" also practiced a profession or owned part of a business.

"Officers" are defined as soldiers who served as a commissioned officer for at least half of their time in the army, or who rose to the rank of major or higher even if they were commissioned for less than half of their service. "Enlisted men" are those who never attained a commission and those who served as officers for less than half of their time, unless they rose to the rank of major or higher.

The "Wiley sample" is a sample of 9,057 soldiers drawn by Bell Irvin Wiley from the company rolls of regiments from Alabama, Arkansas, Georgia, Louisiana, Mississippi, North Carolina, and Virginia. It is as representative of the Confederate army as a whole as we are likely to get, and is included here for comparative purposes. It does not total 100 percent because Wiley included a category of "miscellaneous and unknown" totaling 3.7 percent. The Wiley sample did not distinguish between planters and farmers. I am indebted to the late Professor Wiley for sharing his research data with me.

The occupations of thirty-nine Confederate soldiers could not be determined with certainty, which accounts for the disparity between the number in this table and in Table 1.

Table 4. Occupations of White Union Soldiers

	Sample (%)			U.S. Sanitary Commission Sample (%)
	Officers (N=216)	Enlisted Men (N=364)	Combined (N=580)	
Professional	33.8	2.7	14.3	3.2
White-collar	45.8	21.7	30.7	5.1
Skilled labor	4.6	19.0	13.6	25.1
Unskilled	.04	4.1	2.8	15.9
Farmers	15.3	52.5	38.6	47.5

NOTE: The first three columns of percentages are from the sample of soldiers whose letters and diaries form the basis of this book. They do not total precisely 100 percent in every case because of rounding.

The column labeled "U.S. Sanitary Commission sample" is taken from a study by the Sanitary Commission of the occupations of 666,530 Union soldiers from all Union states except Maryland and Delaware, published in Benjamin A. Gould, *Investigations in Military and Anthropological Statistics of American Soldiers* (New York, 1869). It is included here for comparative purposes. The percentages do not total 100 because the commission included a category of "miscellaneous and unknown."

Examples of "professional" occupations in this and the preceding table for Confederate soldiers include lawyer, physician, clergyman, engineer, college professor, school headmaster, and professional army or navy officer. Examples of "white-collar" occupation include banker, merchant, manufacturer, journalist, clerk, bookkeeper, schoolteacher. Examples of skilled laborers include carpenter, mason, machinist, wheelwright, cooper, shoemaker, smiths of various kinds, and other skilled trades. The line between skilled laborer and white-collar is sometimes blurred; for example, a master cabinetmaker who owns his shop is both a skilled artisan and a businessman; the master cooper may have had a higher status and income than a clerk or bookkeeper. The category of "farmers" includes farm laborers, who in most cases were the sons of farmers working on their fathers' farms.

Soldiers too young to have an occupation, including students in school or college, are designated by their father's occupation when known.

"Officers" and "Enlisted men" are defined here as they are in the Confederate sample in Table 3.

The occupations of sixty-two Union soldiers could not be determined with certainty, which accounts for the disparity between the number in this table and in Table 2.

A NOTE ON SOURCES

THE FINDINGS AND interpretations in this book rest on my reading of letters and diaries in 574 manuscript collections in 22 research libraries and in private possession, plus diaries or sets of letters that were edited and published in 214 books and 403 periodical articles, mostly in state historical journals. The difference in number between this total of 1,191 unpublished and published diaries or collections of letters and the 1,076 soldiers in the samples is explained by: (A) in some cases the same soldier is represented in two or more collections or publications, and (B) the numbers of letters or diary entries by some soldiers were too few to justify inclusion in the samples.

The number of letters in letter collections written by soldiers represented in the samples ranged from about a dozen in the smallest collections to several hundred in the largest. The quality and usefulness of a given soldier's letters varied almost as widely as the quantity, but together these 25,000 to 30,000 letters helped build up the composite portrait of Civil War soldiers that I have tried to portray in this work. In general, letters were more valuable than diaries for this purpose, for many of the latter consisted only of spare factual entries with little or no narrative or reflective commentary. Some diaries, however, were even more valuable than letters in helping me to understand the thoughts, emotions, and convictions of those men in blue and gray.

For help in determining the categories of analysis that frame my study of Civil War soldiers, I am indebted to the studies of combat motivation and behavior in other wars that are cited frequently in my endnotes. These works are too numerous to cite again here, but I must single out John Keegan's *The Face of Battle* (New York, 1976), which helped to inspire me to undertake this Face of Battle for the American Civil War.

I also owe a scholarly debt far beyond my means to repay to historians who have preceded me in writing about Civil War soldiers. I am not the first to ask many of the questions that I try to answer in this book nor the first to offer an interpretation of what motivated those citizens in uniform. Without the foundation laid by others, I could not have built the structure of analysis in *For Cause and Comrades*.

These studies fall into four categories. The first consists of books that survey the full range of Civil War soldiers' experiences and attitudes. The classics in this genre are Bell Irvin Wiley's *The Life of Johnny Reb: The Common Soldier of the Confederacy* (Indianapolis, 1943) and *The Life of Billy Yank: The Common Soldier of the Union* (Indianapolis, 1952). They are supplemented by a fine book from one of Wiley's students, James I. Robertson, Jr., *Soldiers Blue and Gray* (Columbia, S.C., 1988). These three books discuss many topics in addition to combat motivation: camp life, training, discipline, amusements, music, food, weapons, daily routines, winter quarters, soldier crime and punishment, medical care, homesickness, religion, the POW experience, and others. All three rely on soldiers' personal letters and diaries for most of their evidence, though they also cite sometimes suspect memoirs and rewritten diaries for color. Anyone wishing to understand the physical and mental worlds of Civil War soldiers should start with these accounts.

A second category of studies focuses on a narrower range of themes but explores them more deeply. Reid Mitchell's *Civil War Soldiers* (New York, 1988) probes the psychology of the men in blue and gray: their perceptions of themselves and their enemies, their understanding of the meaning of this war, their coming of age as men in the crucible of war, their conceptualizations of the geographical and social "landscape" as Northern soldiers invaded the South and Confederate soldiers raided into Pennsylvania. Mitchell has also sensitively analyzed the ties among Union soldiers and family, community, and nation in

The Vacant Chair: The Northern Soldier Leaves Home (New York, 1993), a study with important implications for combat motivation because it roots patriotism in the soldier's identification with home and community. Both of Mitchell's books are fine social as well as military history, and are important reading for those who want to understand the organic relationship between the armies and the societies for which they fought. Mitchell relies almost entirely on letters and diaries for his primary sources. The same is true of Randall C. Jimerson, *The Private Civil War: Popular Thought During the Sectional Conflict* (Baton Rouge, 1988), which concentrates on the ideological and political issues at stake in the war—nationalism, liberty, republicanism, and slavery. Earl J. Hess, *Liberty, Virtue, and Progress: Northerners and Their War for the Union* (New York, 1988), includes the perspective of civilians on the home front as well as soldiers in the army and emphasizes most strongly the continuum between political ideology and war aims.

In a third category are two books that analyze mindsets, motives, and behavior of soldiers in two specific Civil War armies: Joseph T. Glatthaar, *The March to the Sea and Beyond: Sherman's Troops in the Savannah and Carolinas Campaign* (New York, 1985), and Larry J. Daniel, *Soldiering in the Army of Tennessee: A Portrait of Life in a Confederate Army* (Chapel Hill, 1991). Glatthaar's book, like those by Reid Mitchell, combines social and military history in a deft fashion. It shows how the social background and political culture of these Union soldiers manifested themselves in Sherman's march to the sea and through the Carolinas. A different kind of book about a much different army is Larry Daniel's narrative of the hard-luck Army of Tennessee, which tends to follow Wiley's format in analyzing a broad range of soldier attitudes and behavior patterns mostly internal to the army itself. The principal sources for both Glatthaar and Daniel are soldiers' letters and diaries leavened by a judicious use of memoirs. The trilogy on the Army of the Potomac by Bruce Catton might also fit into this category of books about soldiers in particular armies: *Mr. Lincoln's Army* (Garden City, N.Y., 1951); *Glory Road* (Garden City, 1952); and *A Stillness at Appomattox* (Garden City, 1953). But these volumes are narratives of campaigns and battles, of strategy and tactics, and of commanders and command decisions as much as or more than they are studies of soldiers. Nevertheless, they helped awaken my interest in Civil War soldiers and I have learned a great deal from them.

Finally, a fourth category consists of books with a specific focus on combat motivation and experience. In addition to many recent narratives of individual battles too numerous to mention here, which contain much material on the perceptions and actions of the rank and file, there are two studies that discuss several of the themes treated in *For Cause and Comrades*. Joseph Allan Frank and George A. Reaves, *"Seeing the Elephant": Raw Recruits at the Battle of Shiloh* (New York, 1989), uses letters and diaries as well as memoirs and regimental histories to analyze in close detail the training, motivation, combat behavior, and responses to fear and stress of soldiers on both sides at the bloodiest single battle in the first seventeen months of the war. Gerald Linderman's *Embattled Courage: The Experience of Combat in the American Civil War* (New York, 1987) is a provocative, thesis-driven book that argues for a major transformation in the soldiers' perceptions of combat from an initial set of romanticized ideals to a weary, disillusioned repudiation of those ideals by the latter half of the war. I have made clear the differences between some of Linderman's interpretations and my own in the foregoing pages. In addition, it is perhaps worth noting that Linderman relies heavily on memoirs, regimental histories, and other writings from a postwar perspective as well as on wartime letters and diaries, and that some of this evidence does not seem to support his thesis. Nevertheless, I have found *Embattled Courage* immensely important in stimulating my own thinking about the will to combat in the Civil War.

ABBREVIATIONS

IN NOTES

AHQ	*Alabama Historical Quarterly*
CWH	*Civil War History*
FCHS	Filson Club Historical Society, Louisville
FLPU	Firestone Library, Princeton University
GHQ	*Georgia Historical Quarterly*
GLC PML	Gilder Lehrman Collection, Pierpont Morgan Library, New York
HEH	Henry E. Huntington Library, San Marino, California
HML LSU	Hill Memorial Library, Louisiana State University
IJH	*Iowa Journal of History*
IMH	*Indiana Magazine of History*
ISHL	Illinois State Historical Library, Springfield
KHS	Kentucky Historical Society, Frankfort
LC	Library of Congress
MD HS	Maryland Historical Society, Baltimore
MHI	U.S. Army Military History Institute, Carlisle, Pennsylvania
MN HS	Minnesota Historical Society, St. Paul
MO HS	Missouri Historical Society, St. Louis
MVHR	*Mississippi Valley Historical Review*
NCHR	*North Carolina Historical Review*
OHS	Ohio Historical Society, Columbus
PLDU	Perkins Library, Duke University
PMHB	*Pennsylvania Magazine of History and Biography*

RHSP   *Rochester Historical Society Publications*
SCMH   *South Carolina Magazine of History*
SHC UNC   Southern Historical Collection, University of North Carolina, Chapel Hill
SHQ   *Southwestern Historical Quarterly*
SHS MO   State Historical Society of Missouri, Columbia
THQ   *Tennessee Historical Quarterly*
TSL   Tennessee State Library, Nashville
VHS   Virginia Historical Society, Richmond
VMHB   *Virginia Magazine of History and Biography*
WHS   Wisconsin Historical Society, Madison
WLEU   Woodruff Library, Emory University, Atlanta
WMH   *Wisconsin Magazine of History*
WPMH   *Western Pennsylvania Magazine of History*
WRHS   Western Reserve Historical Society, Cleveland

NOTES

1. For an exhaustive statistical profile of the Union army, see Benjamin A. Gould, *Investigations in Military and Anthropological Statistics of American Soldiers* (New York, 1869). Nothing comparable exists for the Confederate army; the closest thing to a statistical analysis can be found in Bell Irvin Wiley, *The Life of Johnny Reb: The Common Soldier of the Confederacy* (Indianapolis, 1943), 322–37, based on the muster rolls of a sample of forty-two companies of twenty-one regiments from six states. Many years ago Professor Wiley generously provided me with copies of his research data based on a larger sample of 9,057 Confederate soldiers from seven states.

2. Amy E. Holmes, "Widows and the Civil War Pension System," in Maris A. Vinovskis, ed., *Toward a Social History of the Civil War* (Cambridge, 1990), 174. See also Emily J. Harris, "Sons and Soldiers: Deerfield, Massachusetts and the Civil War," *Civil War History* 30 (1984): 168, which found that 32 percent of the soldiers from Deerfield were married.

CHAPTER 1. THE WAR IS A CRUSADE

1. Quoted in Bruce Catton, *A Stillness at Appomattox* (Garden City, 1954), 127.

2. Roger Durham quoted in James Reston, Jr., *Sherman's March and Viet-*

nam (New York, 1984), 97–100; Wickham quoted in a conversation with the author by Edwin Bearss, chief historian of the National Park Service, who guided General Wickham's visit to Antietam.

3. Roy R. Grinker and John P. Spiegel, *Men Under Stress* (Philadelphia, 1945), 37–38; John William De Forest, *A Volunteer's Adventures: A Union Captain's Record of the Civil War,* ed. James Croushore (New Haven, 1946), 123–24. Emphasis added.

4. Roy P. Basler, ed., *The Collected Works of Abraham Lincoln,* 9 vols. (New Brunswick, N.J., 1952–55), VI: 446; Cornelius Tenure to John H. Tenure, March 28, 1864, in *Civil War Letters of the Tenure Family,* ed. Larry H. Whiteaker and W. Calvin Dickinson (New City, N.Y., 1990), 62; Joshua L. Chamberlain, *The Passing of the Armies* (New York, 1915), 20.

5. Uriah Parmelee to father, Jan. 13, 1865, Parmelee Papers, PLDU; Sanford McCall to Helen McCall, July 29, 1862, McCall Papers, in private possession; Edward Wightman to brother, Dec. 14, 1862, *From Antietam to Fort Fisher: The Civil War Letters of Edward King Wightman, 1862–1865,* ed. Edward G. Longacre (Rutherford, N.J., 1983), 91.

6. Edward M. Burrus to father, Feb. 8, 1862, Burrus Papers, HML LSU.

7. Dudley D. Marvin to "Sister Liz," Nov. 21, 1863, and to "Brother Ralph," Dec. 1, 1863, Marvin Family Papers, MHI; "The Reluctant Warrior: The Diary of N. K. Nichols," ed. T. Harry Williams, *CWH* 3 (1957): 36.

8. Thomas J. Elliott to wife, July 15, Sept. 26, 1862, Elliott Papers, PLDU; Stephen Frazier to wife, Jan. 11, 1864, Frazier Papers, PLDU.

9. Charles Wills to family, March 26, 1862, *Army Life of an Illinois Soldier, Letters and Diary of the Late Charles Wills* (Washington, 1906), 74; Henry J. Colyer to mother, July 16, 1863, Colyer Papers, HEH; George W. Tillotson to Elizabeth Tillotson, July 9, 1864, Tillotson Papers, GLC PML; Amos Steere to sister, May 2, 1862, Misc. Civil War Collection, MHI. These comments were written, respectively, by a lieutenant in the 7th Illinois Cavalry, a corporal in the 157th New York, a sergeant in the 89th New York, and a private in the 25th Massachusetts.

10. Darius Starr to mother, March 18, 1863, Starr Papers, PLDU; Nelson Miles to Nelson Miles (uncle), Aug. 26, 1863, Miles Papers, MHI.

11. Samuel A. Stouffer et al., *The American Soldier,* 2 vols. (Princeton, 1949), II: *Combat and Its Aftermath,* 35–36; Grinker and Spiegel, *Men Under Stress,* 11; Peter Watson, *War on the Mind: The Military Uses and Abuses of Psychology* (New York, 1978), 49.

12. George W. Tillotson to Elizabeth Tillotson, May 24, 1864, Tillotson Papers, GLC PML; Edwin Payne to Kim Hudson, Aug. 5, 1862, Jan. 3, 1863, Payne Papers, ISHL; Robert Patrick, diary entry of Jan. 29, 1863, *Reluctant Rebel: The Secret Diary of Robert Patrick, 1861–1865,* ed. Jay F. Taylor (Baton Rouge, 1959), 83–84.

13. George W. Beidelman to father, Nov. 18, 1863, in *The Civil War*

Letters of George Washington Beidelman, ed. Catherine H. Vanderslice (New York, 1978), 147–48; Charles H. Brewster to Mary Brewster, Dec. 31, 1862, *When This Cruel War Is Over: The Civil War Letters of Charles Harvey Brewster,* ed. David W. Blight (Amherst, 1992), 207.

14. Walter Clark to mother, Sept. 26, 1862, in *The Papers of Walter Clark,* ed. Aubrey Lee Brooks and Hugh Talmage Lefler, 2 vols. (Chapel Hill, 1948–50), I: 79.

15. Henry Martyn Cross to parents, June 4, 1863, in "A Yankee Soldier Looks at the Negro," ed. William Cullen Bryant II, *CWH* 7 (1961): 146; Ephraim S. Holloway to Margaret Holloway, Jan. 9, 1863, Holloway Papers, OHS; Eugene Kingman to family, Oct. 24, 1864, *Tramping Out the Vintage, 1861–1864: The Civil War Diaries and Letters of Eugene Kingman,* ed. Helene C. Phelan (Almond, N.Y., 1983), 324.

16. James E. Glazier to Annie Monroe, April 19, 1862, Glazier Papers, HEH.

17. *The Bayonets of the Republic: Motivation and Tactics in the Army of Revolutionary France, 1791–1794* (Urbana, Ill., 1984), 35–36, 177–82.

18. Edward W. Cade to Allie Cade, July 9, Nov. 19, 1863, *A Texas Surgeon in the C.S.A.,* ed. John Q. Anderson (Tuscaloosa, Ala., 1957), 67–68, 81; Alfred L. Hough to Mary Hough, Oct. 28, 1863, March 13, 1864, *Soldier in the West: The Civil War Letters of Alfred Lacey Hough,* ed. Robert G. Athearn (Philadelphia, 1957), 165, 178.

CHAPTER 2. WE WERE IN EARNEST

1. James to John Welsh, May 12, June 2, 1861, John to James Welsh, May 23, 1861, in "A House Divided: The Civil War Letters of a Virginia Family," ed. W. G. Bean, *VMHB* 59 (1951): 399–401.

2. James to Charles Steedman, Dec. 30, 1860, Jan. 6, 1861, Charles Steedman to "My Dear Hudson," April 21, 1861, Charles Steedman Papers, PLDU.

3. *Life, Letters, and Journals of George Ticknor,* 2 vols. (Boston, 1876), II: 433–34; Josiah Favill, diary entry of April 15, 1861, in *Diary of a Young Officer* (Chicago, 1909), 12.

4. "The Diary of Sidney George Fisher, 1861," *PMHB* 88 (1964): 82; "Education of an Artist: The Diary of Joseph Boggs Beale, 1856–1862," ed. Nicholas B. Wainwright, *PMHB* 97 (1973): 500.

5. Robert S. Fletcher, *History of Oberlin College,* 2 vols. (Oberlin, 1943), II: 845; Levi Graybill Diary, entries of April 16 and 18, 1861, HEH.

6. Robert E. Sterling, "Civil War Draft Resistance in the Middle West" (Ph.D. dissertation, Northern Illinois University, 1974), 15–16; James Bell to Augusta Hallock, April 27, 1861, Bell Papers, HEH.

7. Henry T. Shanks, *The Secession Movement in Virginia, 1847–1861*

(Richmond, 1934), 268n; William Howard Russell, *My Diary North and South*, ed. Fletcher Pratt (New York, 1954), 52.

8. Harry St. John Dixon, Diary, entry of April 17, 1861; Henry Ewing to Harry St. John Dixon, May 1, 1861, Dixon Papers, SHC UNC.

9. Henry W. Howe to family, April 20, 1861, *Passages from the Life of Henry Warren Howe, Consisting of Diary and Letters Written During the Civil War* (Lowell, Mass., 1899), 86; Thomas Keith, Diary, entries of Aug. 27 and 30, 1861, MO HS.

10. Ira Gillaspie, diary entry of Aug. 20, 1861, in *The Diary of Ira Gillaspie of the Eleventh Michigan Infantry*, ed. Daniel B. Weber (Mount Pleasant, Mich., 1965), 7; Saxon DeWolf to sister, Oct. 18, 1861, DeWolf Papers, MHI.

11. Roy B. Basler, ed., *The Collected Works of Abraham Lincoln*, 9 vols. (New Brunswick, N.J., 1953–55), IV: 268; George W. Beidelman to father, May 15, 1861, in *The Civil War Letters of George Washington Beidelman*, ed. Catherine H. Vanderslice (New York, 1978), 15; Walter Q. Gresham to Tillie Gresham, April 28, 1861, Gresham Papers, LC; Titus Crenshaw to father, Nov. 10, 1861, March 28, 1862, in Charlotte Erickson, *Invisible Immigrants: The Adaptation of English and Scottish Immigrants in Nineteenth-Century America* (Coral Gables, Fla., 1972), 348, 351.

12. Thomas T. Taylor to Antoinette Taylor, May 23, June 18, 1861, Taylor Papers, OHS; James M. Goff to father, Dec. 14, 1861, James M. Goff to brother, Jan. 29, 1862, Goff-Williams Collection, HEH. The original 12th Ohio was a three-months regiment; when Thomas Taylor reenlisted in the 47th Ohio for three years, his wife was even more upset.

13. John Q. A. Campbell, Diary, entry of July 6, 1861, WRHS; Tully McCrea to Belle McCrea, June 1, 1861, in *Dear Belle: Letters from a Cadet & Officer to his Sweetheart, 1858–1865*, ed. Catherine S. Crary (Middletown, Conn., 1965), 98; John W. Ames to mother, Nov. 12, 1861, Ames Papers, MHI.

14. William M. Thomson to Warner A. Thomson, Dec. 22, 1860, Feb. 2, 1861, Thomson Papers, WLEU; W. R. Redding to "Lizzie," Aug. (no day) 1861, Redding Papers, SHC UNC; Lunsford Yandell, Jr., to Sally Yandell, April 22, 1861, Yandell Papers, FCHS.

15. Basler, ed., *Collected Works of Lincoln*, II: 250; Samuel Johnson, "Taxation No Tyranny," in *Samuel Johnson's Political Writings*, ed. Donald L. Greene (New Haven, 1977), 454.

16. Charles Woodward Hutson to mother, Sept. 14, 1861, Hutson Papers, SHC UNC.

17. Edward Dorr Tracy to wife, June 27, 1861, Tracy Papers, SHC UNC; Hannibal Paine to F. J. Paine, Aug. 30, 1861, Paine Papers, TSL.

18. William Grimball to Elizabeth Grimball, Nov. 20, 1860, Berkley Grimball to Elizabeth Grimball, Dec. 8, 1860, Lewis Grimball to Elizabeth

Grimball, Nov. 27, 1860, John Berkley Grimball Papers, PLDU; Nathaniel H. R. Dawson to Elodie Todd Dawson, June 8, 1861, Elodie Todd Dawson to Nathaniel H. R. Dawson, July 4, 1861, Dawson Papers, SHC UNC.

19. Paul A. McMichael to Margaret McMichael, Feb. 19, 1862, McMichael Papers, SHC UNC; Harry St. John Dixon to father, April 15, 1861, Dixon Papers, SHC UNC; John Lee Holt to Ellen Holt, May 2, 1862, in *I Wrote You Word: The Poignant Letters of Private Holt* (Lynchburg, 1993), 79.

20. Richard W. Simpson to Caroline Miller, Sept. 20, 1861, *"Far, Far from Home": The Wartime Letters of Dick and Tally Simpson, Third South Carolina Volunteers,* ed. Guy R. Everson and Edward H. Simpson, Jr. (New York, 1994), 72; Henry Orr to his sister, Oct. 31, 1861, in *Campaigning with Parsons' Texas Cavalry Brigade, CSA* (Hillsboro, Tex., 1967), 10.

21. John Keegan, *The Face of Battle* (New York, 1976), 164–65; Anthony Kellett, *Combat Motivation: The Behavior of Soldiers in Battle* (Boston, 1982), 175–76.

22. George K. Miller to Celestine McCann, June 10, 1861, Miller Papers, SHC UNC; Val Wynne to mother, n.d. (May 1861), in "Civil War Letters to Wynnewood," ed. Walter T. Durham, *THQ* 34 (1975): 35; George L. Gordon to Mary Gordon, July 3, 1861, Gordon Papers, SHC UNC; George Blakemore to "Melissa," Nov. 15, 1861, Blakemore Papers, TSL.

23. William Fisher Plane to Helen Plane, June 1, 1861, in "Letters of William Fisher Plane, C.S.A. to his Wife," ed. S. Joseph Lewis, Jr., *GHQ* 48 (1964): 217.

24. Eugene Blackford to mother, March 26, 1861, Gordon-Blackford Papers, MD HS; Thomas B. Webber to mother, June 15, 1861, Webber Papers, MHI.

25. Charles Haydon, diary entry of May 6, 1861, in *For Country, Cause & Leader: The Civil War Journal of Charles B. Haydon,* ed. Stephen W. Sears (New York, 1993), 4; Simeon McCord to mother, May 25, 1861, McCord Letters, Earl Hess Collection, MHI; Tully McCrea to Belle McCrea, June 1, 1861, in *Dear Belle,* 97; William Wyckoff to Frances Ives, undated (June 1861), William Wyckoff Letters, in private possession. For the Victorian cultural context of the Civil War generation, see Anne C. Rose, *Victorian America and the Civil War* (Cambridge, 1992).

26. John Pellett to parents, Aug. 4, 16, 1861, Pellett Papers, MHI; Charles P. Bowditch to Jonathan I. Bowditch, Aug. 5, 1862, in "War Letters of Charles P. Bowditch," *Massachusetts Historical Society Proceedings* 57 (1923–24): 417–18; James King to Sarah (Jenny) Babcock, Oct. 18, 1861, copy provided by Leland Thornton.

27. John A. Gillis, Diary, entry of Nov. 11, 1861, MN HS; Benjamin F. Stevenson to sister, Dec. 26, 1861, in *Letters from the Army* (Cincinnati, 1884), 8; Plympton A. White to J. L. Beers, May 10, 1861, in "Notes and Documents," *WPMH* 37 (1954): 60.

28. Hugh L. Honnell to sister, Dec. 17, 1861, Aug. 16, 1862, Honnell Papers, WLEU. For a thorough analysis of the place of honor in Southern culture, see Bertram Wyatt-Brown, *Southern Honor* (New York, 1982).

29. Samuel D. Sanders to Mary Sanders, Nov. 27, 1861, March 22, 1862, in " 'If Fortune Should Fail': Civil War Letters of Dr. Samuel D. Sanders," ed. Walter Rundell, Jr., *SCMH* 65 (1964): 133–34, 135; James T. Armstrong to Ladie Armstrong, Aug. 5, 1861, Armstrong Papers, SHC UNC.

30. Walter G. Keeble to Fanny Keeble, Jan. 17, 1862, Keeble Papers, MHI; Nimrod W. E. Long to wife, July 2, 1862, Long Papers, WLEU.

31. Henry L. Abbott to father, May (no day) 1861 in *Fallen Leaves: The Civil War Letters of Major Henry Livermore Abbott*, ed. Robert Garth Scott (Kent, Ohio, 1991), 32 (20th Massachusetts, later killed in action); George Hopper to James Hopper, Aug. 5, 1861, Hopper Papers, MHI (10th New York); John T. McMahon, diary entry of Aug. 7, 1862, in *John T. McMahon's Diary of the 136th New York 1861–1865*, ed. John Michael Priest (Shippensburg, Pa., 1993), 23–24; Thomas Kilby Smith to Elizabeth Smith, Oct. 10, 1861, March 2, 1862, Smith Papers, HEH (54th Ohio).

32. Charles Francis Adams, Jr., to Charles Francis Adams, June 10, 1861, Charles Francis Adams, Jr., to Henry Adams, January (no day) 1862, in *A Cycle of Adams Letters*, 2 vols., ed. Worthington C. Ford (Boston, 1920), I: 10–11, 103; Rutherford B. Hayes, diary entry of May 5, 1861, in *Diary and Letters of Rutherford Birchard Hayes*, vol. II: *1861–1865*, ed. Charles Richard Williams (Columbus, Ohio, 1922), 17.

33. Hans Mattson to Cherstie Mattson, Oct. 3, 1861, Mattson Papers, MN HS.

34. Allen M. Geer, diary entry of June 9, 1861, in *The Civil War Diary of Allen Morgan Geer*, ed. Mary Ann Anderson (Denver, 1977), 3; Edwin E. Harris to Margaret Harris, Nov. 24, 1861, Harris Papers, GLC PML; Samuel Cormany, diary entry of Sept. 9, 1862, in *The Cormany Diaries: A Northern Family in the Civil War* (Pittsburgh, 1982), 229; William N. Adams to father, Jan. 8, 1862, McClelland Family Papers, SHC UNC.

35. Samuel J. Alexander to Agnes Alexander, Sept. 1, 1861, Alexander Papers, MHI; Richard Henry Watkins to Mary Watkins, Sept. 23, 1861, Watkins Papers, VHS; Philo Gallup to John S. Gallup, May 8, 1861, in "The Second Michigan Volunteer Infantry Joins the Army of the Potomac: Letters of Philo H. Gallup," ed. Chester M. Destler, *Michigan History* 41 (1957): 388.

36. John Babb, Jr., to John Babb, Aug. 16, 1862, Babb Papers, WLEU. For the various meanings of manhood in that era, see E. Anthony Rotundo, *American Manhood: Transformations in Masculinity from the Revolution to the Modern Era* (New York, 1993), and Mark C. Carnes and Clyde Griffen, eds., *Meanings for Manhood: Constructions of Masculinity in Victorian America* (Chicago, 1990).

37. James H. Langhorne to mother, June 26, 1861, Langhorne Papers, VHS; Bell Irvin Wiley, *The Life of Johnny Reb* (Indianapolis, 1943), 17; Wiley, *The Life of Billy Yank* (Indianapolis, 1952), 37. For discussions of this theme, see J. Glenn Gray, *The Warriors: Reflections on Men in Battle* (New York, 1959), 29–31; Frank M. Richardson, *Fighting Spirit: A Study of Psychological Factors in War* (London, 1978), 143; and Kellett, *Combat Motivation*, 295–97.

38. Joseph Griner to mother, June 6, 1861, in Daniel H. Woodward, "The Civil War of a Pennsylvania Trooper," *PMHB* 87 (1963): 41; Charles Woodward Hutson to mother, June 10, Aug. 26, 1861, Hutson Papers, SHC UNC; Ira Pettit to father, Sept. 10, 1862, in *The Diary of a Dead Man: Letters and Diary of Private Ira S. Pettit,* ed. Jean P. Ray (n.p., 1972), 65.

39. John H. Fain to mother, June 1, 1861, Feb. 5, 1863, Archibald E. Henderson Papers, PLDU; W. R. Redding to "Lizzie," Aug. 18, 1861, Redding Papers, SHC UNC; Peter Vredenburgh to mother, Sept. 19, 1862, Vredenburgh Papers, Monmouth County (N.J.) Historical Society, typescript copy supplied by Bernard Olsen.

40. James M. McCaffrey, *Army of Manifest Destiny: The American Soldier in the Mexican War, 1846–1848* (New York, 1992), 31.

41. William A. Clark to parents, Aug. 9, 1863, in " 'Please Send Stamps': The Civil War Letters of William Allen Clark," ed. Margaret Black Tatum, *IMH* 91 (1995): 297; Samuel Merrill to Emily Merrill, Jan. 22, 1863, in "Letters from a Civil War Officer," ed. A. T. Volwiler, *MVHR* 14 (1928): 510.

42. Frank Wells to Philip Wells, Sept. 8, 1861, in *Letters from a Union Soldier,* ed. Alfred Wells (n.p., 1993), 3.

43. Constant Hanks to mother, Dec. 14, 1861, Hanks Papers, PLDU; John T. Dale to Sarah Honnell, Aug. 6, 1862, Honnell Papers, WLEU; Jacob Heffelfinger, Diary, entry of April 27, 1862, MHI.

CHAPTER 3. ANXIOUS FOR THE FRAY

1. Hamilton Branch to mother, July 20, 1861, in "Three Brothers Face Their Baptism of Battle, July 1861," ed. Edward G. Longacre, *GHQ* 61 (1977): 163; William G. Morris to wife, Feb. 15, 1862, Morris Papers, SHC UNC; Leonidas Torrence to father, July 20, 1861, in "The Road to Gettysburg: The Diary and Letters of Leonidas Torrence of the Gaston Guards," ed. Haskell Monroe, *NCHR* 36 (1959): 480.

2. William Ames to father, June 28, 1861, in "Civil War Letters of William Ames, from Brown University to Bull Run," ed. William Greene Roelker, *Rhode Island Historical Society Collections* 33 (1940): 82; James Goff to father, Jan. 23, 1862, Goff Papers, HEH; Stephen Keyes Fletcher, diary entry of Oct. 16, 1861, in "The Civil War Journal of Stephen Keyes Fletcher," ed. Perry McCandless, *IMH* 54 (1958): 145–46.

3. Charles B. Haydon, diary entry of July 12, 1861, in *For Country, Cause & Leader: The Civil War Journal of Charles B. Haydon,* ed. Stephen W. Sears (Boston, 1993), 45; Jacob Heffelfinger to Jennie Heffelfinger, Sept. 18, 1861, in " 'Dear Sister Jennie' 'Dear Brother Jacob': Correspondence Between a Northern Soldier and His Sister," ed. Florence C. McLaughlin, *WPHM* 60 (1977): 121; Hugh L. Honnoll to parents, Nov. 24, 1861, Honnoll Papers, WLEU.

4. E. Watt Webber to mother, Aug. 11, 1861, Webber Papers, MHI; Joseph Stockton, diary entry of Nov. 10, 1862, in *War Diary (1862–5) of Brevet Brigadier General Joseph Stockton* (n.p., 1910), 4.

5. Thomas N. Stevens to Carrie Stevens, June 29, 1863, in *"Dear Carrie"* . . . *The Civil War Letters of Thomas N. Stevens,* ed. George M. Blackburn (Mt. Pleasant, Mich., 1984), 122; Henry L. Abbott to father, Sept. 11, 1861, in *Fallen Leaves: The Civil War Letters of Major Henry Livermore Abbott,* ed. Robert Garth Scott (Kent, Ohio, 1991), 45.

6. James Griffin to Leila Griffin, Aug. 11, 1861, in *"A Gentleman and an Officer": A Military and Social History of James B. Griffin's Civil War,* ed. Judith N. McArthur and O. Vernon Burton (New York, 1996), 118; Robert B. Cornwell to parents, Feb. 26, 1862, Cornwell Papers, MHI; Charles H. Cox to Frank Lord, Aug. 28, Sept. 25, 1863, in "The Civil War Letters of Charles Harding Cox," ed. Lorna Lutes Sylvester, *IMH* 68 (1972): 64–65, 70.

7. Frederick E. Lockley to Elizabeth Lockley, June 1, 1863, Lockley Papers, HEH; James Griffin to Leila Griffin, Jan. 5, 1862, in McArthur and Burton, eds., *"A Gentleman and an Officer,"* 132; John W. De Forest to wife, June 15, 1862, in *A Volunteer's Adventures: A Union Captain's Record of the Civil War,* ed. James Croushore (New Haven, 1946), 25.

8. Cyrus C. Carpenter to Kate Burkholder, March 12, 1863, Cyrus C. Carpenter to Emmett Carpenter, June 23, 1864, in "A Commissary in the Union Army: Letters of C. C. Carpenter," ed. Mildred Throne, *IJH* 53 (1955): 71, 74.

9. Roy R. Grinker and John P. Spiegel, *Men Under Stress* (Philadelphia, 1945), 44.

10. Joseph Diltz to Mary Diltz, Jan. 19, Sept. 21, 1862, Diltz Papers, PLDU; James Overcash to Joseph Overcash, Aug. 11, 1861, Joseph Overcash Papers, PLDU.

11. Samuel T. Foster, diary entries of Jan. 9, 11, 1863, in *One of Cleburne's Command: The Reminiscences and Diary of Capt. Samuel T. Foster, Granbury's Texas Brigade* (Austin, 1980), 15, 19, 20; James Binford to "Carrie and Annie," Aug. 13, 1862, Binford Papers, VHS.

12. William N. Adams to father, June 28, 1862, McClelland Family Papers, SHC UNC; Adam Bright to Emanuel Stotler, July 7, 1862, in *"Respects to All": Letters of Two Pennsylvania Boys in the War of the Rebellion* (Pitts-

burgh, 1962), 26; Charles Brewster to mother, June 2, 1861, in *When This Cruel War Is Over: The Civil War Letters of Charles Harvey Brewster,* ed. David W. Blight (Amherst, Mass., 1992), 146.

13. John McCreery to mother and father, Oct. 13, 1864, McCreery Letters, John Sickles Collection, MHI.

14. Nathaniel H. R. Dawson to Elodie Todd Dawson, Aug. 29, 1861, Dawson Papers, SHC UNC; A. Fred Fleet to mother, June 13, 1862, in *Green Mount: A Virginia Plantation Family During the Civil War* (Lexington, Ky., 1962), 137.

15. William H. Murray to sister, undated, early 1863, Murray Papers, MD HS; Frederick E. Lockley to wife, May 14, 1864, Feb. 27, 1865, Lockley Papers, HEH.

16. Josiah Chaney to wife, July 28, 1862, Chaney Papers, MN HS; Darius Starr to mother, Nov. 10, 1862, Starr Papers, PLDU; Samuel F. Tenney to Alice Toomer, April 18, 1863, in "War Letters of S. F. Tenney, A Soldier of the Third Georgia Regiment," *GHQ* 57 (1973): 293.

17. Quoted in Stephen E. Ambrose, *Band of Brothers: E Company, 506th Regiment, 101st Airborne from Normandy to Hitler's Eagle's Nest* (New York, 1992), 117.

18. John Babb, Jr., to mother, May 22, 1863, Babb Papers, WLEU; Edmund Packard to wife, undated, Packard Papers, East Bridgewater, Mass., Library, copy furnished by Betty Burchell; Henry W. McNatt to family, undated (summer 1862), McNatt Papers, copy supplied by John Morrow.

19. A. Fisk Gore to Kate Gore, April 12, May 19, 1862, Gore Papers, MO HS; William L. Saunders to "Miss Mary," Oct. 3, 1862, Saunders Papers, SHC UNC.

20. Chauncey Cooke to mother, Jan. 29, April 10, 1863, Cooke to father, July 2, 1863, in "A Badger Boy in Blue: The Letters of Chauncey H. Cooke," *WMH* 4 (1920): 214, 333–34, 446; Edwin E. Harris to Margaret Harris, May 2, 1863, Harris Papers, GLC PML; William Calder to Robert Calder, May 22, 1863, William Calder Papers, SHC UNC.

21. John O. Collins to wife, Sept. 6, 1861, Collins Papers, VHS; Thomas W. Osborn to Abraham Osborn, May 12, 1862, in *No Middle Ground: Thomas Ward Osborn's Letters from the Field (1862–1864)* (Hamilton, N.Y., 1993), 30.

22. Harvey Reid to sisters, Feb. 27, 1863, in *The View from Headquarters: Civil War Letters of Harvey Reid* (Madison, 1965), 35; Symmes Stillwell to mother, Feb. 13, 1862, Stillwell Papers, FLPU; Samuel J. Harrison to parents, May 23, 1862, Harrison Papers, OHS.

23. Hayes diary entry of Sept. 10, 1861, in *Diary and Letters of Rutherford Birchard Hayes,* ed. Charles Richard Williams, vol. II: *1861–1865* (Columbus, 1922), 88; James H. Chamberlayne to Sally Grattan, Aug. 19, 1862, in *Ham Chamberlayne Virginian: Letters and Papers of an Artillery Officer* (Rich-

mond, 1932), 95; George H. Cadman to Esther Cadman, Cadman Papers, SHC UNC.

24. Edward Wightman to brother, Oct. 1, 1862, in *From Antietam to Fort Fisher: The Civil War Letters of Edward King Wightman, 1862–1865* (Rutherford, N.J., 1983), 47.

25. Edmund Patterson, diary entry of May 6, 1862, in *Yankee Rebel: The Civil War Journal of Edmund DeWitt Patterson,* ed. John G. Barrett (Chapel Hill, 1966), 19; William Calder to mother, June 29, 1862, Calder Papers, SHC UNC; George Whitman to mother, Feb. 9, 1862, in "Civil War Letters of George Washington Whitman from North Carolina," ed. Jerome M. Loving, *NCHR* 50 (1973): 76.

26. Alfred Bell to wife, Jan. 11, 1863, Aug. 19, 1864, Bell Papers, PLDU; Richard L. Pugh to May Pugh, April 16, 1862, Pugh Papers, HML LSU.

27. Francis E. Pierce to Edward Chapin, Sept. 15, 1862, in "Civil War Letters of Francis Edwin Pierce of the 108th N.Y. Vol. Infantry," *RHSP* 22 (1944): 152; A. Fred Fleet to Benny Fleet, April 15, 1862, in *Green Mount,* 121.

28. Elisha Hunt Rhodes, diary entry of June 5, 1863, in *All for the Union,* ed. Robert Hunt Rhodes (New York, 1991), 112; Drayton Haynes, diary entry of May 31, 1862, *The Field Diary of a Confederate Soldier,* ed. William G. Haynes, Jr. (Darien, Ga., 1963), 3; Charles E. Wilcox, diary entry of May 22, 1863, in "With Grant at Vicksburg: From the Civil War Diary of Charles E. Wilcox," ed. Edgar L. Erickson, *Journal of the Illinois Historical Society* 30 (1938): 479–80.

29. Benjamin Aschenfelter to mother, Dec. 31, 1862, Aschenfelter Papers, MHI; George W. Tillotson to Elizabeth Tillotson, May 4, 1863, Tillotson Papers, GLC PML; Horatio Newhall to mother, Dec. 22, 1862, Newhall Papers, MHI.

30. William Pitt Chambers, diary entry of Aug. 4, 1864, in "My Journal: The Story of a Soldier's Life Told by Himself," *Publications of the Mississippi Historical Society,* Centenary Series V (1925): 332; William Ames to father, July 27, 1861, in "Civil War Letters of William Ames," 13; Robert McAllister to Ellen McAllister, Feb. 8, 1865, in *The Civil War Letters of Gen. Robert McAllister,* ed. James I. Robertson, Jr. (New Brunswick, N.J., 1965). These singing soldiers were from New Jersey.

31. Squire Tuttle to family, undated (early June 1862), Tuttle Papers, MHI; James Wiswell to sister, Aug. 31, 1861, Wiswell Papers, PLDU.

32. Francis E. Pierce to Edward Chapin, Sept. 25, 1862, in "Civil War Letters of Pierce," 154; William A. Walker to James Walker, Feb. 9, April 2, 1862, Walker Papers, FLPU.

33. Paul A. Oliver to Dudley Oliver, July 21, 1862, Oliver Papers, FLPU; Darius Starr to mother, Aug. 25, 1863, Starr Papers, PLDU.

34. John H. Burrill to parents, July 11, 1862, July 13, 1863, Burrill Pa-

pers, MHI; Charles Wainright Diary, entries of May 5, 1862, July 2, 1863, HEH.

35. The most succinct discussion of this physiological process is Elmar Dinter, *Hero or Coward: Pressures Facing the Soldier in Battle,* trans. from German by Tricia Hughes (London, 1985), 13–15, 37–38. See also Willard Gaylin, *The Rage Within: Anger in Modern Life* (New York, 1984), esp. 17–19.

36. Edward Wightman to brother, June 16, 1864, in *From Antietam to Fort Fisher,* 193; Harvey M. Medford, diary entry of April 8, 1864, in "The Diary of H. C. Medford, Confederate Soldier, 1864," eds. Rebecca W. Smith and Marion Mullins, *SHQ* 34 (1930): 218; John W. Ames to mother, May 7, 1863, Ames Papers, MHI.

37. Thomas T. Taylor to Antoinette Taylor, July 26, 1864, Taylor Papers, OHS; John V. Hadley to Mary J. Hill, June 20, 1862, in "An Indiana Soldier in Love and War: The Civil War Letters of John V. Hadley," ed. James I. Robertson, Jr., *IMH* 59 (1963): 214; Charles H. Brewster to mother, July 5, 1862, in *When This Cruel War Is Over,* 345.

38. James J. Archer to mother, Jan. 12, 1863, in "The James J. Archer Letters: A Marylander in the Civil War," ed. C. A. Porter Hopkins, *Maryland Historical Magazine* 56 (1961): 140–41; Eben T. Hale to mother, May 5, 1863, Hale Papers, SHC UNC.

39. Oliver W. Norton to family, July 4, 1862, Norton to "Cousin L.," July 5, 1862, Norton to brother and sister, July 26, 1862, in Oliver Willcox Norton, *Army Letters 1861–1865* (Chicago, 1903), 91, 93, 107–9.

40. Joseph Allan Frank and George A. Reaves, in *"Seeing the Elephant": Raw Recruits at the Battle of Shiloh* (Westport, Conn., 1989), 118; Bradford Perkins, "Impressions of Wartime," *Journal of American History* 77 (1990): 566.

41. Nelson Chapin to wife, April 23, 1862, Chapin Papers, MHI; James P. Douglas to Sallie White Douglas, July 23, 1864, in *Douglas's Texas Battery, CSA,* ed. Lucia Rutherford Douglas (Waco, 1966), 116; John Q. A. Campbell, Diary, entry of Sept. 20, 1862, WRHS.

42. Joseph H. Saunders to mother, June 13, 1862, Saunders Papers, SHC UNC; Charles M. Coit to family, May 17, 19, 1864, Coit Papers, GLC PML; Harry St. John Dixon, Diary, entry of May 29, 1864, Dixon Papers, SHC UNC.

43. Jacob Heffelfinger to Jennie Heffelfinger, Aug. 11, 1862, in *"Dear Sister Jennie,"* 208–9.

44. James Connolly to Mary Connolly, Oct. 14, 1862, in *Three Years in the Army of the Cumberland: The Letters and Diary of Major James A. Connolly,* ed. Paul Angle (Bloomington, Ind., 1962), 25; John W. Ames to parents, July 5, 1862, Ames Papers, MHI; Francis E. Pierce to Edward Chapin, July 27, 1863, in "Civil War Letters of Pierce," 171–72.

45. James Williams to Lizzie Williams, April 20, 1862, in *From That Terrible Field: Civil War Letters of James M. Williams,* ed. John Kent Folmar (University, Ala., 1981), 60; Phillips Bond to James Bond, April 23, 1862, in "Record of the Alabama State Artillery from Its Organization in May 1836 to the Surrender in April 1865," *AHQ* 20 (1958): 319.

46. John McGrath to Lavinia McGrath, Jan. 13, 1863, McGrath Papers, HML LSU; Charles Brewster to mother, June 2, 1862, in *When This Cruel War Is Over,* 145.

47. William H. Phillips to mother, Aug. 13, 1861, Phillips Papers, PLDU; William Fisher Plane to Helen Plane, July 8, June 5, 1862, in "Letters of William Fisher Plane, C.S.A. to His Wife," ed. S. Joseph Lewis, Jr., *GHQ* 48 (1964): 223, 222.

48. Uriah Parmelee to mother, July 15, 1864, Parmelee Papers, PLDU; George Hopper to James Hopper, Dec. 21, 1862, Hopper Papers, MHI.

49. Paddy Griffith, *Battle Tactics of the Civil War* (New Haven, 1989), 50. See also Richard Holmes, *Acts of War: The Behavior of Men in Battle* (New York, 1985), 214–18.

50. *John Dooley Confederate Soldier: His War Journal,* ed. Joseph T. Durkin (Georgetown, DC, 1945), 99, undated journal entry, probably written in prison at Johnson's Island after his capture at Gettysburg.

CHAPTER 4. IF I FLINCHED I WAS RUINED

1. Richard F. Ebbins to sister, Dec. 25, 1862, Ebbins Papers, MHI.

2. Nelson Chapin to wife, April 23, 1862, Chapin Papers, MHI; David Nichol to father, Sept. 10, 1863, Nichol Papers, MHI; Leonidas L. Polk to Sallie Polk, Nov. 4, 1863, Polk Papers, SHC UNC.

3. Oscar Ladley to mother and sisters, May 22, 1861, in *Heart and Knapsack: The Ladley Letters, 1857–1880,* ed. Carl M. Becker and Ritchie Thomas (Athens, Ohio, 1988), 5; Joseph D. Shields to father, Jan. 5, 1862, Shields Papers, HML LSU.

4. Alfred Holcomb to family, Jan. 28, 1864, Holcomb to Sister Emma, Feb. 14, 1864, Holcomb Papers, MHI, copies supplied by Henry C. Lind; John H. Hartman to Partha Hartman, Feb. 6, 1864, Hartman Papers, PLDU.

5. Shaw to Francis G. Shaw, Aug. 29, 1862, in *Blue-Eyed Child of Fortune: The Civil War Letters of Robert Gould Shaw,* ed. Russell Duncan (Athens, Ga., 1992), 238; Champion to wife, June 9, 1864, Champion Papers, PLDU. Shaw later became colonel of the 54th Massachusetts, a black regiment, and was killed in the assault on Fort Wagner in July 1863.

6. Letter of John J. Sherman, undated, in George E. and William F. Murphy, "The Eighth New York Heavy Artillery," *Niagara Frontier* 10 (1963): 82.

7. Robert Carter to father, July (no day) 1861, in *Four Brothers in Blue:*

Or, Sunshine and Shadows of the War of the Rebellion (Austin, Tex., 1978), 9; Bryan Grimes to wife, Sept. 20, 1864, Grimes Papers, SHC UNC.

8. A. F. Davis to F. D. Davis, April 21, 1862, Davis Letters, SHS MO.

9. John Timmerman to Mary Timmerman, Dec. 22, 1862, Timmerman Papers, MHI; Richard H. Watkins to Mary Watkins, June 1, 1862, Watkins Papers, VHS; John H. Burrill to parents, Aug. 8, 1862, Burrill Papers, MHI.

10. William Calder to mother, May 10, 1863, Calder Papers, SHC UNC. See also Harry Lewis to mother, May 15, 1863, Lewis Papers, SHC UNC. Lewis's brother was in a company of the 16th Mississippi that performed the same function for its brigade at Chancellorsville.

11. William Henry Cooley to father, Jan. 6, 1863, Cooley Papers, SHC UNC.

12. Henry Richard Swan to Abbie Swan, June 7, 1864, Swan Papers, MHI. For information on the multiple functions of the provost guards, see Kenneth Radley, *Rebel Watchdog: The Confederate States Army Provost Guard* (Baton Rouge, 1989) and *Inside Lincoln's Army: The Diary of Marsena Rudolph Patrick, Provost Marshal General, Army of the Potomac*, ed. Davis S. Sparks (New York, 1964).

13. Isaiah Robison to sister, May 16, 1863, in *Dear Pa—And So It Goes*, ed. Gertrude K. Johnston (Harrisburg, 1971), 249; Michael Dresbach to Louisa Dresbach, March 28, 1865, Dresbach Papers, MN HS; Isaac L. Taylor, diary entries of Feb. 13, 1863, Nov. 13, 1862, in "Campaigning with the First Minnesota: A Civil War Diary," ed. Hazel C. Wolf, *Minnesota History* 25 (1944): 247, 233.

14. John Dooley, diary entry of March 9, 1863, in *John Dooley Confederate Soldier: His War Journal*, ed. Joseph T. Durkin (Georgetown, D.C., 1945), 83; Irby Goodwin Scott to mother, April 14, 1863, Scott Papers, PLDU.

15. Alonzo Kingsbury to parents, April 18, 1862, in *The Hero of Medfield: Journals and Letters of Allen Alonzo Kingsbury* (Boston, 1862), 71–72.

16. Theodore Mandeville to Carlie, Sept. 2, 1861, Mandeville Papers, HML LSU.

17. Eugene Blackford to mother, Sept. 5, 1861, Gordon-Blackford Papers, MD HS; Thomas T. Taylor to Antoinette Taylor, Jan. 22, 1862, Taylor Papers, OHS; Lyndorf Ozburn to Diza Ozburn, April 6, 1862, in "Letters from Two Wars," ed. Barbara Burr, *Journal of the Illinois Historical Society* 30 (1937): 153.

18. Olney Andrus to Mary Andrus, April 26, 1863, in *The Civil War Letters of Sergeant Olney Andrus*, ed. Fred A. Shannon (Urbana, Ill., 1947), 53.

19. John Keegan, *The Face of Battle* (New York, 1976), 113–14, 181–82; Elmar Dinter, *Hero or Coward: Pressures Facing the Soldier in Battle*, trans. from German by Tricia Hughes (London, 1985), 18–19.

20. William Henry Wyckoff to Richard R. Perry, July 19, 1862, Wyckoff Papers, in private possession; Chauncey Cooke to father, Aug. 4, 1864, in "A Badger Boy in Blue: The Letters of Chauncey H. Cooke," *WMH* 5 (1921): 95; Richard W. Corbin to father, June 10, 1864, in *Letters of a Confederate Officer to His Family in Europe* (Paris, n.d.), 28–29. The principal ingredient in Civil War-era gunpowder was saltpeter. Readers who recall stories from their youth of cooks in the school cafeteria or at summer camp who were alleged to put saltpeter in the food, and the rumored reason for doing so, will be particularly amused at these reports of soldiers hyped up by whisky and gunpowder.

21. James Drish to wife, undated (Aug. 1864), Drish Papers, ISHL.

22. Samuel A. Stouffer et al., *The American Soldier,* 2 vols. (Princeton, 1949), vol. II: *Combat and Its Aftermath,* 118–34; Anthony Kellett, *Combat Motivation: The Behavior of Soldiers in Battle* (Boston, 1982), 153–63; Edward Shils, "Primary Groups in the American Army," in Shils, *Center and Periphery: Essays in Sociology* (Chicago, 1950), 393–97; Roy R. Grinker and John P. Spiegel, *Men Under Stress* (Philadelphia, 1945), 46–48; Francis C. Steckel, "Morale and Men: The Motivation and Service of the American Soldier in World War II" (Ph.D. dissertation, University of Alabama, 1992), 83–98.

23. Thomas Kilby Smith to mother, Jan. 11, 1862, Smith Papers, HEH; William A. Walker to James Walker, Dec. 23, 1861, Walker Papers, FLPU.

24. John Q. Winfield to Sallie Winfield, May 19, 1861, Winfield Papers, SHC UNC; William L. Broaddus to Reuben Broaddus, July 7, 1863, Broaddus Papers, PLDU.

25. Alexander Caldwell to brother, Oct. 3, 1864, Caldwell Papers, MHI; Cadwalader J. Iredell to wife, Dec. 17, 1864, Iredell Papers, SHC UNC.

26. Uriah Parmelee to mother, March 4, 1862, Parmelee Papers, PLDU; Governeer Legg to Crisey Legg, May 16, 1863, in *This Regiment of Heroes: A Compilation of Primary Materials Pertaining to the 124th New York State Volunteers,* ed. Charles J. LaRocca (Montgomery, N.Y., 1991), 144; William Patton to father, Sept. 19, 1864, Patton Family Papers, SHC UNC.

27. William H. H. Clayton to brother, Nov. 13, 1862, Clayton Papers, Smiley Library, Redlands, Calif.; William H. Wyckoff to Nathan S. Wyckoff, Oct. 10, 1862, Wyckoff Papers, in private possession; Edwin Brookfield to mother, Dec. 7, 1863, Brookfield Papers, SHS MO.

28. Uriah Parmelee to mother, March 23, 1864, Parmelee Papers, PLDU; Oscar Ladley to mother and sisters, May 22, 1861, in *Hearth and Knapsack,* 5.

29. Solon A. Carter to Emily Carter, Jan. 11, 1863, Carter Papers, MHI; Jenkin Lloyd Jones, diary entry of Nov. 18, 1864, in *An Artillery Man's Diary,* ed. Carl Russell Fish (Madison, Wis., 1914), 273.

30. George Knox Miller to wife, April 10, 1864, Miller Papers, SHC

UNC; Andrew J. White to wife, Jan. 17, 1863, White Papers, PLDU; William G. Gridley to Elizabeth Gridley, Jan. 21, 1862, Gridley Papers, VHS.

31. Cyrus F. Boyd, diary entry of April 24, 1862, in "The Civil War Diary of C. F. Boyd, Fifteenth Iowa Infantry," ed. Mildred Throne, *IJH* 50 (1952), 159; Robert T. McMahan Diary, entry of Sept. 10, 1862, SHS MO; George N. Bliss to David Gerald, Mar. 18, 22, April 1, 1862, "Chaos Still Reigns in This Camp—Letters of Lieutenant George N. Bliss, 1st New England Cavalry, March–Sept. 1862," *Rhode Island History* 36 (1977), 18, 19, 22.

32. Henry P. Andrews to Susan Andrews, May 27, 1862, Andrews Papers, ISHL; Joseph R. Ward, Jr., diary entry of Sept. 25, 1863, in *An Enlisted Soldier's View of the Civil War: The Wartime Papers of Joseph Richardson Ward*, ed. D. Duane Cummins and Daryl Hohweiler (West Lafayette, Ind., 1981), 58.

33. William H. Martin to Elizabeth Martin, June 7, 1863, Martin Papers, MHI; Edward Pippey to Benjamin Pippey, May 19, 1863, William T. Pippey Papers, PLDU.

34. Paul Fussell, *Wartime: Understanding and Behavior in the Second World War* (New York, 1989), 79–95; William H. Lloyd to wife, Dec. 18, 1864, Lloyd Papers, WRHS, courtesy of Mark Grimsley; John F. Leonard to mother, June 16, 1863, Leonard Papers, SHC UNC; James D. Dargan, diary entries of Nov. 8, 1862, March 17, 1863, typescript copy of diary at California State University, Northridge.

35. Bergun Brown to mother, June 8, 1862, Brown Papers, SHS MO; Jenkin Lloyd Jones, diary entry of Jan. 25, 1864, in *An Artillery Man's Diary*, 168.

36. Some examples: William C. H. Reeder to mother and father, Nov. 21, 1861, Reeder Papers, MHI; John H. Burrill to parents, March 23, 1862, Burrill Papers, MHI; James Glazier to Annie Monroe, March 1, 1863, Glazier Papers, HEH.

37. William H. Walling to "cousins and sisters," Jan. 30, 1862, Walling Papers, in private possession.

38. John Ellis, *The Sharp End: The Fighting Man in World War II* (New York, 1980), 227; Darius Starr to mother, March 23, 1862, Starr Papers, PLDU; John M. Campbell to family, April 27, 1863, Campbell Letters, in private possession.

39. Robert Carter to father, July (no day) 1861, in *Four Brothers in Blue*, 9; Thomas T. Taylor to wife, July 13, 1862, Taylor Papers, OHS.

40. Tristim L. Skinner to Eliza Skinner, Oct. 13, 1861, Skinner Papers, SHC UNC; William Nugent to Eleanor Nugent, Sept. 19, 1862, in *My Dear Nellie: The Civil War Letters of William L. Nugent*, ed. William M. Cash and Lucy Somerville Howarth (Jackson, Miss., 1977), 97; William G. Hinson, diary entries of Aug. 18 and 20, 1864, in "The Diary of William G. Hinson During the War of Secession," ed. Joseph I. Waring, *SCMH* 75 (1974): 22.

41. John A. Gillis, Diary, entry of Aug. 30, 1863, MN HS; James Glazier to parents, Feb. 16, 1862, Glazier Papers, HEH.

42. William Henry Cocke to parents, July 14, 1862, Cocke Papers, VHS; Jasper N. Searles to family, July 25, 1861, Searles Papers, MN HS; Josiah Cheney to Melissa Cheney, June 14, 1862, Cheney Papers, MN HS.

43. Charles E. Perkins to Whiting Haskell, Aug. 3, 1862, Perkins Papers, MHI; Lyman K. Needham to "My friends at home," Nov. 9, 1862, ISHL; John H. Crowley to Mr. Cartwright, June 11, 1864, Cartwright Papers, MHI.

44. Felix Brannigan to sister, undated fragment, July or Aug. 1863, Brannigan Papers, LC.

45. John W. Hagan to Amanda Hagan, June 21, 1864, in "The Confederate Letters of John W. Hagan," ed. Bell Irvin Wiley, *GHQ* 38 (1954): 277.

CHAPTER 5. RELIGION IS WHAT MAKES BRAVE SOLDIERS

1. William D. Kendall to mother, Nov. 29, 1862, Kendall Papers, HEH; Angus McDermid to parents, May 21, 1864, in "Letters from a Confederate Soldier," ed. Benjamin Roundtree, *Georgia Review* 18 (1964): 286.

2. Franklin Howard to brother and sister, Feb. 7, 1863, Howard Papers, WHS.

3. Attributed to Father William Thomas Cummings, who used this phrase in a field sermon on Bataan in 1942. See Francis C. Steckel, "Morale and Men: The Motivation and Service of the American Soldier in World War II" (Ph.D. dissertation, University of Alabama, 1992), 339.

4. Frank M. Richardson, *Fighting Spirit: A Study of Psychological Factors in War* (London, 1978), 44.

5. Samuel A. Stouffer et al., *The American Soldier,* 2 vols. (Princeton, 1949), vol. II: *Combat and Its Aftermath,* 172–75; Allen Jordan to parents, June 5, 1862, in "The Thomas G. Jordan Family During the War Between the States," *GHQ* 59 (1975): 135; Amos Steere to Lucy Steere, May 2, 1862, Steere Papers, Lewis Leigh Coll., MHI.

6. A. Fisk Gore to Katie Gore, May 9, 1862, Gore Papers, MO HS; Robert Bowlin to father, March 15, 1863, Bowlin Papers, in private possession; William F. Benjamin to sister, June 10, 1864, Benjamin Papers, MHI.

7. Joseph D. Thompson to Mary Thompson, April 10, 1862, in "The Battle of Shiloh: From the Letters and Diary of Joseph Dimmit Thompson," ed. John G. Biel, *THQ* 18 (1958): 271; Frederick Pettit to sister, June 1, 1864, Feb. 28, 1863, Pettit Papers, MHI.

8. Edward Acton to Mary Acton, April 9, 1862, in " 'Dear Mollie': Letters of Captain Edward A. Acton to His Wife, 1862," *PMHB* 89 (1965): 8. Five months after writing this letter Acton was killed at the second battle of Bull Run.

9. John Bratton to wife, Dec. 10, 1862, Bratton Papers, SHC UNC; John A. Everett to mother, May 5, 1864, Dec. 18, 1861, Everett Papers, WLEU.

10. William F. Margraff to brother and sister, Jan. 1, 1862, in *A Civil War Soldier's Last Letters,* ed. Paul Janeski (New York, 1975), 32–33; Edward Dorr Tracy to wife, June 4, 1861, Tracy Papers, SHC UNC.

11. Sarah Rosetta Wakeman to parents, April 13, 1863, in *An Uncommon Soldier: The Civil War Letters of Sarah Rosetta Wakeman, alias Private Lyons Wakeman,* ed. Lauren Cook Burgess (Pasadena, Md., 1994), 28.

12. Charles I. Graves to Maggie Lea, April 16, 1862, Graves Papers, SHC UNC; Joshua L. Chamberlain to Frances Chamberlain, Oct. 25, Nov. 3, 1862, quoted in William M. Wallace, *Soul of the Lion: A Biography of General Joshua Lawrence Chamberlain* (New York, 1960), 46, 49.

13. William L. Nugent to Eleanor Nugent, Aug. 19, 1861, March 19, 1862, in *My Dear Nellie: The Civil War Letters of William L. Nugent,* ed. William M. Cash and Lucy Somerville Howarth (Jackson, Miss., 1977), 46, 53; Thomas T. Taylor to Antoinette Taylor, April 28, 1862, Taylor Papers, OHS.

14. Thomas W. Stephens, Diary, entry of Nov. 29, 1863, SHS MO; Felix Brannigan to sister, July 26, 1862, Brannigan Papers, LC.

15. Ted Barclay to sister, Dec. 5, 1863, in *Ted Barclay, Liberty Hall Volunteers: Letters from the Stonewall Brigade,* ed. Charles W. Turner (Rockbridge, Va., 1992), 116; Peter Welsh to Margaret Welsh, March 31, 1863, in *Irish Green and Union Blue: The Civil War Letters of Peter Welsh,* ed. Laurence Frederick Kohl and Margaret Cosse Richard (New York, 1986), 82–83.

16. William Cartter to mother, Nov. 30, 1861, Cartter Family Papers, LC; Eldred Simkins to Eliza Trescott, Oct. 17, 1863, Simkins Papers, HEH; James Love to Molly Wilson, March 13, Oct. 17, 1862, Love Papers, MO HS.

17. James Rush Holmes to Jane Holmes, Jan. 25, 1863, in "The Civil War Letters of James Rush Holmes," ed. Ida Bright Adams, *WPMH* 44 (1961): 118; Charles Coit to family, March 16, Nov. 10, Dec. 14, 1862, Coit Papers, GLC PML.

18. Thomas Kilby Smith to Elizabeth Smith, April 13, 15, 1862, Smith Papers, HEH; Dennis J. McCarthy to cousin, Sept. 18, 1862, McCarthy Papers, HEH.

19. Robert Lemmon to mother, June 4, 1861, Lemmon Papers, MD HS; James Glazier to Annie G. Monroe, Oct. 14, 1862, Glazier Papers, HEH; George Lowe to Elizabeth Lowe, May 1, 1862, Lowe Papers, HEH.

20. William H. Martin to Elizabeth Martin, April 1, 1864, Martin Papers, MHI; Mathew Andrew Dunn to wife, July 6, 1864, in "Mathew Andrew Dunn Letters," ed. Weymouth T. Jordan, *Journal of Mississippi History* 1 (1939): 119.

21. Eldred Simkins to Eliza Trescott, Aug. 9, 1863, Simkins Papers,

HEH; William Johnson to sister and aunt, Jan. 14, 1863, Harriet Johnson Papers, PLDU.

22. Stephen A. Forbes to sister, Jan. 15, 1864, Forbes to Francis Snow, June 11, 1864, Forbes Letters, ISHL; Charles I. Graves to Maggie Lea, May 9, 1862, Graves Papers, SHC UNC.

23. Josiah Perry to Phebe Perry, Oct. 9, 1862, April 17, 1863, Perry Papers, ISHL; Daniel Faust to brother, May 7, 1863, Faust Papers, MHI; William H. Berryhill to Mary Berryhill, Aug. 5, 1864, in *The Gentle Rebel: The Civil War Letters of William Harvey Berryhill* (Yazoo City, Miss., 1982), 68.

24. Charles E. Smith, Diary, entries of Dec. 7, June 28, 1863, in private possession.

25. *The Civil War Letters of George Washington Beidelman*, ed. Catherine H. Vanderslice (New York, 1978), 202–3.

26. Ted Barclay to sister, May 2, 1864, in *Liberty Hall Volunteers*, 144; Peter M. Wright to Sarah Wright, April 16, 1862, Wright Letters, PLDU; Jonas Bradshaw to Nancy Bradshaw, June 1, 1862, Bradshaw Papers, PLDU.

27. Benjamin Guffey to Caroline Guffey, April 21, 1862, Guffey Papers, SHS MO; Richard Henry Watkins to Mary Watkins, Feb. 23, 1862, Watkins Papers, VHS; Allen T. Suddarth to parents, July 19, 1861, Civil War Collection, TSL.

28. Thaddeus J. Hyatt to Mary Hyatt, Aug. 4, 31, 1864, in "Letters Written During the Years 1863–1864 to His Wife, Mary," ed. Hudson Hyatt, *Ohio Archaeological and Historical Quarterly* 53 (1944): 174, 181.

29. James Bell to Augusta Hallock, Dec. 28, 1862; statement dated Oct. 5, 1863, in Bell Collection, HEH.

30. William Martin to "Friend," undated, 1861, Civil War Collection, MO HS; William M. Martin to Elizabeth Martin, Nov. 6, 1862, Martin Papers, MHI; George W. Lennard to Clara Lennard, Dec. 31, 1863, in "Give Yourself No Trouble About Me': The Shiloh Letters of George W. Lennard," ed. Paul Hubbard and Christine Lews, *IMH* 76 (1980): 26.

31. Eric J. Leed, *No Man's Land: Combat and Identity in World War I* (Cambridge, 1979), 108–9; Anthony Kellett, *Combat Motivation: The Behavior of Soldiers in Battle* (Boston, 1982), 294–95.

32. Samuel L. A. Marshall, *Men Against Fire* (New York, 1947), 71–78; Frederick Smoler, "The Secret of the Soldiers Who Didn't Shoot," *American Heritage* 40 (March 1989): 36–45; John Marshall, *Reconciliation Road: A Family Odyssey of War and Honor* (Syracuse, 1993).

33. DeWitt C. Smith to "Dear Ones at Home," July 30, 1861, Smith Papers, in private possession; Martin Lennon to sister, April 9, 1862, in "Letters and Extracts from the Diary of Captain Martin Lennon," *5th Annual Report of the Chief of the Bureau of Military Statistics* (Albany, 1868), 715; James E. Love to Molly Wilson, Jan. 8, 1863, Love Papers, MO HS.

34. Winston Stephens to Octavia Stephens, March 16, 1863, in " 'Rogues

and Black Hearted Scamps': Civil War Letters of Winston and Octavia Stephens, 1861–1863," ed. Ellen E. Hodges and Stephen Kerber, *Florida Historical Quarterly* 57 (1978): 82; James West Smith, diary entry of May 29, 1863, in "A Confederate Soldier's Diary: Vicksburg in 1863," *Southwest Review* 28 (1943): 296, 299–300; Stoughton H. Dent to wife, Feb. 6, 1863, Sept. 10, 1864, in Ray Mathis, ed., *In the Land of the Living: Wartime Letters by Confederates from the Chattahoochee Valley of Alabama and Georgia* (Troy, Ala., 1981), 62, 110–11.

35. Jacob Heffelfinger to Jennie Heffelfinger, Feb. 27, 1862, in " 'Dear Sister Jennie' 'Dear Brother Jacob': Correspondence Between a Northern Soldier and His Sister," ed. Florence C. McLaughlin, *WPHM* 60 (1977): 127; William H. Walling to sisters, May 29, 1862, Walling Papers, in private possession; James Stephens, Diary, entry of May 6, 1864, SHS MO.

36. James Beard to brother and sister, March 6, 1864, Beard Papers, MHI; W. R. Redding to wife, undated, early 1862, Redding Papers, SHC UNC.

37. Edgar Embley to brother and sister, April 28, 1862, Embley Letters, MHI; Nixon's diary entry of April 6, 1862, in "An Alabamian at Shiloh: The Diary of Liberty Independence Nixon," ed. Hugh C. Bailey, *Alabama Review* 11 (1958): 152.

38. Alpheus S. Williams to "My Dear Daughters," July 15, 1864, in *From the Cannon's Mouth: The Civil War Letters of Alpheus S. Williams,* ed. Milo M. Quaife (Detroit, 1959), 330; Samuel Beardsley to Frederick Beardsley, Sept. 12, 1861, Beardsley Papers, MHI.

39. Eldred Simkins to Eliza Trescott, Aug. 19, 1863, Simkins Papers, HEH; Darius Starr to father, Oct. 15, 1862, Starr Papers, PLDU.

40. Theodore Upson, diary entry of March 21, 1865, in *With Sherman to the Sea: The Civil War Diaries & Reminiscences of Theodore F. Upson* (Baton Rouge, 1943), 159–60.

41. For discussions of this phenomenon, see especially Bell Irvin Wiley, *The Life of Johnny Reb* (Indianapolis, 1943), 180–84; Drew Gilpin Faust, "Christian Soldiers: The Meaning of Revivalism in the Confederate Army," *Journal of Southern History* 53 (1987): 63–90; Larry J. Daniel, *Soldiering in the Army of Tennessee* (Chapel Hill, 1991), 115–25. There had been revivals in Confederate armies before this time, but those of 1863–64 dwarfed what had happened earlier.

42. Elias Davis to Georgia Davis, Oct. 30, 1863, March 9, 1864, Davis Papers, SHC UNC; John McGrath to Lavinia McGrath, June 12, 1864, McGrath Papers, HML LSU; Mathew A. Dunn to wife, Aug. 22, 1864, in "Mathew Andrew Dunn Letters," 125.

43. Chancey Welton to parents, May 30, 1864, Welton Papers, SHC UNC; Stephen P. Chase, Diary, entry of March 31, 1865, MHI.

44. Stouffer et al., *The American Soldier,* II: 175.

CHAPTER 6. A BAND OF BROTHERS

1. Samuel L. A. Marshall, *Men Against Fire* (New York, 1947), 150.

2. Joseph Kirkland, *The Captain of Company K* (Chicago, 1891), 42; Solon A. Carter to Emily Carter (wife), Dec. 4, 1862, Carter Papers, MHI; Harry Lewis to mother, July 20, 1862, Lewis Papers, SHC UNC.

3. George H. Cadman to Esther Cadman, Oct. 2, 1862, Cadman Papers, SHC UNC.

4. Edward Spencer to Jennie Spencer, Jan. 15, 1863, Saxton Family Collection, HEH; Duncan Thompson to mother, undated, early 1863, Thompson Papers, MHI; Elijah Petty to wife, May 1, 1863, *Journey to Pleasant Hill: The Civil War Letters of Captain Elijah P. Petty* (San Antonio, 1982), 207.

5. Charles Coit to family, Dec. 29, 1861, March 15, 1862, Coit Papers, GLC PML; Jacob Heffelfinger, Diary, entry of June 27, 1862, MHI; Peter Wilson to brother, Feb. 19, 1862, "Peter Wilson in the Civil War," *IJH* 40 (1942): 269.

6. Jesse W. Reid to wife, Aug. 27, 1861, in Jesse W. Reid, *History of the Fourth Regiment of S.C. Volunteers* (Greenville, S.C., 1891), 40; Oscar L. Jackson, diary entry of April 28, 1862, in *The Colonel's Diary*, ed. David P. Jackson (Sharon, Pa., 1922), 56.

7. John W. Barnes to uncle, Dec. 19, 1862, Barnes Papers, PLDU; Joseph D. Thompson to Mary Thompson, April 10, 1862, in "The Battle of Shiloh: From the Letters and Diary of Joseph Dimmit Thompson," ed. John G. Biel, *THQ* 18 (1958): 271.

8. Royal Potter, Diary, entry of Dec. 14, 1862, Potter Papers, in private possession; John M. Campbell to family, Oct. 22, 1863, Campbell Papers, in private possession; Joseph M. Ellison to Camilla Ellison, July 4, 1862, in "Joseph M. Ellison: War Letters," ed. Calvin J. Billman, *GHQ* 48 (1964): 233.

9. Samuel J. Alexander to mother, May 3, 1862, Alexander Papers, MHI; William H. Wykoff to Richard Parry, Jan. 26, 1862, Wykoff Letters, in private possession; Shaw to mother, Aug. 12, 1862, in *Blue-Eyed Child of Fortune: The Civil War Letters of Robert Gould Shaw*, ed. Russell Duncan (Athens, Ga., 1992), 231.

10. Franklin Howard to brother and sister, Jan. 8, 1863, Howard Papers, WHS; William Reeder to parents, Dec. 3, 1863, Reeder Papers, MHI; Ruffin Thomson to father, June 30, 1861, Thomson Papers, SHC UNC.

11. John Lewis to wife, May 14, 1863, Lewis Leigh Collection, MHI; Thomas T. Taylor to Antoinette Taylor, Feb. 9, Aug. 7, 1862, Taylor Papers, OHS.

12. Harvey J. Hightower to Martha Hightower, April 7, 1863, in "Letters from H. J. Hightower, a Confederate Soldier, 1861–1864," ed. Dewey W. Grantham, *GHQ* 40 (1956): 183; Richard M. Saffell to Samuel Saffell, Feb.

18, 1862, Saffell Papers, in private possession; Henry Clay Pardee to father, March 28, 1862, Pardee Papers, PLDU.

13. Edward M. Burrus to father, Jan. 28, 1864, Burrus Papers, HML LSU; Edward Pippey to Benjamin Pippey, Dec. 2, 1862, Pippey Papers, PLDU.

14. Richard Holmes, *Acts of War: The Behavior of Men in Battle* (New York, 1985), 141; Gerald Linderman, *Embattled Courage: The Experience of Combat in the American Civil War* (New York, 1987), esp. chap. 8: "Unraveling Convictions."

15. Charles H. Brewster to mother, June 2, 1864, in *When This Cruel War Is Over: The Civil War Letters of Charles Harvey Brewster*, ed. David W. Blight (Amherst, 1992), 313; John T. Timmerman to wife, Aug. 19, 1864, Timmerman Papers, MHI.

16. John Gillis, Diary, entry of March 24, 1864, MN HS; Wilbur Fisk Diary, entry of May 11, 1864, Fisk Papers, LC.

17. George W. McMillen to "Sister Sue," Jan. 1, 1864, in "Civil War Letters of George Washington McMillen and Jefferson O. McMillen," *West Virginia History* 32 (1971): 183; Samuel Merrill to Emily Merrill, June 13, 15, 1864, in "Letters from a Civil War Officer," ed. A. T. Volwiler, *MVHR* 14 (1928): 518; Eli S. Ricker to Mary Smith, Jan. 8, 1865, in " 'We Left a Black Trace in South Carolina': Letters of Corporal Eli S. Ricker, 1865," ed. Edward G. Longacre, *SCHM* 82 (1981): 214.

18. Charles B. Haydon, diary entry of April 13, 1862, in *For Country, Cause, & Leader: The Civil War Journal of Charles B. Haydon*, ed. Stephen W. Sears (Boston, 1993), 221; James Anderson to family, May 9, 1863, Anderson Papers, WHS.

19. James E. Glazier to Annie Monroe, Dec. 27, 1862, Glazier Papers, HEH.

20. Tristim L. Skinner to Eliza Skinner, Oct. 3, 1861, Skinner Papers, SHC UNC; William L. Saunders to "Florida," Dec. 30, 1862, Saunders Papers, SHC UNC.

21. Willie Root, Diary, entry of Sept. 25, 1864, MHI; Harvey Reid to Libbie Reid, Oct. 9, 1863, in *The View from Headquarters: Civil War Letters of Harvey Reid* (Madison, 1965), 99.

22. Abner Dunham to parents, Dec. 21, 1863, in "Civil War Letters of Abner Dunham," ed. Mildred Throne, *IJH* 53 (1955): 320–21. Reenlistments took place during the winter of 1863–64 even though the terms of some 1861 regiments still had up to ten months to run.

23. Walt Whitman to mother, April 10, 1864, in Whitman, *The Wound Dresser: Letters Written to His Mother from the Hospitals in Washington During the Civil War*, ed. Richard M. Cucke (New York, 1949), 163–64.

24. Paul Oliver to "Quita," Nov. 8, 1864, Oliver Papers, FLPU.

25. The principal studies that developed the primary group cohesion the-

sis are Marshall, *Men Against Fire;* Edward Shils and Morris Janowitz, "Cohesion and Disintegration in the Wehrmacht in World War II," *Public Opinion Quarterly* 12 (1948): 280–315; and Samuel A. Stouffer et al., *The American Soldier,* 2 vols. (Princeton, 1949), esp. vol. II: *Combat and Its Aftermath.* Other works that have made the concept an important part of their analysis are Roy R. Grinker and John P. Spiegel, *Men Under Stress* (Philadelphia, 1945); J. Glenn Gray, *The Warriors: Reflections on Men in Battle* (New York, 1959); Anthony Kellett, *Combat Motivation: The Behavior of Soldiers in Battle* (Boston, 1982); Frank M. Richardson, *Fighting Spirit: A Study of Psychological Factors in War* (London, 1978); John Keegan, *The Face of Battle* (New York, 1976); Holmes, *Acts of War;* John Ellis, *The Sharp End: The Fighting Man in World War II* (New York, 1980); Edward Shils, "Primary Groups in the American Army," in his *Center and Periphery: Essays in Sociology* (Chicago, 1950), 384–402; Stanford Gregory, Jr., "Toward a Situated Description of Cohesion and Disintegration in the American Army," *Armed Forces and Society* 3 (1977): 463–73; and Larry H. Ingraham and Frederick J. Manning, "Cohesion: Who Needs It, What Is It?" *Military Review* 61 (1981): 2–12. The opposition to accepting homosexuals in the American armed forces is based in part on the belief that their presence in a military unit would undermine the cohesion necessary for combat effectiveness; see the front-page story in the *New York Times,* April 1, 1993.

26. Holmes, *Acts of War,* 291; Grinker and Spiegel, *Men Under Stress,* 45.

27. Ellis, *The Sharp End,* 315; William Manchester, *Goodbye Darkness* (New York, 1987), 451.

28. John O. Collins to wife, Dec. 16, 1861, Collins Papers, VHS; Abram McClellan to "Mag," Nov. 2, 1864, McClellan Papers, OHS.

29. James T. Thompson to mother and sisters, March 26, 1862, in "A Georgia Boy with 'Stonewall' Jackson: The Letters of James Thomas Thompson," *VMHB* 70 (1962): 322; Frank Batchelor to George Turner, Oct. 29, 1862, *Batchelor-Turner Letters 1861–1864, Written by Two of Terry's Texas Rangers* (Austin, 1961), 32; Edmund Patterson, diary entry of Oct. 25, 1862, in *Yankee Rebel: The Civil War Journal of Edmund DeWitt Patterson* (Chapel Hill, 1966), 41, 73.

30. Nathan Buck to sister, July 9, 1864, Saxton Collection, HEH.

31. Thomas Kilby Smith to Elizabeth Smith, Aug. 8, 1862, Smith Papers, HEH; Delos Van Deusen to Henrietta Van Deusen, Jan. 1, 1863, Van Deusen Papers, HEH; Oliver N. Norton to "Cousin L.," July 18, 1862, in Norton, *Army Letters 1861–1865* (Chicago, 1903), 104.

32. James E. Glazier to Annie G. Monroe, Oct. 24, 1862, Glazier Papers, HEH.

33. Charles Woodward Hutson to father, May 13, 1862, Hutson Papers, SHC UNC; Henry L. Abbott to father, March 17, 1862, in *Fallen Leaves:*

The Civil War Letters of Major Henry Livermore Abbott, ed. Robert Garth Scott (Kent, Ohio, 1991), 107; Edward A. Acton to Mary Acton, June 16, 1862, in "'Dear Mollie': Letters of Captain Edward A. Acton to His Wife, 1862," *PMHB* 89 (1965): 20.

34. Charles Woodward Hutson to father, Aug. 16, 1862, Hutson Papers, SHC UNC; Thaddeus Capron to family, April 26, 1862, in "War Diary [and Letters] of Thaddeus H. Capron, 1861–1865," *Journal of the Illinois Historical Society* 12 (1919): 348; Henry Kyd Douglas to "Cousin Tippie," Nov. 20, 1864, Douglas Papers, PLDU.

35. Shils and Janowitz, "Cohesion and Disintegration in the Wehrmacht."

36. Omar Bartov, *Hitler's Army: Soldiers, Nazis, and War in the Third Reich* (New York, 1991), 6, 33, 104.

CHAPTER 7. ON THE ALTAR OF MY COUNTRY

1. Samuel A. Stouffer et al., *The American Soldier,* 2 vols. (Princeton, 1949), vol. II: *Combat and Its Aftermath,* 169; Elmar Dinter, *Hero or Coward: Pressures Facing the Soldier in Battle,* trans. from German by Tricia Hughes (London, 1985), 177.

2. John Ellis, *The Sharp End: The Fighting Man in World War II* (New York, 1980), 322; Stouffer et al., *The American Soldier,* II: 107–8, 150.

3. Charles C. Moskos, *The American Enlisted Man* (New York, 1970), 148; Ronald Spector, *After Tet: The Bloodiest Year in Vietnam* (New York, 1992), 71.

4. Moskos, *The American Enlisted Man,* 135–36, 147; Frank M. Richardson, *Fighting Spirit: A Study of Psychological Factors in War* (London, 1978), 12.

5. Bell Irvin Wiley, *The Life of Billy Yank* (Indianapolis, 1952), 39–40. See also Wiley, *The Life of Johnny Reb* (Indianapolis, 1943), 309.

6. Pete Maslowski, "A Study of Morale in Civil War Soldiers," *Military Affairs* 34 (1970): 123; Fred A. Bailey, *Class and Tennessee's Confederate Generation* (Chapel Hill, 1987), 78; *The New Yorker,* May 18, 1992, p. 31.

7. James G. Theaker to brother, Aug. 10, 1863, *Through One Man's Eyes: The Civil War Experiences of a Belmont County Volunteer,* ed. Paul E. Rieger (Mount Vernon, Ohio, 1974), 49; Robert A. Moore, diary entry of Jan. 28, 1862, in "Robert A. Moore: The Diary of a Confederate Private," ed. James W. Silver, *Louisiana Historical Quarterly* 39 (1956): 312.

8. Ted Barclay to sister, March 6, 1864, in *Ted Barclay, Liberty Hall Volunteers: Letters from the Stonewall Brigade,* ed. Charles W. Turner (Rockbridge, Va., 1992), 131; William J. Mims to wife, Sept. 22, 1864, in "Letters of Major W. J. Mims, C.S.A.," *AHQ* 3 (1941): 223.

9. Gustave Paul Cluseret, *Armée et democratie* (Paris, 1869), 101–2, 20. Quote translated by Philip Katz. See also a statement by the Comte de Paris,

who served for a time on General George B. McClellan's staff, quoted in Belle Becker Sideman and Lillian Friedman, eds., *Europe Looks at the Civil War* (New York, 1960), 52–53.

10. *The Civil War Diary of Allen Morgan Geer*, ed. Mary Ann Anderson (Denver, 1977), 142, 145, 147, 149.

11. Thomas W. Stephens Diary, entry of Nov. 25, 1863, SHS MO; Henry Orendorff to William Parlin, Feb. 4, 1864, in *We Are Sherman's Men: The Civil War Letters of Henry Orendorff*, ed. William M. Anderson (Macomb, Ill., 1986), 73; Henry H. Howell to Emily Howell (sister), Dec. 7, 1864, in *This Regiment of Heroes: A Compilation of Primary Materials Pertaining to the 124th New York State Volunteers*, ed. Charles J. LaRocca (Montgomery, N.Y., 1991), 230.

12. Thomas Kilby Smith to Eliza Smith, Feb. 4, 1863, Smith Papers, HEH; Nelson Chapin to wife, March 6, 1864, Chapin Papers, MHI.

13. *Personal Memoirs of U.S. Grant*, 2 vols. (New York, 1885–86), II: 531; John Keegan, *The Mask of Command* (New York, 1987), 191.

14. *Webster's New World Dictionary*, Third College Edition (New York, 1988), 670; Eric Foner, *Free Soil, Free Labor, Free Men: The Ideology of the Republican Party Before the Civil War* (New York, 1970), 4.

15. See in particular Avery Craven, *The Growth of Southern Nationalism, 1848–1861* (Baton Rouge, 1953), and John McCardell, *The Idea of a Southern Nation . . . 1830–1860* (New York, 1979).

16. William B. Coleman to parents, Jan. 19, 1862, Coleman Letters, Civil War Collection, TSL; William Preston Johnston to wife, Aug. 24, 1862, in "A War Letter from William Johnston," ed. Arthur Marvin Shaw, *Journal of Mississippi History* 4 (1942): 44; H. Christopher Kendrick to father and sister, June 2, 1863, Kendrick Papers, SHC UNC.

17. George W. Dawson to wife, April 26, 1862, in "One Year at War: Letters of Capt. Geo. W. Dawson, C.S.A.," ed. H. Riley Bock, *Missouri Historical Review* 73 (1979): 194; John N. Shealy to Eugenia Shealy, June 27, 1862, Shealy Papers, HML LSU.

18. William C. Porter, diary entries of Feb. 8, 1863, Aug. 2, 1862, in "War Diary of W. C. Porter," *Arkansas Historical Quarterly* 11 (1952): 309, 299.

19. John W. Cotton to Mariah Cotton, Aug. 3, 1862, in *Yours Till Death: Civil War Letters of John W. Cotton* (University, Ala., 1951), 14; George K. Miller to Celestina McCann, Sept. 15, 1863, Miller Papers, SHC UNC; Andrew J. White to Margaret White, Jan. 11, 1863, White Papers, PLDU.

20. John Collins to Mary Collins, April 28, 1862, Collins Papers, VHS; George Loyall Gordon to Mary Gordon, June 17, 1862, Gordon Papers, SHC UNC; Charles Minor Blackford to Susan Leigh Blackford, Dec. (no day) 1862, quoted in William C. Wickham, in *Letters from Lee's Army*, ed. Susan Lee Blackford (New York, 1947), 144.

21. James J. Womack, Diary, entry of Feb. 18, 1862, privately printed copy in the Museum of the Confederacy, Richmond; William H. Davis to mother, June 23, 1862, Davis Papers, WLEU; Richard Pugh to Mary Pugh, May 4, 1862, Pugh-Williams Papers, HML LSU.

22. James West Smith, diary entries of June 2 and 15, 1863, "A Confederate Soldier's Diary: Vicksburg in 1863," *Southwest Review* 28 (1943): 304, 312.

23. Paul A. Oliver to mother, Sept. 27, 1862, Oliver Papers, FLPU; Olney Andrus to Mary Andrus (wife), Nov. 9, 1862, in *The Civil War Letters of Sergeant Olney Andrus,* ed. Fred A. Shannon (Urbana, Ill., 1947), 25–26.

24. Edwin E. Harris to Margaret Harris, June 16, 1862, Harris Papers, GLC PML.

25. T. C. Du Pree to wife, Jan. 31, 1864, in *The War-Time Letters of Captain T. C. Du Pree, C.S.A. 1864–1865* (Fayetteville, Ark., 1953), unpaged; Joseph Branch O'Bryan to sister, July 9, 1863, O'Bryan Papers, TSL.

26. Edward M. Burrus to mother, June 14, 1862, Burrus Family Papers, HML LSU; Harry Lewis to mother, Aug. 9, 1862, Harry Lewis Papers, SHC UNC. Emphasis added.

27. William H. Davis to mother, June 23, 1862, Davis Papers, WLEU (emphasis added); Samuel F. Tenneo to Alice Toomer, Jan. 18, 1862, in "War Letters of S. F. Tenney, A Soldier of the Third Georgia Regiment," *GHQ* 57 (1973): 280.

28. Alexander Swift Pendleton to William N. Pendleton, Feb. 25, 1862, in "The Valley Campaign of 1862 as Revealed in Letters of Sandie Pendleton," ed. W. G. Bean, *VMHB* 78 (1970): 332.

29. John B. Jones, diary entry of March 29, 1863, in *A Rebel War Clerk's Diary,* ed. Earl Schenck Miers (New York, 1958), 181; H. C. Medford, diary entries of April 4, 8, 1864, in "The Diary of H. C. Medford, Confederate Soldier, 1864," ed. Rebecca W. Smith and Marion Mullins, *SHQ* 34 (1930): 211, 220; Frederick Bartleson to Kate Bartleson, Feb. 26, 1864, in *The Brothers' War,* ed. Annette Taper (New York, 1988), 187.

30. Paul A. Oliver to Sam Oliver, Jan. 2, 1863, Oliver Papers, FLPU; Richard S. Thompson to sister & brother, Jan. 14, 1863, in *While My Country Is in Danger: The Life and Letters of Lieutenant Colonel Richard S. Thompson,* ed. Gerry Harder Poriss and Ralph G. Poriss (Hamilton, N.Y., 1994), 40–41.

31. John Brobst to Mary Englesby, March (no day) 1863, in *Well, Mary: Civil War Letters of a Wisconsin Volunteer,* ed. Margaret B. Roth (Madison, 1960), 15; James Glazier to parents, Jan. 11, Feb. 5, 1862, Glazier Papers, HEH; A. D. Pratt to Mr. Murdock, Feb. 16, 1863, Murdock Papers, ISHL.

32. Joseph H. Griner to Sophia Griner, Jan. 3, 1863, in Daniel H. Woodward, "The Civil War of a Pennsylvania Trooper," *PMHB* 87 (1963): 51; William Henry Wykoff to Richard R. Parry, May 27, 1862, Wykoff Letters, in

private possession; George Lowe to Elizabeth Lowe, Sept. 18, 1862, Lowe Papers, HEH; Nelson Chapin to wife, Oct. 19, 1863, Chapin Papers, MHI.

33. Ernest Hemingway, *A Farewell to Arms* (New York, 1929), 191; Paul Fussell, *The Great War and Modern Memory* (New York, 1975), 21–22.

34. These figures for both Confederate and Union soldiers are based on enlisted men only; the number of post-conscription men in the sample who became officers is too small for meaningful comparisons.

35. For a sampling of this scholarship, see Bailey, *Class and Tennessee's Confederate Generation*; Stephen E. Ambrose, "Yeoman Discontent in the Confederacy," *CWH* 8 (1962): 259–68; Paul D. Escott, "Southern Yeomen and the Confederacy," *South Atlantic Quarterly* 77 (1978); Steven Hahn, *The Roots of Southern Populism: Yeoman Farmers and the Transformation of the Georgia Upcountry, 1850–1890* (New York, 1983); Wayne K. Durrill, *War of Another Kind: A Southern Community in the Great Rebellion* (New York, 1990); Armstead Robinson, "Bitter Fruits of Bondage: Slavery's Demise and the Collapse of the Confederacy" (unpublished manuscript); Frank L. Klement, *The Copperheads in the Middle West* (Chicago, 1960); Iver Bernstein, *The New York City Draft Riots: Their Significance for American Society and Politics in the Age of the Civil War* (New York, 1990); Grace Palladino, *Another Civil War: Labor, Capital, and the State in the Anthracite Regions of Pennsylvania* (Urbana, Ill., 1990); William F. Hanna, "The Boston Draft Riot," *CWH* 36 (1990): 262–73; and Robert E. Sterling, "Civil War Draft Resistance in the Middle West" (Ph.D. dissertation, Northern Illinois University, 1974).

36. John W. Reese to wife, May 26, 1863, Reese Papers, PLDU; James C. Zimmerman to Adeline Zimmerman, April 13, Aug. 5, 1863, Zimmerman Papers, PLDU; Valentin Bechler to wife, Sept. 17, 1862, in "A German Immigrant in the Union Army: Selected Letters of Valentin Bechler," *Journal of American Studies* 4 (1971): 160.

CHAPTER 8. THE CAUSE OF LIBERTY

1. Roy P. Basler, ed., *The Collected Works of Abraham Lincoln*, 9 vols. (New Brunswick, N.J., 1953–1955), VII: 23; Dunbar Rowland, ed., *Jefferson Davis, Constitutionalist: His Letters, Papers, and Speeches*, 10 vols. (Jackson, Miss., 1923), V: 202.

2. Eugene Blackford to mother, Feb. 22, 1862, Gordon-Blackford Papers, MD HS; James E. Paton, diary entry of July 4, 1862, in "Civil War Journal of James E. Paton," ed. Mrs. Wade Hampton Whitley, *Register of the Kentucky Historical Society* 61 (1963): 228; Edmund D. Patterson, diary entry of July 4, 1863, in *Yankee Rebel: The Civil War Journal of Edmund DeWitt Patterson*, ed. John G. Barrett (Chapel Hill, 1966), 119.

3. James Griffin to Leila Griffin, March 17, 1862, in *"A Gentleman and an Officer": A Military and Social History of James B. Griffin's Civil War*, ed.

Judith N. McArthur and O. Vernon Burton (New York, 1996), 172; William C. Proffit to Andrew J. Proffit, May 10, 1862, Proffit Family Papers, SHC UNC; William Fleming to Georgia Fleming, July 13, 1863, Fleming Papers, SHC UNC.

4. Edmund D. Patterson, diary entry of March 20, 1862, in *Yankee Rebel,* 14; Randal McGavock, diary entry of May 9, 1862, in *Pen and Sword: The Life and Journals of Randal W. McGavock,* ed. Jack Allen (Nashville, 1959), 624.

5. Noah Dixon Walker to father, Feb. 10, 1863, Noah D. Walker Papers, MD HS; Joseph Mothershead Diary, entry of June 13, 1862, TSL.

6. W. H. Williams to Susan Williams, May 19, 1862, Civil War Collection, TSL; James H. Stanley to Mary Stanley, Feb. 28, 1862, Stanley Papers, SHC UNC; Pleas B. Clark to Henry H. Wells, Aug. 7, 1863, Henry Wells Papers, SHC UNC.

7. Lunsford Yandell, Jr., to Sally Yandell, April 22, 1861, Lunsford Yandell, Jr., to father, April 22, 1861, Yandell Papers, FCHS; James B. Griffin to Leila Griffin, Feb. 26, May 21, 1862, in McArthur and Burton, eds., "A Gentleman and an Officer," 163, 221.

8. Edgeworth Bird to Sallie Bird, Aug. 8, 28, 1863, in *The Granite Farm Letters: The Civil War Correspondence of Edgeworth and Sallie Bird,* ed. John Rozier (Athens, Ga., 1988), 132, 135; Richard Lewis to mother, Feb. 9, April 14, 1864, in *Camp Life of a Confederate Boy . . . Letters Written by Lieut. Richard Lewis* (Charleston, S.C., 1883), 82, 92.

9. Richard Henry Watkins to Mary Watkins, Dec. 20, 1861, Watkins Papers, VA HS; Edward O. Guerrant to father, Feb. 15, 1865, Guerrant Papers, FCHS; John Thomas Jones to Edmund Walter Jones, Jan. 20, 1861, Edmund Jones Papers, SHC UNC.

10. William Calder to mother, June 26, 1863, Calder Papers, SHC UNC.

11. John B. Evans to Mollie Evans, June 28, 1863, Jan. 22, 1865, Evans Papers, PLDU.

12. William Nugent to Eleanor Nugent, Sept. 7, 1863, in *My Dear Nellie: The Civil War Letters of William L. Nugent,* ed. William M. Cash and Lucy Somerville Howarth (Jackson, Miss., 1977), 132; Elias Davis to Mrs. R. L. Lathan, Dec. 10, 1863, Davis Papers, SHC UNC.

13. Henry L. Stone to father, Feb. 13, 1863, Stone Papers, KHS; John Welsh to mother and wife, Jan. 26, 1863, in "A House Divided: The Civil War Letters of a Virginia Family," ed. W. G. Bean, *VMHB* 59 (1951): 410; George W. Tillotson to wife, Sept. 24, 1862, Tillotson Papers, GLC PML.

14. Hilton Graves to Charles I. Graves, March 15, 1863, Graves Papers, SHC UNC; Henry K. Burgwyn to father, Feb. 8, 1863, Burgwyn Papers, SHC UNC.

15. Edward Porter Alexander to Bessie Alexander, July 26, 1863, Alexander Papers, SHC UNC; Eldred Simkins to Eliza Trescott, Jan. 27, 1865, Simkins Papers, HEH.

16. George Hamill Diary, n.d. (probably March 1862), in private possession; Jonas Bradshaw to Nancy Bradshaw, April 29, 1862, Bradshaw Papers, PLDU.

17. John G. Keyton to Mary Hilbert, Nov. 30, 1861, Keyton Papers, PLDU; Samuel Walsh to Louisa Proffitt, April 11, 1864, Proffitt Papers, SHC UNC; Chauncey Cooke to parents, May 10, 1864, in "A Badger Boy in Blue: The Letters of Chauncey H. Cooke," *WMH* 5 (1921): 67.

18. Thomas Key, diary entry of April 10, 1864, in *Two Soldiers: The Campaign Diaries of Thomas J. Key, C.S.A., and Robert J. Campbell, U.S.A.,* ed. Wirt Armistead Cate (Chapel Hill, 1938), 70; William Wakefield Garner to Henrietta Garner, Jan. 2, 1864, in "Letters of an Arkansas Confederate Soldier," ed. D. D. McBrien, *Arkansas Historical Quarterly* 2 (1943): 282; Allen D. Candler to wife, July 7, 1864, in "Watch on the Chattahoochee: A Civil War Letter," ed. Elizabeth Hulsey Marshall, *GHQ* 43 (1959): 428.

19. By the end of 1864, however, when Confederate officials began to discuss the possibility of arming slaves to fight for the South, some soldiers expressed a willingness to accept the emancipation of those who fought. See pp. 171–72.

20. Jasper N. Searles to family, Nov. 27, 1861, Searles Papers, MNHS; Horatio D. Chapman, diary entry of Sept. 19, 1863, in *Civil War Diary— Diary of a Forty-Niner* (Hartford, 1929), 35; Joseph Fardell to parents, July 11, 1863, Fardell Papers, MO HS.

21. Benjamin Stevenson to wife, July 5, 1863, in *Letters from the Army* (Cincinnati, 1884), 243.

22. Leander Stem to Amanda Stem, Dec. 15, 1862, in "Stand by the Colors: The Civil War Letters of Leander Stem," ed. John T. Hubbell, *Register of the Kentucky Historical Society* 73 (1975): 408; Philo H. Gallup to John S. Gallup, May 8, 1861, in "The Second Michigan Volunteer Infantry Joins the Army of the Potomac: Letters of Philo H. Gallup," ed. Chester M. Destler, *Michigan History* 41 (1957): 388.

23. Ephraim S. Holloway to Margaret Holloway, June 14, July 11, 1862, March 30, 1864, Holloway Papers, OHS; Josiah Chaney to Melissa Chaney, Oct. 3, 1862, Chaney Papers, MN HS.

24. Thomas Kilby Smith to Elizabeth Smith, Aug. 25, 1862, Thomas Kilby Smith to Eliza Smith, Oct. 7, 1863, Smith Papers, HEH; Basler, ed., *Collected Works of Lincoln,* IV: 268.

25. Dan G. Porter to Maria Lewis, July 24, 1862, in "The Civil War Letters of Captain Andrew Lewis and His Daughter," ed. Michael Barton, *WPMH* 40 (1977): 389; Delos Van Deusen to Henrietta Van Deusen, Dec. 23, 1862, Van Deusen Papers, HEH; John Beatty, diary entry of July 3, 1862, in *Memoirs of a Volunteer, 1861–1865* (1879; rpt., New York, 1946), 115.

26. James H. Goodnow to Samuel Goodnow, Jan. 11, 1863, Goodnow Papers, LC; Samuel Evans to father, Sept. 13, 1863, Evans Family Papers,

OHS. I am indebted to Professor Robert Engs of the University of Pennsylvania for providing me with information about the Evans Papers.

27. Josiah Perry to Phebe Perry, Oct. 3, 1862, Perry Papers, ISHL; Robert Goodyear to Sarah Goodyear, Feb. 14, 1863, Goodyear Letters, MHI.

28. William H. H. Ibbetson, Diary, undated entry sometime in the winter of 1863–64, ISHL; Robert T. McMahan, Diary, entry of Sept. 3, 1863, SHS MO.

29. George H. Cadman to Esther Cadman, March 6, 1864, Cadman Papers, SHC UNC.

30. Peter Welsh to Mary Welsh, Feb. 3, 1863, Peter Welsh to Patrick Prendergast, June 1, 1863, in *Irish Green and Union Blue: The Civil War Letters of Peter Welsh,* ed. Laurence Frederick Kohl and Margaret Cosse Richard (New York, 1986), 65–66, 102; Edmund English to mother, May 27, 1862, English Papers, HEH.

31. John Dollard, *Fear in Battle* (rpt., Westport, Conn., 1977), 40–41.

32. John Dooley, undated diary entry but apparently July 3, 1863, in *John Dooley Confederate Soldier: His War Journal,* ed. Joseph T. Durkin (Georgetown, D.C., 1945), 104–5; William B. Greene, diary entry of May 6, 1864, *Letters from a Sharpshooter: The Civil War Letters of Private William B. Greene,* ed. William H. Hastings (Belleville, Wis., 1993), 203.

33. William G. Morris to wife, Aug. 19, 1862, Morris Papers, SHC UNC; Robert Gooding to brother, April 13, 1862, Gooding Papers, SHS MO; Edwin Payne to Kim Hudson, May 25, June 19, 1863, Payne Papers, ISHL.

34. Henry Crydenwise to parents, July 9, 1863, Crydenwise Papers, WLEU; Henry Warren Howe, diary entry of May 26, 1863, in *Passages from the Life of Henry Warren Howe, Consisting of Diary and Letters Written During the Civil War, 1861–1865* (Lowell, Mass., 1899), 48.

35. James Bell to Augusta Hallock, Jan. 14, 1863, Bell Papers, HEH; Henry H. Perry to mother, Aug. 14, 1864, in private possession.

36. John W. Geary to Mary Geary, Aug. 22, 1863, in *A Politician Goes to War: The Civil War Letters of John White Geary,* ed. William Alan Blair (University Park, Pa., 1995), 110; William E. Dunn to sister, April 2, 1863, Dunn Letters, MHI; James P. Douglas to Sallie White Douglas, Sept. 14, 1864, in *Douglas's Texas Battery, CSA,* ed. Lucia Rutherford Douglas (Waco, 1966), 132.

37. James H. Leonard to Mary Sheldon, Aug. 15, 1861, in "Letters of a Fifth Wisconsin Volunteer," ed. R. G. Plumb, *WMH* 3 (1919): 54.

CHAPTER 9. SLAVERY MUST BE CLEANED OUT

1. Harvey C. Medford, diary entry of April 8, 1864, in "The Diary of H. D. Medford, Confederate Soldier, 1864," ed. Rebecca W. Smith and Marion Mullins, *SHQ* 34 (1930): 220.

2. Bell Irvin Wiley, *The Life of Billy Yank* (Indianapolis, 1952), 40; Chauncey Cooke to Doe Cooke, Jan. 6, 1863, in "A Badger Boy in Blue: The Letters of Chauncey H. Cooke," *WMH* 4 (1920): 212; Walter Poor to George Fox, May 15, 1861, March 1, 1862, in "A Yankee Soldier in a New York Regiment," ed. James J. Heslin, *New York Historical Society Quarterly Bulletin* 50 (1966): 115, 126–27.

3. George W. Lowe to Elizabeth Lowe, Jan. 18, 1862, Lowe Papers, HEH; John A. Gillis, Diary, entry of July 4, 1862, MN HS; Edward H. Bassett to family, Dec. 1, 1861, in *From Bull Run to Bristow Station*, ed. M. H. Bassett (St. Paul, 1962), 12.

4. Oliver W. Norton to "Cousin L.," Jan. 28, 1862, in Norton, *Army Letters 1861–1865* (Chicago, 1903), 43; Henry M. Crydenwise to parents, Aug. 19, 1862, Crydenwise Papers, WLEU.

5. Walter Q. Gresham to Tillie Gresham, March 24, 1862, Gresham Papers, LC; Simeon McCord to Hanna McCord, March 11, Dec. 15, 1863, in "Letters Home: Camp and Campaign Life of a Union Artilleryman," ed. Ruth K. Lynn, typescript in Earl Hess Collection, MHI; John W. Geary to Mary Geary, Jan. 28, 1863, in *A Politician Goes to War: The Civil War Letters of John White Geary*, ed. William Alan Blair (University Park, Pa., 1995), 86–87.

6. Thomas Kilby Smith to Helen Smith, Sept. 15, 1862, Smith Papers, HEH; Charles Brewster to mother, March 4, 1862, in *When This Cruel War Is Over: The Civil War Letters of Charles Harvey Brewster*, ed. David W. Blight (Amherst, 1992), 92.

7. John C. Buchanan to Sophia Buchanan, Oct. 17, 1861, in "The Negro as Viewed by a Michigan Civil War Soldier: Letters of John C. Buchanan," ed. George M. Blackburn, *Michigan History* 47 (1963): 79–80; Franklin B. Howard to brother and sister, March 29, 1862, Howard Papers, WHS.

8. Charles Wills to family, April 16, 1862, Wills to brother, Feb. 25, 1862, in *Army Life of an Illinois Soldier: Letters and Diary of the Late Charles Wills* (Washington, 1906), 83, 158; Henry Andrews to Susan Andrews, Sept. 9, 1862, Andrews Papers, ISHL.

9. George Lowe to Elizabeth Lowe, Aug. 17, 1862, Lowe Papers, HEH; Stephen O. Himoe to wife, June 26, 1862, in "An Army Surgeon's Letters to His Wife," ed. Luther M. Kuhns, *Proceedings of the Mississippi Valley Historical Association* 7 (1914): 311–12; Thomas Kilby Smith to Eliza Smith, July 23, 28, 1862, Smith Papers, HEH.

10. Charles E. Perkins to Whiting Haskell, Aug. 3, 1862, Perkins Papers, MHI; Lucius Hubbard to Mary Hubbard, Sept. 8, 1862, in "Letters of a Union Officer: L. F. Hubbard and the Civil War," ed. N. B. Martin, *Minnesota History* 35 (1957): 314–15.

11. Arthur B. Carpenter to parents, Dec. 5, 1861, quoted in Thomas R. Bright, "Yankees in Arms: The Civil War as a Personal Experience," *CWH* 19

(Sept. 1973): 202; Herman F. Dellinger, Diary, entries of July 19 and 21, 1862, HEH.

12. William T. Pippey to Benjamin Pippey, July 31, 1862, Pippey Papers, PLDU; Charles S. Wainwright, Diary, entries of Jan. 15 and May 29, 1862, HEH.

13. Darius Starr, Diary, entry of Feb. 4, 1863, Starr Papers, PLDU; Thomas W. Stephens, Diary, entry of Jan. 14, 1863, SHS MO; George Breck to Ellen Breck, Jan. 18, 1865, in "George Beck's Civil War Letters from the 'Reynolds Battery,' " *RHSP* 22 (1944): 119–20.

14. Alexander Caldwell to brother, Jan. 11, 1863, Caldwell Papers, MHI; Josiah Chaney to Melissa Chaney, Sept. 24, 1862, Chaney Papers, MN HS.

15. Constant Hanks to mother, April 20, 1863, Hanks Papers, PLDU; John Q. A. Campbell, Diary, entry of Oct. 28, 1862, WRHS.

16. Henry Henney to family, late Dec. 1862, Henney Papers, MHI; David Nichol to father, Jan. 4, 1863, Nichol Papers, MHI.

17. George W. Beidelman to father, Oct. 1, 1862, in *The Civil War Letters of George Washington Beidelman,* ed. Catherine H. Vanderslice (New York, 1978), 116; George Cadman to Esther Cadman, May 9, 1863, Cadman Papers, SHC UNC.

18. Valentin Bechler to wife, Nov. 11, 1862, in "A German Immigrant in the Union Army: Selected Letters of Valentin Bechler," ed. Robert C. Goodell and P. A. M. Taylor, *Journal of American Studies* 4 (1971): 161; John Shank to family, Feb. 17, 1863, in *One Flag One Country and Thirteen Greenbacks a Month: Letters from a Civil War Private,* ed. Edna J. Shank Hunter (San Diego, 1980), 59.

19. Olney Andrus to Mary Andrus, in *The Civil War Letters of Sergeant Olney Andrus,* ed. Fred A. Shannon (Urbana, Ill., 1947), 29; Henry P. Hubbell to Walter Hubbell, Jan. 26, Feb. 7, 1863, Hubbell Papers, FLPU.

20. David T. Massey to father, Feb. 23, 1863, David T. Massey to sister, Jan. 26, 1863, Massey Papers, MO HS; John W. Ford to family, Ford Letters, MHI; John Babb, Jr., to John Babb, Oct. 3, 1862, Babb Papers, WLEU.

21. John Vliet to Mr. Bodge, Feb. 2, 1863, in Thomas W. Sweeny Papers, HEH; Simeon Royse to father, Feb. 14, 1863, Royse Papers, PLDU; John G. McDermott to Isabella McDermott, McDermott Papers, WHS.

22. Cyrus B. Boyd, diary entry of March 6, 1863, in "The Civil War Diary of C. F. Boyd, Fifteenth Iowa Infantry," ed. Mildred Throne, *IJH* 50 (1952): 375.

23. Chauncey B. Welton to "Dear friends at home," Jan. 13, 1863, Welton to mother, Feb. 11, 1863, Welton to uncle, March 20, 1863, Welton Papers, SHC UNC.

24. Chauncey B. Welton to parents, June 15, 1863, to his father, Sept. 19, Oct. 13, 1864, to parents, Feb. 18, 1865, Welton Papers, SHC UNC.

25. Marcus Spiegel to Caroline Spiegel, Jan. 25, April 27, 1863, Jan.

22, Feb. 12, 1864; address by Spiegel to his regiment, Feb. 22, 1863, all in *Your True Marcus: The Civil War Letters of a Jewish Colonel,* ed. Frank L. Byrne and Jean Powers Soman (Kent, Ohio, 1985), 226, 269, 315–16, 320, 244.

26. William H. Martin to James Davidson, May 24, 1863, Martin Papers, MHI; B. W. H. Pasron to A. A. Shafer, March 24, 1863, *Civil War Times Illustrated* Collection, MHI.

27. John F. Marquis to Neeta Haile, July 26, 1863, Neeta Marquis Papers, HEH; John R. Beatty to Laura Maxfield, Feb. 20, 1863, Beatty Papers, MN HS.

28. Alfred Pirtle to sister, Aug. 3, Sept. 8, 1863, Pirtle Papers, FCHS.

29. Aaron J. Benton to father, March 2, 1863, Benton Papers, MHI; Symmes Stillwell to mother, Feb. 21, 1863, Stillwell Papers, FLPU.

30. B. W. H. Pasron to A. A. Shafer, March 24, 1863, *Civil War Times Illustrated* Collection, MHI; Hiram Weatherby to George Huson, Jan. 22, 1863, Nelson Huson Papers, HEH.

31. Edwin Payne to Kim Hudson, May 3, 1863, Payne Papers, ISHL; Joseph G. McNutt to A. F. Scott, June 23, 1863, in private possession.

32. William F. Keeler to Anna Keeler, June 30, 1863, in *Aboard the USS Florida, 1863–1865: The Letters of Paymaster William Frederick Keeler,* ed. Robert W. Daly (Annapolis, 1968), 59–60; James Theaker to sister, Oct. 19, 1863, in *Through One Man's Eyes: The Civil War Experiences of a Belmont County Volunteer,* ed. Paul E. Rieger (Mount Vernon, Ohio, 1974), 63.

33. Thomas W. Stephens, Diary, entry of June 15, 1864, SHS MO; William J. Tomlinson to Emily Tomlinson, Dec. 26, 1864, March 28, 1865, Tomlinson Papers, in private possession.

34. Charles W. Singer to *Christian Recorder,* Sept. 18, 1864, published in *Christian Recorder,* Oct. 8, 1864, reprinted in Edwin S. Redkey, ed., *A Grand Army of Black Men: Letters from African-American Soldiers in the Union Army, 1861–1865* (New York, 1993), 214; Edgar Dinsmore to Carrie Drayton, May 29, 1865, Dinsmore Papers, PLDU.

35. James Henry Hall to *Christian Recorder,* Aug. 3, 1864, in *Christian Recorder,* Aug. 27, 1864, reprinted in Redkey, *A Grand Army of Black Men,* 205; Corporal John H. B. Payne, in a letter to the *Christian Recorder,* May 24, 1864, reprinted in Noah Andre Trudeau, ed., *Voices of the 55th: Letters from the 55th Massachusetts Volunteers* (Dayton, Ohio, 1996), 146; Diary of William B. Gould, quoted by his great-grandson William B. Gould IV, chairman of the National Labor Relations Board, in a speech to the Officers' Club of the U.S. Navy on Feb. 11, 1995, and published in a press release by the NLRB.

36. William C. H. Reeder to parents, Dec. 23, 1863, Reeder Papers, MHI; Benjamin Jones to Lemuel Jones, March 9, 1864, William Jones to Lemuel Jones, Feb. 12, 1864, Misc. Civil War Letters, FCHS; Thomas

Donahue to Almira Mitchell, July 31, 1864, Winchell Papers, GLC PML.

37. Jenkin Lloyd Jones, diary entries of Oct. 31, Dec. 19, 1864, in *An Artillery Man's Diary,* ed. Carl Russell Fish (Madison, 1914), 265, 289–90.

38. Samuel Ely to mother, Aug. 15, 1863, Ely to mother and sister, Dec. 26, 1863, Ely to Anne Ely, July 10, 1864, April 12, 1865, Ely Papers, FLPU; William Tuckey Meredith to Mary Watson, May 10, 1864, Meredith Papers, FLPU.

39. Robert Gooding to brother, May 4, 1863, Gooding Papers, SHS MO; John Q. A. Campbell Diary, entries of Nov. 12, July 4, 1863, WRHS.

40. Phineas Hager to Sabra Hager, March 6, July 14, 1864, Hager Papers, typescript copies supplied by Dave Holmquist.

CHAPTER 10. WE KNOW THAT WE ARE SUPPORTED AT HOME

1. John L. Barnett to sister, Nov. 17, 1862, in "Some Civil War Letters and Diary of John Lympus Barnett," ed. James Barnett, *IMH* 37 (1941): 172; Irby G. Scott to "Dear Ones at Home," Nov. 6, 1861, Scott Papers, PLDU; James H. Leonard to Mary Sheldon, Aug. 15, 1861, in "Letters of a Fifth Wisconsin Volunteer," ed. R. G. Plumb, *WMH* 3 (1919): 54.

2. Henry McDaniel to Hester Felker, June 14, 1863, in *With Unabated Trust: Major Henry McDaniel's Love Letters from Confederate Battlefields* (Monroe, Ga., 1977), 169–70; Charles Francis Adams, Jr., to Henry Adams, Aug. 2, 1863, in *A Cycle of Adams Letters,* 2 vols. (Boston, 1920), II: 68; Charles K. Mervine, diary entry of Jan. 8, 1864, in "Jottings by the Way: A Sailor's Log—1862 to 1864," *PMHB* 71 (1947): 255.

3. Marcus Spiegel to Caroline Spiegel, Feb. 13, July 13, 1862, in *Your True Marcus: The Civil War Letters of a Jewish Colonel,* ed. Frank L. Byrne and Jean Powers Soman (Kent, Ohio, 1985), 37, 128, 129.

4. Roger W. Little, "Buddy Relations and Combat Performance," in Morris Janowitz, ed., *The New Military: Changing Patterns of Organization* (New York, 1964), 219; Edmund Patterson, diary entry of Nov. 23, 1862, in *Yankee Rebel: The Civil War Journal of Edmund DeWitt Patterson* (Chapel Hill, 1966), 83.

5. Lila Chunn to Willie Chunn, May 19, 1863, and Emily Harris, diary entry of Nov. 18, 1864, both quoted in Drew Gilpin Faust, "Altars of Sacrifice: Confederate Women and the Narratives of War," *Journal of American History* 76 (1990): 1222.

6. Sophia Wight to Levi Wight, Nov. 16, 1862, Dec. 5, 1863, in *The Reminiscences and Civil War Letters of Levi Lamoni Wight,* ed. Davis Bitton (Salt Lake City, 1970), 121–22, 142; S.W.W. to "My Dear Charley," undated, in Edward G. Longacre, " 'Come home soon and dont delay': Letters from the Home Front, July 1861," *PMHB* 100 (1976): 400; Leokadia Bechler to Valentin Bechler, June 16, Sept. 13, 1862, in "A German Immigrant in the

Union Army: Selected Letters of Valentin Bechler," ed. Robert C. Goodell and P. A. M. Taylor, *Journal of American Studies* 4 (1971): 157, 159.

7. Charles Wills to sister, Jan. 22, 1863, in *Army Life of an Illinois Soldier, Letters and Diary of the Late Charles Wills* (Washington, 1906), 150; Hans Christian Heg to Thomas Adland, Feb. 15, 1863, in *Civil War Letters of Hans Christian Heg,* ed. Theodore C. Blegen (Northfield, Minn., 1936), 220; Rufus Dawes, *Service with the Sixth Wisconsin Volunteers* (1890; rpt., 1962), 127.

8. Wilbur Fisk, Diary, entry of Feb. 14, 1864, LC; Duren Kelley to Emma Kelley, Oct. 18, 1863, in *The War Letters of Duren F. Kelley 1862–1865,* ed. Richard S. Offenberg and Robert Rue Parsonage (New York, 1967), 73.

9. Richard Watkins to Mary Watkins, Oct. 18, 1862, Watkins Papers, VHS.

10. Ephraim W. Holloway to Margaret Holloway, Dec. 7, 1863, March 30, 1864, Jan. 15, 1865, Ephraim Holloway to John W. Holloway, April 23, 1863, Holloway Papers, OHS.

11. Thomas Taylor to Antoinette Taylor, Feb. 25, June 7, 1862, Taylor Papers, OHS; Joseph W. Collingwood to Rebecca Collingwood, Aug. 12, 1862 (misdated March 12), Collingwood Papers, HEH.

12. Sydney Champion to wife, undated, Oct. or Nov. 1862, Champion Papers, PLDU; Ephraim S. Holloway to Margaret Holloway, July 11, 1862, Holloway Papers, OHS; Tristrim L. Skinner to Eliza Skinner, Nov. 21, 1861, April 6, 1862, Skinner Papers, SHC UNC.

13. R. Curtis Edgerton to Lydia Edgerton, April 21, 1862, Edgerton Papers, HEH; Richard Henry Watkins to Mary Watkins, Feb. 20, 1862, Watkins Papers, VHS; John McGrath to Lavinia McGrath, Jan. 13, 1863, McGrath Papers, HML LSU.

14. James K. Edmondson to wife, Oct. 14, 1862, in *War Letters of Col. James K. Edmondson 1861–1865,* ed. Charles W. Turner (Vernon, Va., 1978), 105; Ellison Capers to Lottie Capers, Dec. 9, 1862, Capers Papers, PLDU; Elisha Paxton to wife, Jan. 26, Oct. 25, 1862, *Memoir and Memorials of Elisha Franklin Paxton,* ed. John G. Paxton (New York, 1905), 48, 68.

15. Ladie Armstrong to James T. Armstrong, April 17, 1862, Armstrong Papers, SHC UNC.

16. Thomas Kilby Smith to Eliza Smith, Feb. 4, June 17, 1863, Smith Papers, HEH; William L. Nugent to Eleanor Nugent, April 20, 1864, in *My Dear Nellie: The Civil War Letters of William L. Nugent,* ed. William M. Cash and Lucy Somerville Howarth (Jackson, Miss., 1977), 168; Hans Christian Heg to Gunild Heg, Aug. 25, 1862, in *Civil War Letters of Heg,* 128.

17. Hillory Shifflet to Lemima Shifflet, Feb. 28, 1862, Shifflet Papers, MO HS; Andrew J. White to Margaret White, June 13, 1862, White Papers, PLDU; James S. Watson to wife, Oct. 5, 1862, Watson Papers, VHS.

18. Quoted in Bessie Martin, *Desertion of Alabama Troops from the Con-*

federate Army (New York, 1932), 148. See also Ella Lonn, *Desertion During the Civil War* (New York, 1928), 12–14, and Drew Gilpin Faust, "Altars of Sacrifice," 1224.

19. W. S. Shockley to Eliza Shockley, Jan. 15, 1863, Shockley Papers, PLDU; John Calvin Gruar to wife, March 20, 1864, Civil War Collection, TSL.

20. Amory Allen to Delphany Allen, March 19, 1863, in "Civil War Letters of Amory K. Allen," *IMH* 31 (1935): 364; Royal Potter to wife, Oct. 19, 1862, Potter Papers, in private possession.

21. Catherine Buckingham to Roswell H. Lamson, June 29, May 16, 1864, Lamson Papers, FLPU.

22. Henry Ackerman Smith to wife, June 19, 1862, Smith Papers, PLDU; Mortimer Leggett to wife, Jan. 1, 1865, Leggett Papers, Lincoln Shrine, A. K. Smiley Public Library, Redlands, California.

23. Hans Christian Heg to Gunild Heg, April 25, 1863, in *Civil War Letters of Heg*, 206; Eldred Simkins to Eliza Trescott, July 27, 1863, Simkins Papers, HEH; Bryan Grimes to Charlotte Grimes, Oct. 8, 1863, Grimes Papers, SHC UNC.

24. Bryan Grimes to Charlotte Grimes, Oct. 13, 1863, Grimes Papers, SHC UNC; James Connolly to Mary Connolly, March 2, 1863, in *Three Years in the Army of the Cumberland: The Letters and Diary of Major James A. Connolly*, ed. Paul Angle (Bloomington, Ind., 1962), 38; Joseph Collingwood to Rebecca Collingwood, Aug. 25, 1861, Collingwood Papers, HEH. The data on combat mortality of married soldiers varied for the Union and Confederate samples. Among Confederates 38 percent of married men and only 26 percent of unmarried soldiers were killed; in the Union sample the figures were 15 percent for married soldiers and 18 percent for single men.

25. Eric J. Leed, *No Man's Land: Combat and Identity in World War I* (Cambridge, 1979), 110–11.

26. Gerald F. Linderman, *Embattled Courage: The Experience of Combat in the American Civil War* (New York, 1987), 216, 218, 239.

27. Charles H. Brewster to mother, May 15, 1864, in *When This Cruel War Is Over: The Civil War Letters of Charles Harvey Brewster*, ed. David W. Blight (Amherst, 1992), 298; David Nichol to father, March 28, 1863, Nichol Papers, MHI; James M. Williams to Elizabeth Williams, Oct. 17, 1864, in *From That Terrible Field: Civil War Letters of James M. Williams*, ed. John Kent Folmar (University, Ala., 1981), 146.

28. Robert A. McClellan to sister, May 13, 1863, McClellan Papers, PLDU; Joab Goodson to Nannie Clements, Aug. 18, 1863, in "The Letters of Captain Joab Goodson, 1862–1864," ed. W. Stanley Hoole, *Alabama Review* 10 (1957): 146–47; Peter McDavid to Nellie McDavid, Aug. 15, 1863, McDavid Papers, PLDU.

29. Abner E. McGarity to Francinia McGarity, March 6, 1865, in "Let-

ters of a Confederate Surgeon: Dr. Abner Embry McGarity, 1862–1865," ed. Edmund Cody Burnett, *GHQ* 30 (1946): 62.

30. Edward Acton to Mary Acton, July 13, 1862, in " 'Dear Molly': Letters of Captain Edward A. Acton to His Wife, 1862," *PMHB* 89 (1965): 37–38; Alfred Lacey Hough to Mary Hough, July 3, 17, 1864, in *Soldier in the West: The Civil War Letters of Alfred Lacey Hough*, ed. Robert G. Athearn (Philadelphia, 1957), 202, 206.

31. James Connolly to Mary Connolly, Aug. 16, 1864, in *Three Years in the Army of the Cumberland*, 255–56.

32. Enos B. Lewis to parents, April 21, 1863, in "The Civil War Letters of Enos Barret Lewis," *Northwest Ohio Quarterly* 57 (1985): 90.

33. Seneca B. Thrall to wife, Nov. 15, 1862, in "An Iowa Doctor in Blue: Letters of Seneca B. Thrall, 1862–1864," ed. Mildred Throne, *IJH* 58 (1960): 109–10; Osiah Moser to wife, March 22, 1863, Civil War Collection, MO HS.

34. Charles M. Coit to family, Jan. 5, 1863, Coit Papers, GLC PML; Charles Wills to sister, Feb. 7, 1863, in *Army Life*, 153–54.

35. Wills, *Army Life*, 154; John Herr to Kate Herr, April (no day), 1864, John Herr to mother, April 29, 1864, Herr Papers, PLDU.

36. John Brobst to Mary Englesby, Sept. 27, 1864, in *Well, Mary: Civil War Letters of a Wisconsin Volunteer*, ed. Margaret B. Roth (Madison, 1960), 93; Robert Bowlin to David Powell, Aug. 11, 1863, Bowlin Papers, in private possession.

37. Alexander Caldwell to brother, March 7, 1863, Caldwell Papers, MHI; Bela Zimmerman to Minnie Zimmerman, June 14, 1863, Zimmerman Letters, in private possession.

38. John Brobst to Mary Englesby, May 27, 1865, in *Well, Mary*, 144; Eugene Kingman to Charles Kingman, Aug. 4, 1863, in *Tramping Out the Vintage 1861–1864: The Civil War Diaries and Letters of Eugene Kingman*, ed. Helene C. Phelan (Almond, N.Y., 1983), 202.

39. John Rumpel to father, Sept. 14, 1863, in "Ohiowa Soldier," ed. H. E. Rosenberger, *Annals of Iowa*, 3rd Ser., 36 (1961): 129–30; James Stallcop to Catherine Varner, Oct. 31, 1863, in "Letters of James Stallcop to Catherine Verner, Charlotte, Iowa, 1863–1865," *North Dakota Historical Quarterly* 4 (1929–30): 122.

40. Constant Hanks to Mary Rose, Nov. 20, 1864, Hanks Papers, PLDU; Amory K. Allen to Delphany Allen, Nov. 26, 1864, in "Civil War Letters of Allen," 383.

CHAPTER 11. VENGEANCE WILL BE OUR MOTTO

1. Hannibal Paine to "Miss Virginia," July 26, 1861, Paine Papers, TSL.

2. H. Christopher Kendrick to sister, Nov. 19, 1861, Kendrick Papers, SHC UNC; Richard M. Saffell to Mrs. John Bogle, Nov. 24, 1861, Saffell

Letters, in private possession; John Q. Winfield to Sallie Winfield, Sept. 2, 1861, Winfield Papers, SHC UNC.

3. Edward K. Ward to sister, April 2, 1864, Ward Papers, GLC PML; Benjamin Batchelor to Julia Batchelor, Dec. 19, 1861, June 2, 1863, in *Batchelor-Turner Letters 1861–1864, Written by Two of Terry's Texas Rangers* (Austin, 1961), 3, 52–53; Elijah Petty to wife, Sept. 11, 1862, May 22, 1863, Elijah Petty to daughter, May 10, 1863, in *Journey to Pleasant Hill: The Civil War Letters of Captain Elijah P. Petty,* ed. Norman D. Brown (San Antonio, 1982), 78–79, 223, 215.

4. Theodorick W. Montfort to Louisa Montfort, March 18, 1862, in "Rebel Lawyer: The Letters of Lt. Theodorick W. Montfort, 1861–1862," ed. Spencer Bidwell King, Jr., *GHQ* 49 (1965): 209; Edwin H. Fay to Sarah Fay, Sept. 19, June 27, July 10, 1863, in *"This Infernal War": The Confederate Letters of Sgt. Edwin H. Fay,* ed. Bell Irvin Wiley (Austin, 1958), 329, 286–87, 292; Samuel Ritchey to Margaret Harris, Nov. 25, 1862, Edwin E. Harris Papers, GLC PML.

5. H. Christopher Kendrick to father, undated, Kendrick to mother, June 6, 1863, Kendrick Papers, SHC UNC; Taliaferro Simpson to Caroline Miller, June 28, 1863, Simpson to Anna Simpson, July 27, 1863, in *"Far, Far from Home": The Wartime Letters of Dick and Tally Simpson, Third South Carolina Volunteers,* ed. Guy R. Everson and Edward H. Simpson, Jr. (New York, 1994), 251, 261–62.

6. Eugene Blackford to Mary L. Minor, undated, probably Sept. 1864, Gordon-Blackford Papers, MD HS.

7. Osmun Latrobe Diary, entry of Dec. 16, 1862, MD HS; Thomas H. Colman to parents, Oct. 5, 1863, Colman-Hayter Family Papers, SHS MO; Ted Barclay to sister, Sept. 29, 1863, in *Ted Barclay, Liberty Hall Volunteers: Letters from the Stonewall Brigade,* ed. Charles W. Turner (Rockbridge, Va., 1992), 107.

8. Richard W. Simpson to Anna T. Simpson, Aug. 22, 1861, in *"Far, Far from Home,"* 64; Edward M. Burrus to parents, n.d. (late September 1862), Burrus Papers, HML LSU; John E. Collins to wife, Aug. 17, 1863, Collins Papers, VHS.

9. Eldred Simkins to Eliza Trescott, Aug. 8, Sept. 14, 17, 1864, Simkins Papers, HEH.

10. George W. Littlefield to Whitfield Harroll, Oct. 26, 1863, in David B. Gracy II, "With Danger and Honor: George W. Littlefield 1861–1864," *Texana* 1 (1963): 139–40; Edmund Patterson, diary entry of Aug. 4, 1863, in *Yankee Rebel: The Civil War Journal of Edmund DeWitt Patterson,* ed. John G. Barrett (Chapel Hill, 1966), 128.

11. Thomas R. Roulhac to mother, March 13, 1864, Ruffin, Roulhac, and Hamilton Family Papers, SHC UNC; William R. J. Pegram to Virginia Pegram, Aug. 1, 1864, Pegram-Johnson-McIntosh Family Papers, VHS.

12. Achilles V. Clark to sister, April 14, 1864, Clark Letters, Civil War Collection, TSL.

13. Louis Alexander Hammontree to James Hammontree, June 6, 1864, in "The Hammontrees Fight the Civil War: Letters from the Fifth East Tennessee Infantry," ed. Lewis A. Lawson, *Lincoln Herald* 78 (1976): 118; John D. Mitchell to Absalom B. Barner, June 6, 1862, in "Selected Civil War Letters from the Collection of Dr. William F. Hawn," *Register of the Kentucky Historical Society* 71 (1973): 297–98.

14. Thomas T. Taylor to Antoinette Taylor, Oct. 16, 1861, Taylor Papers, OHS; Philander Draper to Edwin Draper, July 12, 1861, Draper-McClurg Papers, SHS MO; William and Henry Crawford to "Dear Friends," Aug. 5, 1864, Crawford Letters, SHS MO.

15. Delavan Arnold to mother, April 21, 1862, in *A Kalamazoo Volunteer in the Civil War,* ed. Thomas O. McConnell (Kalamazoo, 1962), 22; Robert Gould Shaw to Annie Haggerty, Aug. 13, 1862, in *Blue-Eyed Child of Fortune: The Civil War Letters of Robert Gould Shaw,* ed. Russell Duncan (Athens, Ga., 1992), 235; Squire Tuttle to parents, June 19, 1864, Tuttle to brother and sister, June 27, 1864, Tuttle Papers, MHI.

16. John Brobst to Mary Englesby, May 20, July 11, 1864, in *Well, Mary: Civil War Letters of a Wisconsin Volunteer,* ed. Margaret B. Roth (Madison, 1960), 56–57, 75.

17. Charles Wills to sister, Sept. 17, 1861, in *Army Life of an Illinois Soldier, Letters and Diary of the Late Charles Wills* (Washington, DC, 1906), 32; John G. McDermott to Isabella McDermott, March 14, 1862, McDermott Papers, WHS; John Beatty to Laura Beatty, July 30, 1864, Beatty Papers, MN HS.

18. Ira Payne to parents, March 1, 1863, Payne Papers, ISHL; Samuel Roper to sister, Aug. 8, 1863, Roper Papers, HEH.

19. Isaac Jackson to Moses and Phebe Jackson, July 13, 1863, in *"Some of the Boys . . .": The Civil War Letters of Isaac Jackson, 1862–1865* (Carbondale, Ill., 1960), 111–12; George M. Wise to John Wise, March 13, 1865, in "Civil War Letters of George M. Wise," ed. Wilfred W. Black, *Ohio Historical Quarterly* 46 (1957): 193.

20. John C. M. Baynes, *Morale: A Study of Men and Courage* (New York, 1967), 237; John Dollard, *Fear in Battle* (rpt., Westport, Conn., 1977), 38–39.

21. Henry P. Andrews to wife, March 25, April 2, May 16, 1862, Andrews Papers, ISHL; Eugene Blackford to mother, May 20, 1862, Gordon-Blackford Papers, MD HS.

22. Charles H. Brewster to mother, Nov. 1, 1862, in *When This Cruel War Is Over: The Civil War Letters of Charles Harvey Brewster,* ed. David W. Blight (Amherst, 1992), 187; Rutherford B. Hayes to S. Birchard, Sept. 22, 1862, in *Diary and Letters of Rutherford Birchard Hayes,* ed. Charles R. Williams, vol. II: *1861–1865* (Columbus, 1922), 359.

23. James Bell to Augusta Hallock, Jan. 21, 1863, Bell Papers, HEH; Edmund Halsey, Diary, entry of Dec. 23, 1862, MHI; Uriah Parmelee to mother, Dec. 26, 1862, Parmelee Papers, PLDU.

24. George W. Tillotson to wife, Feb. 5, 1863, Tillotson Papers, GLC PML; Martin Lennon to sister, Dec. 18, 1862, in "Letters and Extracts from the Diary of Captain Martin Lennon," in 5th Annual Report of the Chief of the Bureau of Military Statistics (Albany, 1868), 725–26; John Pellett to James Pellett, Dec. 29, 1862, Pellett Papers, MHI.

25. Walter Carter to family, May 10, 1863, in Four Brothers in Blue (rpt., Austin, Tex., 1978), 264; Governeer Legg to Crisey Legg, May 16, 1862, in Charles J. LaRocca, This Regiment of Heroes: A Compilation of Primary Materials Pertaining to the 124th New York State Volunteers (Montgomery, N.Y., 1991), 144.

26. Uriah Parmelee to Samuel Parmelee, May 21, 1863, Parmelee Papers, PLDU; Stephen M. Weld to mother, June 10, 1863, in War Diary and Letters of Stephen Minot Weld 1861–1865 (Boston, 1979), 213.

27. Rob Carter to father, July 14, 1863, in Four Brothers in Blue, 334; Cornelius Moore to Adeline Moore, July 21, 1863, in Cornie: The Civil War Letters of Lt. Cornelius C. Moore, ed. Gilbert C. Moore (n.p., 1989), 122.

28. Rufus Dawes to Mary Gates, July 9, 1863, in Service with the Sixth Wisconsin Volunteers (rpt., Madison, 1962), 185; J. Herbert George to parents, Nov. 10, 18, 22, 1863, George Papers, HEH.

29. Marcus Spiegel to Caroline Spiegel, Jan. 8, 1863, in Your True Marcus: The Civil War Letters of a Jewish Colonel, ed. Frank L. Byrne and Jean Powers Soman (Kent, Ohio, 1985), 128–29; Henry G. Ankeny to wife, Dec. 31, 1862, Jan. 6, 1863, in Kiss Josey for Me, ed. Florence M. A. Cox (Santa Ana, Calif., 1974), 115–17.

30. Deloraine P. Chapman to brothers and sisters, April 11, 1863, Chapman Papers, HEH; Isaac Jackson to sister, June 28, 1863, in "Some of the Boys . . .", 108.

31. Richard W. Waldrop to father, July 18, 1863, Waldrop Papers, SHC UNC; William Walsh to cousin, Aug. 3, 1863, Proffit Family Papers, SHC UNC.

32. L. P. Festerman to Caleb Hampton, Sept. 8, 1863, Caleb Hampton Papers, PLDU; William F. Wagner to Nancy Wagner, Aug. 2, 4, 15, 1863, in Letters of William F. Wagner, Confederate Soldier, ed. Joe M. Hatley and Linda B. Huffman (Wendell, N.Y., 1983), 61–63, 65.

33. John A. Barry to sister, Aug. 7, 1863, Barry Papers, SHC UNC.

34. Daniel B. Sanford to sister, July 25, 1863, in private possession.

35. John Euclid Magee, Diary, undated entry in July 1862, PLDU; Cyrus F. Boyd, diary entry of July 7, 1862, in "The Civil War Diary of C. F. Boyd, Fifteenth Iowa Infantry," ed. Mildred Throne, IJH 50 (1952): 171; Henry G. Ankeny to Tina Ankeny, Sept. 13, 1862, in Kiss Josey for Me, 87.

36. James E. Glazier to parents, Jan. 16, 1863, Glazier Papers, HEH; Thomas T. Taylor to Antoinette Taylor, July 15, 1863, Taylor Papers, OHS.

37. Charles Wills to sister, June 6, 1864, in *Army Life of an Illinois Soldier,* 255; John W. Hagan to Amanda Hagan, May 18, July 11, 1864, in "The Confederate Letters of John W. Hagan," ed. Bell Irvin Wiley, *GHQ* 38 (1954): 272; William A. Stephens to wife, July 22, 1864, in Chattahoochee Valley Historical Society, *War Was the Place: A Centennial Collection of Confederate Soldier Letters,* Bulletin 5 (Columbus, Ga., 1961): 100.

38. Thomas Connolly to Mary Connolly, Sept. 11, 1864, in *Three Years in the Army of the Cumberland: The Letters and Diary of Major James A. Connolly,* ed. Paul Angle (Bloomington, Ind., 1962), 258; John H. Morse to "Dear folks at home," Dec. 24, 1864, in *Civil War: The Letters of John Holbrook Morse, 1861–1865,* ed. Bianca Morse Federico (Washington, 1975), 171.

39. James E. Glazier to Annie Monroe, June 12, July 17, 1864, James E. Glazier to Joseph Glazier, Aug. 3, 1864, Glazier Papers, HEH.

40. Lewis Foster to Amelia Clapper, Oct. 22, 1864, in Charles M. Snyder, "A Teen-Age G.I. in the Civil War," *Proceedings of the New York State Historical Association* 52 (1954): 25–26; John M. Gould, diary entry of Dec. 31, 1864, in Gould, *History of the First-Tenth-Twenty-Ninth Maine Regiment* (Portland, 1871), 566.

41. Henry St. John Dixon, Diary, entries of Dec. 28, 1864, March 23, 1865, St. John Dixon Papers, SHC UNC.

42. David Thompson to mother, Jan. 9, Feb. 10, 1865, Samuel Thompson Papers, SHC UNC; James M. Wright to Louisa F. Wright, Nov. 27, 1864, Wright Papers, in private possession.

CHAPTER 12. THE SAME HOLY CAUSE

1. Charles Moran, *The Anatomy of Courage* (London, 1945), 61, 63–64. Several studies contain useful analyses of psychiatric casualties in war: Abram Kardiner, *The Traumatic Neuroses of War* (New York, 1941); Frank M. Richardson, *Fighting Spirit: A Study of Psychological Factors in War* (London, 1978); Peter G. Bourne, *Men, Stress, and Vietnam* (Boston, 1970); and Zahava Solomon, *Combat Stress Reaction: The Enduring Toll of War* (New York, 1993).

2. Henry D. McDaniel to Hester Felker, March 17, 1863, in *With Unabated Trust: Major Henry McDaniel's Love Letters from Confederate Battlefields* (Monroe, Ga., 1977), 137–38.

3. James K. Edmondson to wife, June 3, 1862, in *War Letters of Col. James K. Edmondson 1861–1865,* ed. Charles W. Turner (Verona, Va., 1978), 96–97; Irby G. Scott to "Dear Ones at Home," July 7, 1862, Scott Papers, PLDU; Tally Simpson to Anna Simpson, July 27, 1862, in *"Far, Far from Home": The Wartime Letters of Dick and Tally Simpson, Third South Carolina*

Volunteers, ed. Guy R. Everson and Edward H. Simpson, Jr. (New York, 1994), 140.

4. Michael Murray Miller to Elizabeth Miller, July 11, 1862, in Robert K. Murray and Warren W. Hassler, Jr., "Gettysburg Farmer," *CWH* 3 (1957): 185; Charles H. Brewster to Mary Brewster, July 9, 1862, in *When This Cruel War Is Over: The Civil War Letters of Charles Harvey Brewster,* ed. David W. Blight (Amherst, 1992), 164; Samuel Selden Partridge to Francis Macomber, July 6, 1862, in "Civil War Letters of Samuel S. Partridge of the 'Rochester Regiment,'" *RHSP* 22 (1944): 87–88.

5. Peter Meador Wright to Susan James Wright, Nov. 8, 1862, Wright Papers, in private possession; Henry L. Abbott to father, Nov. 20, 1862, in *Fallen Leaves: The Civil War Letters of Major Henry Livermore Abbott,* ed. Robert Garth Scott (Kent, Ohio, 1991), 143.

6. Holmes to parents, June 24, 1864, in *Touched with Fire: Civil War Letters and Diary of Oliver Wendell Holmes, Jr., 1861–1864,* ed. Mark De Wolfe Howe (Cambridge, Mass., 1946), 149–50; Adams to Charles Francis Adams, June 19, 1864, in *A Cycle of Adams Letters,* 2 vols., ed. Worthington C. Ford (Boston, 1920), II: 154. For a suggestive study of post-traumatic stress disorder in Civil War veterans, see Eric Dean, "We Will All be Lost and Destroyed: Posttraumatic Stress Disorder and the Civil War," *CWH* 37 (June 1991): 138–53.

7. Frederick Pettit to parents, June 13, 1864, Pettit Papers, MHI; William C. H. Reeder to parents, June 27, 1864, Reeder Papers, MHI; Peter Vredenburgh to "Dear Doctor," June 25, 1864, Vredenburgh Papers, Monmouth County Historical Society, New Jersey, typescript copy supplied by Bernard Olsen.

8. Peter Watson, *War on the Mind: The Military Uses and Abuses of Psychology* (New York, 1978), 231.

9. Charles W. Wainwright, Diary, entry of June 17, 1864, HEH; Frederick Lockley to Elizabeth Lockley, Aug. 7, 1864, Lockley Papers, HEH; H. L. Patten to George M. Macy, June 29, 1864, in "Reports, Letters and Papers Appertaining to the 20th Mass. Volunteer Infantry," Vol. I, Boston Public Library, quoted in John E. Talbott, "Combat Trauma in the American Civil War," *History Today* 46 (March 1996): 45.

10. William T. Casey to James Casey, June 30, 1864, William T. Casey to "my dear cousin," July 20, 1864, Casey Papers, PLDU; Irby G. Scott to "Loved ones at home," June 8, 1864, Scott Papers, PLDU; Thomas J. Strayhorn to Harriet Strayhorn, July 18, 1864, in "Letters of Thomas Jackson Strayhorn," ed. Henry McGilbert Wagstaff, *NCHR* 13 (1936): 317.

11. Charles H. Brewster to mother, May 15, 1864, in *When This Cruel War Is Over,* 298.

12. Chauncey Cooke to parents, May 20, June 2, 1864, in "A Badger Boy in Blue: The Letters of Chauncey H. Cooke," *WMH* 5 (1921): 74, 82; George

Knox Miller to wife, May 20, 1864, Miller Papers, SHC UNC; Henry Clay Weaver to Cornelia Wiley, Aug. 14, 1864, in "Georgia Through Kentucky Eyes: Letters Written on Sherman's March to Atlanta," ed. James M. Merrill and James F. Marshall, *Filson Club Historical Quarterly* 30 (1956): 332.

13. Charles Wills to sister, July 1, 1864, in *Army Life of an Illinois Soldier, Letters and Diary of the Late Charles Wills* (Washington, 1906), 272.

14. Hiram Smith Williams, diary entry of April 4, 1864, in *This War So Horrible: The Civil War Diary of Hiram Smith Williams*, ed. Lewis N. Wynne and Robert A. Taylor (Tuscaloosa, 1993), 43–44.

15. Gerald F. Linderman, *Embattled Courage: The Experience of Combat in the American Civil War* (New York, 1987), 2, 240; Leif Torkelsen, "Forged in Battle: The Evolution of Small Unit Cohesion in the Union Voluntary Infantry Regiments, 1861–1865" (Senior thesis, Princeton University, 1991), 5.

16. Stephen A. Forbes to Frances Snow, Jan. 12, 1865, Forbes Papers, ISHL; Abial Edwards to Anna Conant, Dec. 16, 1863, in *"Dear Friend Anna": The Civil War Letters of a Common Soldier from Maine*, ed. Beverly Hayes Kallgren and James L. Crothamel (Orono, Me., 1992), 71.

17. William J. Tomlinson to Emily Tomlinson, July 16, 1864, Tomlinson Papers, in private possession; William L. Nugent to Eleanor Nugent, Nov. 22, 1863, in *My Dear Nellie: The Civil War Letters of William L. Nugent*, ed. William M. Cash and Lucy Somerville Howarth (Jackson, Miss., 1977), 148.

18. William W. Ward to James B. Hale, Oct. 15, 1864, in *"For the Sake of my Country": The Diary of Col. W. W. Ward, 9th Tennessee Cavalry*, ed. R. B. Rosenburg (Murfreesboro, 1992), 145; Urban G. Owen to Laura Owen, March 1, April 8, 1864, in "Letters of a Confederate Surgeon in the Army of Tennessee to His Wife," *THQ* 4 (1945): 154, 161.

19. David Thompson to mother, Feb. 25, 1865, Samuel Thompson Papers, SHC UNC; John A. Everett to mother, Feb. 7, March 16, 1865, Everett Papers, WLEU.

20. John Beatty to Elizabeth Beatty, Jan. 12, 1865, Beatty Papers, MN HS; George Hopper to brother and sister, Dec. 16, 1864, Hopper Papers, MHI; Sarah D. B. Chamberlain to Joshua L. Chamberlain, Jan. 1, 1865, Joshua L. Chamberlain to Joshua Chamberlain (father), Feb. 20, 1865, Joshua L. Chamberlain to Sarah Bristow Chamberlain, March 9, 1865, in Alice Rains Trulock, *In the Hands of Providence: Joshua L. Chamberlain and the American Civil War* (Chapel Hill, 1992), 225–27.

21. Neal F. Heendy to Bryant Wright, Feb. 14, 1864, Wright Papers, PLDU; Joseph F. Maides to mother, Sept. 23, 1864, Maides Papers, PLDU; Sydney S. Champion to wife, June 1, 1864, Champion Papers, PLDU.

22. James Crowder to brother, March 13, 1864, in *In the Land of the Living: Wartime Letters by Confederates from the Chattahoochee Valley of Alabama and Georgia*, ed. Ray Mathis (Troy, Ala., 1981), 85; Thomas J. Key, diary entries of Aug. 8, 1864, Feb. 5, 1865, *Two Soldiers: The Campaign*

Diaries of Thomas J. Key, C.S.A., and Robert J. Campbell, U.S.A. (Chapel Hill, 1938), 111, 187; T. B. Kelly to L. A. Honnoll, April 25, 1864, Honnoll Papers, WLEU.

23. William L. Nugent to Eleanor Nugent, Aug. 8, Dec. 26, 1864, in *My Dear Nellie,* 197, 229.

24. Joseph Thompson to mother, Feb. 15, 1865, Samuel Thompson Papers, SHC UNC.

25. William B. Bate to William H. T. Walker, Jan. 19, 1864, Civil War Collection, HEH; *Jackson Mississippian,* reprinted in *Montgomery Weekly Mail,* Sept. 9, 1863, in Robert F. Durden, *The Gray and the Black: The Confederate Debate on Emancipation* (Baton Rouge, 1972), 31–32.

26. R. Howard Browne to wife, undated (Nov. 1864), Browne Papers, SHC UNC; James Wingard to Simon Wingard, Jan. 4, 1865, Wingard Papers, PLDU.

27. Ethan Pennell, Diary, entry of April 8, 1865, MO HS; Joseph F. Maides to mother, Feb. 18, 1865, Maides Papers, PLDU.

28. Thomas J. Goree to Mary Frances Goree Kittrell, Oct. 21, 1864, in *Longstreet's Aide: The Civil War Letters of Major Thomas J. Goree,* ed. Thomas W. Cutrer (Charlottesville, 1995), 137; Robert Patrick, diary entry of Jan. 18, 1865, in *Reluctant Rebel: The Secret Diary of Robert Patrick, 1861–1865,* ed. Jay F. Taylor (Baton Rouge, 1959), 250; Richard W. Corbin to father, Dec. 29, 1864, in *Letters of a Confederate Officer to His Family in Europe* (Paris, n.d.), 89.

29. James Branch O'Bryan to sister, Jan. 20, 1865, O'Bryan Papers, TSL; Walter Taylor to Bettie Saunders, Feb. 16, 1865, in *Lee's Adjutant: The Wartime Letters of Colonel Walter Herron Taylor, 1861–1865,* ed. R. Rockwood Tower (Columbia, S.C., 1995), 223–24.

30. John V. Hadley to Mary J. Hill, Feb. 24, 1863, in "An Indiana Soldier in Love and War: The Civil War Letters of John V. Hadley," ed. James I. Robertson, Jr., *IMH* 59 (1963): 230; John D. Shank to family, March 12, April 13, 1863, in *One Flag One Country and Thirteen Greenbacks a Month: Letters from a Civil War Private,* ed. Edna J. Shank Hunter (San Diego, 1980), 61, 68; Cornelius Moore to Adeline Moore, July 7, 1864, in *Cornie: The Civil War Letters of Lt. Cornelius L. Moore,* ed. Gilbert C. Moore (n.p., 1989), 192.

31. John A. Gillis, Diary, entries of Jan. 1, March 17, 1864, MN HS; Henry Crydenwise to parents, Jan. 31, June 7, 1864, Crydenwise Papers, WLEU; John G. McDermott to Isabella McDermott, March 10, 1864, McDermott Papers, WHS.

32. Josiah M. Favill, diary entry of Jan. 1, 1864, in *The Diary of a Young Officer* (Chicago, 1909), 273; Bliss Morse to mother, Aug. 29, 1864, and diary entry of Nov. 8, 1864, in *War Diaries and Letters of Bliss Morse,* ed. Loren J. Morse (Tahlequah, Okla., 1985), 150, 165.

33. Edward Wightman to Fred Wightman, Aug. 28, 1864, in *From Antietam to Fort Fisher: The Civil War Letters of Edward King Wightman, 1862–1865* (Rutherford, N.J., 1983), 206; Edmund English to mother, undated (1864) and April 22, 1864, English Papers, HEH.

34. *London Daily News,* Sept. 27, 1864, quoted in Allan Nevins, *The Organized War to Victory* (New York, 1971), 141–42.

35. Delos Van Deusen to Henrietta Van Deusen, Aug. 21, 1864, Van Deusen Papers, HEH; John Berry to Samuel L. M. Barlow, Aug. 27, 1864, Barlow Papers, HEH; Thomas N. Stevens to Carrie Stevens, Sept. 19, 1864, in *"Dear Carrie" . . . The Civil War Letters of Thomas N. Stevens,* ed. Georg M. Blackburn (Mt. Pleasant, Mich., 1984), 250.

36. John Hamer to Eveline Hamer, Aug. 5, 1864, Hamer Papers, MHI; James Love to Molly Wilson, Sept. 24, 1864, Feb. 14, 1865, Love Papers, MO HS; Benjamin Stevens to mother, Sept. 8, 1864, in "The Civil War Letters of an Iowa Family," ed. Richard N. Ellis, *Annals of Iowa,* 3rd Series, 39 (1969): 585.

37. Samuel J. Harrison Diary, OHS.

38. Henry Kauffman to Katherine Kreitzer, Oct. 15, 1864, in *The Civil War Letters (1862–1865) of Private Henry Kauffman,* ed. David McCordick (Lewiston, N.Y., 1991), 89. For studies of the soldier vote in 1864, see Oscar O. Winther, "The Soldier Vote in the Election of 1864," *New York History* 25 (1944): 440–58, and Josiah Henry Benton, *Voting in the Field: A Forgotten Chapter of the Civil War* (Boston, 1915).

39. Henry Crydenwise to parents, Oct. 25, 1864, Crydenwise Papers, WLEU; Delos Lake to mother, July 12, Nov. 1, 1864, Lake Papers, HEH.

40. Lowell to Josephine Shaw Lowell, Sept. 1, 1864, Lowell to Charles E. Perkins, Oct. 17, 1864, in *Life and Letters of Charles Russell Lowell,* ed. Edward W. Emerson (Boston, 1907), 333, 362; Nathan Buck to sister, July 9, 1864, Saxton Family Collection, HEH.

41. William B. Sniffen to mother, Oct. 18, 1864, Sniffen Papers, MHI; John H. Morse to Belle Morse, Oct. 25, 1864, in *The Letters of Morse,* 155; Chauncey B. Welton to father, Oct. 1, 1864, Welton Papers, SHC UNC.

42. William F. Keeler to Anna Keeler, Nov. 9, 1864, in *Aboard the USS Florida, 1863–1865: The Letters of Paymaster William F. Keeler,* ed. Robert W. Daly (Annapolis, 1968), 200; Justus Silliman to mother, Nov. 9, 1864, in *A New Canaan Private in the Civil War: Letters of Justus M. Silliman, 17th Connecticut Volunteers,* ed. Edward Marcus (New Canaan, 1984), 83.

43. John N. Sherman to parents, Feb. 10, 1865, Sherman Papers, MHI; Robert McAllister to Ellen McAllister, April 9, 1865, in *The Civil War Letters of General Robert McAllister,* ed. James I. Robertson, Jr. (New Brunswick, N.J., 1965), 608.

44. Ephraim S. Holloway to John W. Holloway, Aug. 7, 1864, Holloway Papers, OHS.

INDEX

Frémont, John C., 93
Fussell, Paul, 57, 100

Glatthaar, Joseph T., 185
Glory
  as motive for enlistment, 26–27
  disillusionment with, 28–29, 33, 44
Gooding, James, 10
Gorman, Willis, 60
Grant, Ulysses S., 94
  1864 military campaign of, 146, 165
  Vicksburg campaign of, 158
Graves, Robert, 58
Grimes, Bryan, 49

Haley, John, 10
Hallock, Augusta, 71
Hammond, James, 154
Hardee, William, 46
Hayes, Rutherford B., 25, 37, 156
Heartsill, William, 10
Hemingway, Ernest, 100
Henry, Patrick, 21
Hess, Earl, 185
Holmes, Oliver Wendell, Jr., 49, 165
Homefront
  importance of support for soldiers,
    131–33, 155
  and married soldiers, 133–40
  estrangement between, and soldiers,
    140–47
Honor
  as combat motive, 5, 6, 31, 76
  as motive for enlistment, 8, 13, 23–
    25, 76
  and desire to avoid the dishonor of
    cowardice, 77–82
  and regimental and state pride, 83–
    84
  sustaining motivation and, 131
  competing ideals of, for married
    soldiers, 134–40
  persistence of, 142, 168–70
  and vengeance, 148
Hood, John Bell, 97
Hooker, Joseph, 156

Ideology. See also Patriotism; Slavery;
    Emancipation
  as motive for enlistment, 13, 18–21,
    27–28

and sustaining motivation, 90–94,
    104–14, 131, 135
  definition of, 94
  relation to combat motivation, 114–
    16
  persistence of, 168, 170–73, 175–76
  and Union reenlistments, 173–74
  and 1864 election, 176–78
Immigrant soldiers. See Foreign-born
    soldiers
Irish-American soldiers, 9, 66
  and ideology, 113–14

Jackson, Thomas J. ("Stonewall"), 136,
    164
Jefferson, Thomas, 20
Jimerson, Randall C., 185
Johnson, Samuel, 20
Johnston, Joseph E., 156
Jones, John, 98

Keegan, John, 94, 184
Kirkland, Richard, 151

Latrobe, Benjamin, 150
Leadership
  and combat motivation, 46, 53, 58–
    61
Lee, Robert E.
  defense of Virginia, 22
  creates provost guards, 50
  surrender at Appomattox, 117, 178
  and Gettysburg campaign, 132, 150,
    157
  and Antietam campaign, 160
  supports enlistment of slaves, 171–72
Liberty. See also Slavery; Emancipation
  and slavery, Confederate soldiers on,
    20–21, 106–7, 171
  theme of, in Confederate ideology,
    104–6, 114, 170–71
  theme of, in Union ideology, 104–5,
    110–114, 135, 175–76
  and relationship to slavery, 116
Lincoln, Abraham, 113
  on motives for enlistment, 6
  election of in 1860, 14
  calls out militia, 17
  and slavery, 19, 20
  on theme of constitutional liberty,
    104, 112

Lincoln, Abraham (*continued*)
and emancipation, 121
Emancipation Proclamation of, 107–
8, 120–26
Proclamation of Amnesty and
Reconstruction, 109
reelection in 1864, and soldier vote,
129, 146, 162, 176–78
Lincoln, Mary Todd, 20
Linderman, Gerald, 141, 168, 186
Liquor
as form of liquid courage, 52–53,
202n. 20
Longstreet, James, 150
Lowell, Charles Russell, 177
Lynn, John A., 12

McClellan, George B., 123, 156, 176–
78
Madison, James, 22
Mail
importance of in sustaining morale,
132–33
Manchester, William, 86
Manhood
and combat motivation, 6, 13, 31,
76, 78
as motive for enlistment, 13, 25–26,
76
competing ideals of for married
soldiers, 134–40
persistence of, 170
Married soldiers
percentage of, viii
and theme of honor, 23–24, 134–38
tension with wives, 111, 133–40
casualty rates of, 140, 223n. 24
Marshall, John, 22
Marshall, S. L. A., 72, 77
Masculinity. *See* Manhood; Honor
Mauldin, Bill, 168
Mitchell, Reid, 184–85
Morale
relation to victory and defeat, 155–62
Morgan, John Hunt, 107
Motivation
three categories of, 12–13, 114–16,
131

Nationalism. *See* Patriotism
Negro soldiers. *See* Black soldiers

North Carolina
and state pride, 83
degree of patriotic motivation of
soldiers from, 101

Officers
overrepresented in sample, ix, 101
and function of discipline, 48
coercion by, 49–50
drinking problems of, 52, 56–57
leadership qualities of, 53–55
criticisms of, by enlisted men, 55–
58
importance of courage in, 58–60
importance of honor, 137

Patriotism. *See also* Ideology
as motive for enlistment, 6, 8, 13,
17–18, 27–28
and sustaining motivation, 90, 94–
102, 131
persistence of, 142, 168, 170–73,
175–76
and Union reenlistments, 173–74
and 1864 election, 176–78
Peace Democrats. *See* Copperheads
Pegram, William R. J. ("Willie"), 152
Pendleton, Alexander Swift ("Sandie"),
98
Pendleton, George, 176–77
Pickett, George E., 3, 10, 115
Post-traumatic stress disorder, 44, 165,
229n. 6.
See also Combat stress reaction
Promotion, ambition for, and combat
motivation, 52
Provost guards, as file closers, 50–
51

Reaves, George A., 186
Rage militaire, stimulates enlistment,
16–17
Religion
helps soldiers face threat of death,
63–71, 76, 114
injunction against killing, 71–72
just-war rationale, 72–73, 148
self-defense rationale, 73–74
religious revivals in Confederate
armies, 75–76, 159, 207n. 41
Revenge. *See* Vengeance